ELEMENTARY HEBREW

ELEMENTARY HEBREW

by

E. Leslie Carlson, A.M., Th.D.,

Professor of Old Testament Introduction and
Interpretation,

Southwestern Baptist Theological Seminary
Fort Worth, Texas

BAKER BOOK HOUSE

Grand Rapids 6, Michigan

1956

PHOTOLITHOPRINTED BY CUSHING - MALLOY, INC.
ANN ARBOR, MICHIGAN, UNITED STATES OF AMERICA
1956

INTRODUCTION

This textbook is an endeavor to simplify the study of the Hebrew language, and still to use the inductive method in a modified form. Twenty-three years of using this method in teaching Hebrew, careful study of all new textbooks using the deductive method, and experience with students previously taught by this latter method increase my faith in the superiority of a modified inductive method.

This course is divided into four quarters of study, each quarter having twenty-four lessons. Every third lesson will be a review of the previous two lessons. The first fourteen chapters of Genesis are covered. The number of verses used in each lesson should be determined by the teacher as is felt necessary.

We acknowledge our debt of deepest and sincerest gratitude to our colleague, Dr. B. A. Copass, who through the years has inspired us in this endeavor, and likewise to Dr. Clinton Lockhart, of Texas Christian University, Fort Worth, Texas, for his encouragement. To Dr. Robt. T. Daniel we acknowledge his part in helping in charts used in the study of nouns and helpful suggestions.

E. LESLIE CARLSON
March, 1956

i

TABLE OF CONTENTS

Guide to pronunciation of vowels in English equivalents

ā and â   are as ä in cälm, fär.

  ă   is as   ă in ăct, infănt.

  é   is as   ĕ in mĕt, ĕnd.

ē and ê   are as ā in fāte, lābor.

  ĕ   is as   ĕ in mĕt, ĕnd.

  î   is as   ē in ēve, deēr.

  ĭ   is as   ĭ in ĭll, habĭt.

ō and ô   are as ō in ōld, nōte.

  ŏ   is as   ŏ in ŏdd, nŏt.

  û   is as   ú in únite, húmane.

  ŭ   is as   ŭ in hŭt, circŭs

Guide to interpretation of abbreviations used

abs.   = absolute state

adj.   = adjective.

adv.   = adverb.

(c)   = common gender.

cf.   = compare.

conj.   = conjunction.

const.   = construct state.

(f) or fem.   = feminine gender.

impft.   = imperfect action.

inf.   = infinitive.

impv.   = imperative.

juss.   = jussive.

(m) or mas.   = masculine gender.

no.   = number.

p., pp.   = page, pages.

part.   = participle.

per.   = person.

pft.   = perfect action.

plu.   = plural number.

prep.   = preposition.

sec.   = section.

sing.   = singular number.

š.   = s h   iii

PART ONE — LESSON ONE

I. Importance of the study of the Hebrew language

1. It is the principal one of the original languages in which the Old Testament was written.

2. It is the basis for knowledge of the New Testament. Jesus and the New Testament writers, except Luke, were Jews. They thought and wrote in the mind and language of the Jew.

3. This is a study of the Word of God and of the language in which He spoke to the Old Testament writers. It is a high and holy privilege to study and to learn what was really said in the Old Testament.

II. Complete mastery of material assigned in each lesson is essential.

III. Reading Lesson — Gen. 1:1.

For discussion of consonants see pages 8, 9 and of vowels see page 9.

Consonants used are:

1.   בְּרֵאשִׁית
     TH SH ' R B
       î   ē   ⓔ
     beginning in

ב (bēth)   — B as in *b*at

ר (rēsh)   — R as in *r*un

א (ālĕph) — A consonant but equivalent to a soft breathing in Greek, allowing a syllable to begin or

1

close with a vowel
sound.

שׁ (shîn)   — SH as in *sh*in

תּ (tāw)   — TH as in benea*th*

Vowels used are:

ְ (sh^ewa)   — the shortest vocal sound
possible — a grunt.

ֵ (sēre)   — ē as "ay" in hay or
"ey" in th*ey*.

ִי (hîrek)   — î as in machine.

2.   בָּרָא

' R B
ā ā
created

All consonants in No. 1.

Vowels used are:

ָ (kāmĕts)   — ā as in calm. Both ָ
are the same.

3.   אֱלֹהִים

M H ōL '
     î   Ⓔ
God (s)

Consonants used are:

א   — See 1.

ל (lāmĕdh)   — L as in *l*ow

ה (hē)   — H as in *h*ay

ם (mēm)   — M as in ha*m*. (This is
a final form used at the
end of a word.)

Vowels used are:

ֱ   — This is a form of Sh^ewa
used under gutturals
giving a quick sound of
ĕ.

ֹ (hōlĕm)   — ō as in n*o*te

ִי (hîrĕk)   — î as in ma*chi*ne

4.   אֵ ת

TH '
   ē
———

As to consonants and vowels see No. 1. This is a word not translated as it indicates here that the following noun is the definite and direct object of the transitive verb.

5.   הַשָּׁמַיִם

M Y M SH SH H
   ĭ ă   ā   ă
  heavens   the

Consonants used:

ה (hē)   — H as in *h*at

שׁ (shîn)   — SH as in *Sh*in. The dot — daghes-forte, p. 14 doubles the consonant and always has a short vowel before it.

מ (mēm)   — M as in *m*ay. This is the initial and medial form.

י (yōdh)   — y as in *y*ear

ם (mēm)   — final form of M.

Vowels used:

— (păthăch) — a as in *h*at

—ָ kāmĕts) — a. See No. 2.

—ִ (hĭrĕk)   — i as in *h*it.

ֽ This is an accent mark indicating that the penultimate syllable receives the accent.

6.   וְ אֵ ת

TH ' W
 ē   ⓔ
——— *and*

Consonants used:

ו (wāw)   — w as in *w*aste

אֵת   — See No. 4.

Vowels used:

ָ   — See No. 1.

7.   הָאָרֶץ   Consonants used:

TS R ' H
 ĕ ā ā
earth the

ה   — See No. 3. א See No. 1

ר   — See No. 1.

ץ (tsādĕ)   — *ts.* This is a final form used at the end of a word.

Vowels used:

ָ   — See No. 2.

ֶ (sĕghōl)   — e as in b*e*t.

׀   — This perpendicular line is used to indicate the final accent of a sentence.

׃   — This sign is the equivalent of a period closing a sentence. It is called the "soph pasukh" (end of verse).

IV. Grammar

1. Position of the verb.

The finite verb generally precedes the subject. Late Hebrew, however, shows influence of the Babylonian in often having the subject first.

2. Syllables.

a. Every syllable begins with a consonant except וֹ. See rule on p. 35, II, 4, b. Note the use of אַ as a silent consonant, enabling a syllable to begin with a vowel sound.

b. There are as many syllables in a word as there are *full* vowels; i. e. vowels other than half-vowels, called Sheʷwa's. Begin at the end of a word to count its syllables. It is easier to note them in this way.

c. Words are accented either on the last syllable (ultima) or on the next-to-last syllable (penult). When the penult receives the accent, or "tone," it is indicated ordinarily by " ֽ " placed at the left of the vowel of that syllable.

V. The use of the name of God

In Gen. 1:1 אֱלֹהִים in the plural coincides in its usage with the New Testament teaching of the triune God. The simpler form אֱלוֹהַּ is used fifty-seven times in the Old Testament. The plural is used about three thousand times. The noun is derived from a verb root meaning "lasting, firm, or strong," hence the plural means "eternal powers." It is employed in the plural form to denote one God, and always, when speaking in this term, of Jehovah, the God of Israel. The verb used as predicate is always singular.

VI. Vocabulary

1.	רֵאשִׁית beginning (f)	6.	שָׁמַיִם heavens (always plural) (m)
2.	רֹאשׁ head (m)		
3.	אֱלֹהִים Gods (m)	7.	אֶרֶץ earth (f)
4.	אֱלוֹהַּ God (m)	8.	הָאָרֶץ the earth
5.	אֵל God (m)	9.	בָּרָא he created

in, on (see rule
p. 24, 1, a)

11.   הָ   הַ·   the (see rule
pp. 18, 19, 3, a,
c)

12.   אֵת   sign of the definite
and direct object
(see rule p. 10)

13.   וְ and (see rule
p. 35, 4)

PART ONE — LESSON TWO

I. Reading Lesson — Gen. 1:2a.

8.   וְהָאָרֶץ
TS R ' H W
ĕ ā ā ⓔ
earth the and

Consonant used is:
ו (wāw) — w as in *w*aste
Vowel used is:
ְ (simple shᵉwa) ⓔ. This is the least
sound to which any short vowel may be
reduced. In every instance the sound
is the same, hence called "simple" shᵉwa.
For the remainder of the word see Lesson One — III, 7.

9.   הָיְתָה
H TH Y H
ā ⓔ ā
was (she)

Consonants used are ה (hē), י (yōdh),
ת (tāw), ה (hē) used at the close of a
word is silent as in English, hence called
in this position, a vowel letter.
Vowels used are: ָ =ā, ְ =ⓔ and
ָ =ā.
This is a feminine form of the verb
agreeing with the subject.

10.   תֹהוּ
H ᵒTH
û
desolation

Consonants used are ת (tāw) and ה
(hē).
Vowels used are ֹ =ō as in note and

וֹ = û as *oo* in b**oo**n and called "shūrrĕk."
The accent (ˌ) is on the penult.

11. וָבֹהוּ
H ōBH(ᵥ) W
û   ā
waste   and

Consonants used are וֹ (wāw), בּ (bēth)—
BH equivalent to v, and הֹ (hē).
Vowels used are — (ā), ⁻ (ō) and וֹ (û).
The ⁻ (sh°wā) under וֹ (wāw) is sometimes lengthened to — (ā) before the
accent. Accent (ˌ) here is on the
penult.

12. וְחֹשֶׁךְ
K SH ōCH W
ĕ   ℮
darkness   and

Consonants used are : וֹ (wāw), חֹ (hēth)
as ch in German, a harsh sound deep in
the throat; שׁ (shîn) and ךְ (kăf) as
χ in Greek.
Vowels used are —, ⁻ = (ō) and ⁻ =
(ĕ). The accent (ˌ) is on the penult.

13. עַל־פְּנֵי
N P L '
ê ℮ ă
faces of   upon

Two words connected by a hyphen
called makkef. (Page 10.)
Consonants used are ע (ayin) and designated by the rough breathing sign ' as
in Greek. The pronunciation of this consonant is so difficult that it is not at-
tempted. ל (lamedh), פּ (pē) as in *p*in,
and נ (nun) as in *n*oon. Vowels used
are ⁻ (ă), — (℮), ⁻ (ê) as *ay* in say.

14a. תְהוֹם
M H TH
ô   ℮
abyss.

Consonants used חֹ (tāw), הֹ (hē) and
ם (final form of mēm).
Vowels used are — (℮) and וֹ (ô) as
in h**o**me.

ᴧ — the pausal accent which is called Athnah. (See p. 19, No. 5).

As to the usage of פְּנֵי and תְהוֹם see page 10. "The Construct State".

II. Grammar

1. Master writing of the alphabet.

a. Consonants

א	א — Ālĕph	— (as a soft breathing)		ך	ך — Kăf	— kh (final form)
ב	ב — Bēth	— b		ל	ל — Lāmĕdh	— l
ב	ב — Bēth	— v		מ	מ — Mēm	— m
ג	ג — Gîmĕl	— g		ם	ם — Mēm	— m (final form)
ג	ג — Gîmĕl	— gh		נ	נ — Nūn	— n
ד	ד — Dālĕth	— d		ן	ן — Nūn	— n (final form)
ד	ד — Dālĕth	— dh (like "th" in "this")		ס	ס — Sāmĕkh	— s
ה	ה — Hē	— h		ע	ע — Ăyĭn	— (not pronounced)
ו	ו — Wāw	— w		פ	פ — Pē	— p
ז	ז — Zăyĭn	— z		פ	פ — Pē	— pf or f
ח	ח — Hēth	— ch		ף	ף — Pē	— pf (final form)
ט	ט — Tēth	— t		צ	צ — Tsādĕ	— ts
י	י — Yōdh	— y		ץ	ץ — Tsādĕ	— ts (final form)
כ	כ — Kăf	— k				
כ	כ — Kăf	— kh				

ק ק — Kōf   — q   ת ת — Tāw   — t

ר ר — Rēsh   — r   ת ת — Tāw   — th (like

שׁ שׁ — Shîn   — sh   "th" in

שׂ שׂ — Sîn   — s   "thin")

b. Vowels

Class	Long		Name	Short	Name	Reduced		Name
A	ā) *as in â) } calm		Kāmĕts	ă as in hat	Păthăch	⁝ ⓔ	as in below	Simple Sheʷâ
	é **as in net		Seghôl			ⱶ ⓐ	very short ă sound	Hătĕf- Păthăch
I	î as in machine		Hîrĕk	ĭ as in hit	Hĭrĕk	ⱶ ⓔ	very short	Simple Sheʷa
	ē) as "ey" ê } in they	Sērē		ĕ as in hem	Seghôl	ⱶ ⓔ	ĕ sound	Hătĕf- Seghôl
U	û as "oo" in boon	Shûrrĕk		ŭ as in hut	Kĭbbûts	ⱶ ⓞ	very short	Simple Sheʷa
	ō) as in ô } note	Hôlĕm		ŏ as in hot	Kāmĕts- hātûf	ⱶ ⓞ	ŏ sound	Hătĕf- Kāmĕts

*Most grammars use ° over the vowel to indicate tonelong but in this textbook the short horizontal line as above other tonelong vowels will be used.
**This ⷮ⷟ becomes ⷀ in pause.

c. Vowel letters

There are four consonants that function as vowel letters when final in a syllable. They lose their consonantal force and the syllables in which they are final are considered open.

(1) א   usually used with ā.

(2) ה   usually used with ā, ê, or ô.

(3) י   used with î or ê.

(4) וֹ used with ô or û.

Both יֹ and לֹ are treated as consonants when doubled. When final הֹ is a consonant, a point called "Mappik" is placed in it: הּ.

2. Syllables.

Open syllables end with a vowel or vowel letter, i. e. the vowel sound continues until stopped by consonant of next syllable or word. Closed syllables close with a consonant, i. e. when the consonantal sound is final in the syllable.

3. The construct state.

When two nouns are in such relation that the first depends upon the second for its full meaning, the first is said to be in the construct state and the second in the absolute. It is the first of the two nouns that suffers change; e. g. פְּנֵי   תְהוֹם

abyss   faces of.

The noun in the construct state is dependent upon the following noun for: (1) its meaning; (2) its tone, or accent; (3) its definiteness.

4. The use of the hyphen.

The hyphen, called 'Makkef", is the same in form and usage as in English. E. g. עַל־פְּנֵי.

5. The use of אֶת.

The definite and direct object of a transitive verb should be preceded by אֶת. Note its use in vs. 1.

6. In the writing of the Hebrew sentences for written exercises, note the following example:

בְּרֵאשִׁית בָּרָא אֱלֹהִים:

III. Vocabulary

14. הָיָה he was or became   22. פְּנֵי faces of (construct
15. הָיְתָה she was   state)
16. בֹּהוּ waste (m)   23. מָשַׁל he ruled
17. תֹּהוּ desolation (m)   24. מְשֹׁל rule, dominion (m)
18. תְּהוֹם abyss (c)   25. שָׁמַר he kept
19. חָשַׁךְ to be dark, dim   26. עַל upon
20. חֹשֶׁךְ darkness (m)
21. פָּנִים faces (always plu.)
      (m)

PART ONE — LESSON THREE

I.   Review reading thoroughly, noting syllables and vowels con-
     tained in each word.

II. Review grammar and vocabulary.

III. Be able to write out in full the alphabet and table of vowel
     signs.

IV. Sentences to be translated into Hebrew and written in
     exercise book:

     1. In beginning God was in heavens.
     2. He created the heavens and the faces of the earth.
     3. God (is) in earth.
     4. God ruled the heavens.
     5. The earth became in beginning.
     6. Desolation ruled in earth.
     7. Upon faces of abyss was darkness.
     8. God kept the faces of the heavens.

9. Darkness was upon the earth.

10. Waste was upon the abyss.

11. Darkness ruled upon the faces of the abyss.

12. God kept the darkness upon the earth.

PART ONE — LESSON FOUR

I. Reading Lesson — Gen. 1:2b–3.

14 b.   וְ ר וּ חַ
      CH R W
      (ă)   û   ⓔ
      Spirit of and

Consonants used are:

ר (rēsh) and ח (hēth).

Vowels used are:

⸲ Simple shᵉwa (ⓔ) and וּ (û). The ⸲ used under ח is not a vowel but merely a transitional sound used under final ח and ע to facilitate pronunciation. One closed syllable — (Why?). See p. 10, No. 2.

15.   אֱ ל הִ י ם

See No. 3 in Lesson One. For usage of רוּחַ with אֱלֹהִים see page 10, "The Construct State."

16.   מְ רַ חֶ פֶ ת
   TH PH CH R M
    ĕ   é   ă   ⓔ
    brooding

Consonants used are:

מ (mēm), ר (rēsh), ח (hēth), פ (without dot called daghēš-lene, it is PH or F), ת (tāw).

Vowels used are:

⸲ (Simple shᵉwa), ⸲ (ă), ⸲ a form of long ā always accented on penult and pronounced as short ĕ; ⸲ (ĕ). This verb form is a participle. There are one open and two closed syllables — (Why?)

17.   עַל ־ פְּ נֵ י

See No. 13 in Lesson Two. There are one closed and one open syllables — (Why?)

18.   הַ מָּ יִ ם
M Y M M H
  ĭ   ā   ă
waters   the

Consonants used are:

הֵ (hē), מ (mēm) — here doubled by a dot called Daghĕs-forte. See p. 14, II, 2. י (yodh), ם (final form of Mēm).

Vowels used:

ַ (ă), ָ (ā), ִ (ĭ). See page 18, II, 3 as to the forms and use of the Article. ָ was lengthened from ַ because it received the final accent called silluk. There are two closed and one open syllables. — (Why?)

19.   וַ יֹּ א מֶ ר
R M ' ō Y Y W
  ĕ   ă·
He said   and

Consonants used are:

ו (wāw), י (yodh), א ('), מ (mēm), ר (rēsh).

Vowels used are:

ַ (ă), ֹ (ō), ֶ (ĕ). וַ is a form of the conjunction. See p. 16, No. 5. There are two closed and one open syllables — (Why?)

20.   יְ הִ י ־ אוֹ ר
R ' - H Y
  ô   î   ⓔ
light Let or will be

Consonants used are:

י (yodh), ה (hē), א ('), ר (rēsh).

Vowels used are:

─ (Simple Shᵉwa ⓔ), ˒─ (î), וֹ (ô),

יְהִי is the simple imperfect, masculine singular. ᴧ is an accent mark called athnah. (See p. 19, No. 5). There are one open and one closed syllables — (Why?)

21.   וַיְהִי ־ אוֹר
R ' – H Y W
ô   î   ⓔ   ă
light   it was and

As to consonants and vowels see above Nos. 19 and 20. וַ is the same conjunction and used in the same way as in No. 19. There are two closed and one open syllables — (Why?)

II. Grammar

1. Classification of letters.

    a. Labials: בּ, ו, מ, פּ.

    b. Dentals: ד, ז, ט, ל, נ, ס, צ, שׁ, שׂ, ת.

    c. Palatals: י.

    d. Velars: ג, כ, ק.

    e. Gutturals: א, ר, ע, ה, ח.

      The gutturals are divided into two classes, weak: א and ר; and strong: ה and ח; with ע as variable, more often weak.

2. Daghes̆-forte.

    a. This is a point placed in the bosom of all consonants, except gutturals, to indicate doubling. This occurs only when it is preceded by a full short vowel. The hard and not the soft sound of spirant consonants is doubled. A final consonant always, and a medial consonant sometimes, omit the daghes-forte. In the strong gutturals ה and ח and sometimes ע, doubling is implied, and the preceding vowel remains un-changed. Before א, ר, and usually ע, the vowel is heightened to the corresponding long vowel to indicate the refusal of the guttural to be doubled.

b. The omission of Daghes-forte

(1) It is always omitted from a final vowelless consonant, except אַתְּ (thou) and נָתַתְּ (thou gavest); e. g. וַיְכַל (2:2),(and he finished.)

(2) It is often omitted from <u>medial</u> consonants with Sheʷwa. Spirant consonants are exceptions and always retain it. E. g. וַיְהִי (1:3) for וַיְּהִי; בְּדְלָה(be divided.)

(3) It is omitted from gutturals. E. g. הָאָרֶץ for הָּאָרֶץ.

3. Daghes̆-lene.

Certain consonants, called spirants, have two sounds. These spirants are ב, ג, ד, כ, פ, ת, and are called "Begadkaphath" letters to better remember them. The hard sound is indicated by a point called daghes̆-lene, which these spirants receive when they do not immediately follow a vowel or half-vowel.

4. Quantity of vowels in syllables.

a. The vowel of an unaccented, pretonic, open syllable must be long; if ante-pretonic or more, it must reduce to Sheʷwa.

b. The vowel of an unaccented closed syllable must be short.

c. The vowel of an accented open or closed syllable may be either long or short.

5. In verse 3, in וַיֹּאמֶר the form of the conjunction is וַ, which is not only conjunctive, but also conversive in that it changes the action of the verb from imperfect to perfect.

Begin in

←——————

the Perfect, and to continue in the Perfect with the conjunction, use the Imperfect form with וַ. The waw conversive only affects the verb to which it is attached.

See page 43 for the use of Waw Conversive with the Perfect.

III. Vocabulary

27. רוּחַ spirit (construct same in form) f.

28. רָחַף he brooded, hovered

29. מְרַחֶפֶת brooding

30. מַיִם waters (always plural) (m). Const. — מֵי

31. אָמַר he said

32. יֹאמַר he will say

33. וַיֹּאמֶר and he said

34. אֹמֶר saying, word, utterance, (m)

35. אוֹר to shine

36. אוֹר light (m)

37. אוּר flame, blaze (m)

38. יְהִי he will be or let be

39. וַיְהִי and he was.

PART ONE — Lesson Five

I. Reading Lesson — Gen. 1:4.

22.   וַיַּרְא
    ' R Y Y W
      ă   ă
    he saw and

No new consonants or vowels. Since there are two full vowels there are two syllables. Both syllables are closed. Why? — See page 10, No. 2. The character looking like Simple Sheʷa is a syllable divider, placed under all medial and some final consonants when they close a syllable. It is not vocal, i. e. not pronounced. This is the simple imperfect form of the verb used with ·וֹ. See p. 16, No. 5.

23. אֶת ־ הָ א וֹ ר
R ' H-HT '
ô ā   ĕ
light   the   ———

Three words in Hebrew but pronounced as one due to use of the Măkkēf (hyphen). There are three full vowels, hence there are three syllables, one open and two closed. Since אֶת is attached to the following by use of the makkef (hyphen) it loses its accent. The ‒‒ (ē) thus in an unaccented closed syllable is shortened to ‒‒ (ĕ). See p. 15, No. 4.

24. כִּי ־ ט וֹ ב
V   T – K
ô   î
good – that

Two words united by makkef, the first is open and the second closed as to their syllables. Note use of the tone (accent) sign ʌ (ăthnāh).

25. וַיַּבְדֵּל
L D V Y Y W
ē   ă   ă
he divided   and

One new consonant ד (dālĕth). D as in *d*en. There are three syllables (Why?) and all are closed. The character under בּ is not vocal Shᵉwa. (Why?) See p. 15, No. 3. The daghĕš in ד is not daghĕš-forte (Why?). See p. 14, No. 2, a. It is called "daghĕš-lēnĕ."

26. בֵּין
N B
ê
between

One new consonant ן (nūn), N as in de*n*. There are two forms of nūn, נ which is initial or medial and ן (here used) is the final form used at the end of a word. Why is the daghes̆-lene used in בֵ?

27. וּבֵין
N V
ê û
between and

The conjunction וְ is here written וּ. See p. 35, No. 4, b.

28. הַחֹשֶׁךְ
K SH ŏCH H
ĕ ă
darkness the

This is the 3rd way in which the article (הַ) is used. See II, 3, b, below.

II. Grammar

1. Thoroughly review grammar to date.

2. The syllable divider.

This character, which is the same in form as a simple Sh^ewa, is placed under consonants, medial spirants without a daghes̆-lene, or final spirants with a daghes̆-lene, when they close a syllable. It is not placed under vowel letters. Some grammarians call this character a silent Sh^ewa. E. g. וַיִּבְדֵּל.

3. The article.

The article formerly was הַל, but the ל was lost and the loss compensated by the use of daghes̆-forte. ל is retained in the Arabic.

a. The usual form is הַ with daghes̆-forte in the following letter . . . . הַּ·

E. g. הַשָּׁמַיִם,(the heavens,)

b. Before strong gutturals, הַ and חַ, doubling is implied . הַ

E. g. הַחֹשֶׁךְ,(the darkness.)

c. Before weak gutturals א, ר, and ע, loss of daghes-forte is
compensated by lengthening — to ָ . . . . . . הָ

E. g. הָאוֹר,(the light.)

d. Before הָ and before unaccented הָ and עָ, the — is deflected
to ֶ for sake of dissimilarity. . . . . הֶ

E. g. הֶהָרִים,(the mountains.)

e. The inseparable prepositions בְּ, לְ, and כְּ, when used with the
article, combine with it, taking its vowel; the Sheʷa of the
preposition and the ה of the article being dropped. E. g.
בְּהָאָרֶץ becomes בָּאָרֶץ.

4. **The comparison of simple Sheʷa with the syllable divider.**

They are unlike in usage though same in form. No vocal
Sheʷa can follow another one, and the first of the two must
change to a full vowel. In וַיַּבְדֵּל ַ is not a vocal Sheʷa since
a spirant follows with a daghes-lene and the unaccented penultimate syllable has a short vowel.

5. **The common accents.**

Sentences in Hebrew may be divided into two or three parts,
each part closing with an additional accent, called "pause."

The stressed, or pausal, accent, when occurring under the last
accented syllable of a sentence is called "Silluk", and is indicated
by a short perpendicular line, ׀.

The second part of the sentence has its pausal accented
syllable shown by "Athnah," which is indicated by ᵥ.

If a third part, this pausal accent is shown by "Segholta"

and indicated by a character ⸚ placed above the accented syllable. If the latter accented syllable is penultimate, two Segholtas are used.

All sentences are closed with the same sign, : , called "Sōphpāsûk" (end of verse).

Accents are divided into two classes, namely: disjunctives and conjunctives. The disjunctives denote a separation so distinct that if the word following this type of accent begins with a spirant consonant, that spirant consonant receives a daghes-lene. The conjunctives denote as their name implies — connection.

III. Table of Accents

1. Disjunctives

a. אֽ — Silluk, always indicating final accented syllable of a sentence.

b. אַ — Athnah, indicating close of second part of a sentence.

c. אֱ — Segholta, indicating close of third part of a sentence.

The above are the primary accents. The following indicate divisions within the above larger parts of a sentence. They are equivalent to some usages of the semi-colon and all usages of the comma.

d. אֱ — Shelsheleth

e. אֱ — Zakef Katon

f. אֱ — Zakef gadol

g. אֱ — Reviach

h. אֱ — Pashta

i. אֶ — Yethiv

j. אֱ — Tifcha

k. אֱ — Tevir

l. אֱ — Zarka

m. אֱ — Geresh

n. אֵ — Gerashayim   q. אַ — Karne Farah

o. אֵ — Legarmeh   r. אֵ — Tilisha Gedolah

p. אֵ — Pazer

2. Conjunctives.

a. אֵ — Merkha   e. אֵ — Mahpakh

b. אֵ — Merkha Khefula   f. אֵ — Telisha Qetanna

c. אֶ — Darga   g. אֵ — Yerah ben yomo

d. אֵ — Qadma   h. אֵ — Meayyela

These accents are called "servants" to the disjunctives, and are placed on the words that stand immediately before or in close relation with those upon which the disjunctives are placed. These accents must have had a musical significance.

IV. Vocabulary

40. רָאָה he saw

41. וַיַּרְא and he saw

42. רֹאֶה seer, prophet (m)

43. בָּדַל he divided

44. יַבְדִּיל he will cause to divide

45. וַיַּבְדֵּל and he caused to divide

46. לָמַד he learned

47. לִמּוּד accustomed, trained, taught (adj.)

48. תַּלְמִיד learner, disciple (m)

49. טוֹב to be good, to please

50. טוֹב good (adj.)

51. טוּב goodness (m)

52. טוֹבָה good, blessing, benefit (f)

53. בֵּין between, among

54. כִּי that, because, when

55. וַ and (conversive form with imperfect).

PART ONE — Lesson Six

I. Review all reading thoroughly and apply grammar learned.

II. Review grammar given to date.

III. Be able to write out the words numbers 27–56 of vocabulary from memory.

IV. Sentences to be translated into Hebrew and written in exercise book:

1. God ruled the earth and the heavens and the waters.
2. Man saw the light upon the faces of the heavens.
3. And said God, In beginning let be the light.
4. The spirit of God (was) brooding upon the earth.
5. The man of God saw the light of the heavens.
6. He saw a good learner (learner good).
7. God created the heavens and caused a division between the earth and between the waters.
8. He learned that the man was good (the man that good).
9. He saw a good man.
10. God's man saw the light of the heavens.
11. In beginning God's spirit was brooding upon the waters.
12. Let there be a division between the light and the darkness.

PART ONE — Lesson Seven

I. Reading Lesson — Gen. 1:5.

29.   וַיִּקְרָא

' R Q YY W

ā   ĭ   ă

he called, and

One new consonant — ק (kōf) as q in clique. This is the simple imperfect with the waw conversive. יִקְרָא – "he will call" but וַיִּקְרָא – "and he called." Three syllables — one open and two closed. Why is ָ‍ under ק silent? See p. 18, II, No. 2.

30. לָאוֹר
R ' L
ô ā
light, to the

The inseparable preposition לְ and the article הַ have combined, the preposition taking the vowel of the article. See p. 19, No. 3, e. Two syllables — one closed and one open.

31. יוֹם
M   Y
ô
day

Note the use of final form of mem, (ם). One closed syllable.

32. וְלַחֹשֶׁךְ
K SHᵒCH L W
ĕ   ā   ⓔ
darkness to the and

A combination of the inseparable preposition לְ with the article הַ becoming לַ. Three syllables, one closed and two open.

33. קָרָא
' R Q
ā ā
he called

The simple perfect of the verb. Two syllables, both open.

34. לַיְלָה
H L Y L
ā ⓔ ā
night

The ָ‍ which regularly belongs in the penultimate syllable receiving the additional tone (accent) ʌ, has lengthened to ָ (ā). Two syllables, both open.

35. עֶרֶב
V R '
ĕ é
evening

The penultimate vowel is a tone long ā only found in the penultimate syllable and pronounced as ĕ. Two syllables, one closed and one open.

36.   בֹּקֶר   Two syllables, one closed and one open.
R Q ŏV
ĕ
morning

37.   אֶחָד   Note ד without the daghes-lene.
DH CH   '   (Why?) and pronounced as *th* in "they."
ā   ĕ
one   Two syllables, one closed and one open.

II. Grammar

1. The inseparable prepositions

These prepositions are three in number, namely בְּ, in or on; לְ, to, or unto; and כְּ, as, like, or according to. They are always prefixed to the words they govern:

a. Regularly with simple Sh^ewa reduced from — . . . —
    e. g. בְּשָׁמַיִם(in heavens).

b. Before consonants having simple Sh^ewa with —
    thinned or attenuated from — . . . . —
    e. g. בִּרְקִיעַ(in expanse of).

c. Before gutturals having compound Sh^ewa with
    the corresponding short vowel . . . . . —, —, —
    e. g. לַעֲשׂוֹת(to do).

d. Before the article, with the vowel of the article. —, —, —
    e. g. בָּאָרֶץ,(in the earth).See p. 19, 3, e.

e. Before tone, or accented, syllable, sometimes with
    tone-long —, lengthened from original — . . . . —
    e. g. לְמַיִם(to waters).

2. The simple active verb

The Hebrew verb is composed of three root consonants. There are some grammarians that hold to some roots having only two consonants, but this latter view is doubtful. To the root, vowels were added to make it pronounceable. The simple active Perfect is called the "Kal" stem and indicates completed action; as קָטַל = "he killed." Gender and number are expressed by affixes.

3. The two kinds of long vowels

There are two kinds of long vowels differing in origin, character, and writing (except "A" class). What would be diphthongs are contracted with their vowel letters making one character.

NATURALLY LONG	TONE LONG
1. Characteristic or natural verbal or nominal forms. This keeps the original form, as in תְּהוֹם.	Original short vowel given, or standing before, the tone.

2. Contraction, as

ORIGIN   a   plus w = ô
            ָ   plus וֹ = וֹ
            i   plus y = î
            ִ   plus י = י ִ

3. Compensation, as הָאָרֶץ
becoming הָאָרֶץ, daghes-
forte being rejected. Cf.
מֵעַל for מִן עַל, the ֵ is
defectively written.

Fully, as	Defectively, as:

Fully, as

â — ָ
î — ִי

How
Written ê — ִי

û — וּ

ô — וֹ

Defectively, as:

Original short form		Resultant tone-long form
ă, ַ	becoming	ָ, ā / ֵ, ê
ĕ, ֶ ĭ, ִ	becoming	ֵ, ē
ŭ, ֻ ŏ, ָ	becoming	ֹ, ō

Character	Unchangeable	Changeable

III. Vocabulary

57. קָרָא he called
58. יְקְרָא he will call
59. וַיְּקְרָא and he called
60. קְרָאָה a meeting (f)
61. יָשַׁב he sat, dwelt
62. יוֹם day (m)
63. יוֹמָם daily (adv.)
64. שֵׁם name (m)
65. שָׁם there (adv.)

66. לַיְלָה night (m)
67. עָרַב it became or grew
dark
68. עֶרֶב evening (m)
69. עֹרֵב raven (m)
70. בָּקַר he cut, broke forth
71. בֹּקֶר morning (m)
72. אֶחָד one (adj.)

PART ONE — LESSON EIGHT

I. Reading Lesson — Gen. 1:6.

38. רָ קִ י עַ
‘ Q R
(ā) î ā
expanse

Two syllables, one closed and one open. The — under עַ is the same as under חַ in רוּחַ (Spirit of). See No. 14b. Remember that this — is not a vowel but merely an aid to help pronounce a final ח or ע. See p. 28, II, 1.

39. בְּ ת וֹ ךְ
K TH B
ô   ⓔ
midst of in

One closed syllable. This noun form תוֹךְ is a construct form used with הַמָּיִם which is in the absolute state.

·40. וִ י הִ י
H W
î   î
let be and

Two open syllables. יְהִי is the shortened simple imperfect form. Here the conjunction וְ is used with it. Since no two vocal Sheʷas can stand together there is here a contraction since the first — was attenuated from an original — making וְיְהִי. The ‘ being also a corresponding vowel letter combines with — making ‘—. The second — is lost since its consonant becomes a part of ‘—. Cf. וַיְהִי (and it or there was).

41. מַ בְ דִּ י ל
L D V M
î   ă
dividing

This is the participial form of the same stem of the verb וַיַּבְדֵּל. (See No. 25.) Two closed syllables.

42. מַ יִ ם
M Y M
ĭ ă
waters

Two syllables, one closed and one open.

43. לְ מָ יִ ם
M Y M L
ĭ ā ā
waters to

Three syllables, one closed and two open. The inseparable preposition sometimes takes ⟨ ָ ⟩ before an accented syllable especially when pausal. ⟨ ָ ⟩ under מ is lengthened from ⟨ ְ ⟩ since it receives the pausal accent.

II. Grammar

1. The Pathach Furtive.

When words end in ע, ה or ח, the long vowel, except ⟨ ָ ⟩ in the syllable, is followed under these consonants by a Pathach which is called "Pathach Furtive". This is a transitional sound that is permitted to steal in to facilitate pronunciation and is not considered a vowel either full or half. E. g. רוּחַ,(spirit); רָקִיעַ, (expanse).

2. Review of pausal accents.

a. Regularly מֵיִם; but in pause becomes מָיִם

b. Regularly הַמֵּיִם; but in pause becomes הַמָּיִם

c. Regularly לְמֵיִם; but in pause becomes לְמָיִם

d. Regularly לַמֵּיִם; but in pause becomes לַמָּיִם

3. Learn thoroughly syllables: their kinds; quantity of vowels contained with and without tone; and kinds of vowels as to origin, writing, and character. This is one of the chief keys to mastering Hebrew.

III. Vocabulary

73. רָקַע he beat or spread out

74. רָקִיעַ expanse (m)

75. תָּוֶךְ midst, middle (m)

76. תּוֹךְ midst of (const.)

77. מַבְדִּיל division (causative participle of בָּדַל)

78. אִישׁ man, husband (m)

PART ONE — LESSON NINE

I. Review all reading to date.

II. Practice orally pronunciation of words, emphasizing syllables.

III. Be able to write from memory the table of vowel signs.

IV. Sentences to be translated into Hebrew and written in exercise book:

1. He saw the light in the morning.

2. God created the earth and said, Let be the light in the heavens.

3. He called to the light, day, and He called to the darkness, night.

4. The beginning of the day (is) morning, and the beginning of the night (is) evening.

5. He dwelt between the earth and between the heavens.

6. God said, Let be a division between the light and between the darkness in day one.

7. He ruled upon the waters and divided between waters to the waters.

8. He learned the name of the man.

9. God created the man in the evening.

10. In day second the man saw the waters and the abyss and the waste.

11. The name of the darkness is night, and the name of the light is day.

12. He kept the good light in the midst of the expanse.

PART ONE — Lesson Ten

I. Reading Lesson — Gen.1:7, 8.

44.   וַ יַּ עַ שׂ

S ' Y Y W

ǎ ǎ   ǎ

he made   and

A new consonant— שׂ "s" as in *sin*. Cf. (SH). •וֹ is the waw conversive that both connects and converts the imperfect form of the verb to perfect in meaning only. (See p. 16, II, 5.) This is a shortened form of the imperfect of the verb עָשָׂה (No. 79 in vocabulary).

45.   הָ רָ קִ יַ עַ

' Q R H

(ǎ) î ā â

expanse,   the

The article is used here as in הָאָרֶץ. (See p. 19, II, 3, c.) Note use of pathach furtive. (See p. 28, II, 1.). ∴ indicates the third part of a sentence and is a pausal accent. (See pp. 19, 20, II, 5).

46.   אֲ שֶׁ ר

R SH '

ĕ Ⓐ

which

A new half vowel, a compound Shᵉwa called Hatef Pathach. It is a very short "a" sound. (See chart, p. 9.) This is the relative pronoun which is indeclinable, having no gender or number. (See p. 32, II, 1.)

47.　מִתַּחַת
TH CH T T M
　ă　ă　ĭ
under from

This is composed of two prepositions תַּחַת and מִן. When used together they are combined into one word, the נ of מִן being assimilated and shown by a dagheš forte in תּ. (See p. 32, II, 2.)

48.　לָרָקִיעַ
‘　Q R L
(ā)　î　ā　â
expanse　to the

The inseparable preposition לְ takes the vowel of the article הָ becoming לָ. (See p. 19, II, 3, e.).

49.　מֵעַל
L ‘ M
　ă　ê
upon　from

This is the same type of combination as No. 47, only that the ע refusing the daghes-forte caused the lengthening of ⸗ (ĭ) to ⸗ ê) for compensation. This ⸗ is unchangeably long though defectively written.

50.　כֵּן
N K
　ē
so

A monosyllabic adverb.

51.　שָׁמָיִם
M Y M SH
　ĭ　ā　ā
heavens

This word is here without the article (cf. No. 5.) The ⸗ is here lengthened to ⸗ because it has received the pausal accent.

52.　שֵׁנִי
N SH
î　ē
second

Note that the accented syllable, here final, received the pausal accent.

II. Grammar

1. The relative pronoun.

The relative pronoun is אֲשֶׁר (who, which, that), occasionally shortened to · שַׁ or · שֶׁ. It is indeclinable and thus this one form is for all genders and cases, both singular and plural.

2. The preposition מִן

This preposition means "from." It is written **fully** before nouns with the article; otherwise it combines with the first letter of the following word, the נ being assimilated and shown by a daghes-forte. If the consonant is a strong guttural, it is doubled by implication; and if a weak guttural, the ⟶ is lengthened to ⟶. E. g. מִתַּחַת and מֵעַל.

3. Affixes for gender and number of nouns.

a. Masculine singular nouns have no special ending for either the absolute or the construct state.

b. Masculine plural ending absolute is ◌ִים and construct is ◌ֵי.

c. Feminine singular ending is usually ה◌ָ and construct is ת◌ַ. Many feminine nouns in the absolute end in ת, which was the original ending for all feminine nouns in singular absolute.

d. Feminine plural ending both absolute and construct is וֹת.

III. Vocabulary

79.	עָשָׂה	he made	82.	אֲשֶׁר who, which
80.	יַעֲשֶׂה	he will make	83.	שֵׁנִי second
81.	וַיַּעַשׂ	and he made	84.	תַּחַת under
		(shortened form of	85.	מִן from
		imperfect used)	86.	כֵּן so, thus.

PART ONE — Lesson Eleven

I. Reading Lesson — Gen. 1:9, 10.

53.   יִקָּווּ

W Q Q Y
û   ā   ĭ

Let or shall be collected

This is the plural passive imperfect masculine — the plural indicated by the ו and the passive indicated by the dagheš-forte in ק that shows the assimilation of נ which is the sign of the passive. (See p. 34, II, 1.)

54.   אֶל ־

L   '
  ĕ

unto

A preposition with meaning "unto" or "to". It is not necessarily written with a makkef nor is it inseparable in usage as לְ.

55.   מָקוֹם

M Q M
ô   ā

place

The noun is based on the verb root קוּם meaning to "rise or stand". (See No. 91 in vocabulary.)

56.   וְתֵרָאֶה

H ' R TH W
ĕ ā ē ℮

let or shall be seen and

This is the singular passive imperfect feminine, compared to plural masculine in No. 53. (See p. 34, II, 1.)

57.   הַיַּבָּשָׁה

H SH B B Y Y H
ā   ā   ă   ă

dry(land)   the

This is a feminine adjective as seen by the ending הָ and treated as a noun referring to land.

58.   לַיַּבָּשָׁה

dry land   to the

The same form as above (No. 57) except that the article ·הַ is used with the preposition לְ making ·לַ. (See p. 19, II, 3, e.)

59.   אֶ רֶ ץ
TS R '
ĕ é
earth

This is the regular form but changed when used with the article. הָאָרֶץ Note that — becomes —. This is an exceptional usage so used always with this noun.

60.   וּ לְ מִ קְ וֵ ה
H W Q M L
ē   ĭ   ⓔ û
*(the) collection to and
of*

וּ (and), regularly וּ is written thus before consonants supported by a half vowel, i. e. Shᵉwa. (See p. 35, II, 4, b.) This noun is the construct form because the — under ו stands in open syllable and hence lengthened to —. Why? (See p. 10, II, 3.)

61.   יַ מִּ י ם
M M M Y
î   ă
seas

This is the plural of יָם (sea). The daghes̆-forte in the מ is due to the fact that the verb root is יםם (to roar, rage). Cf. use of ים—ּ in אֱלֹהִים.

II. Grammar

1. In verse 9 the simple passive forms of the verb are used. This verb stem is called "Nifal," and its chief characteristic is the consonant נ.

Note use in Imperfect, third person, mas. sing. יִקָּוֶה where the נ is assimilated. So in third person, fem. sing. תִּקָּוֶה and in the third person, masc. plural יִקָּוּ.

In the second verb there are gutturals in the root, hence rejection of daghes̆-forte and lengthening of vowel; as

3d mas. sing. יֵרָאֶה — he will be seen.
3d fem. sing. תֵּרָאֶה — she will be seen.
3d mas. plu. יֵרָאוּ — they will be seen.

2. It is to be noted in וַתֵּרָאֶה that there is a secondary accent mark used. It is called "Metheg", is shown by ֽ , and is generally used on the second syllable before the tone, sometimes on the third if the second is closed.

3. Know "Key to Hebrew" (See p. 5, 2, a, b, c; p. 10, 2; p. 15, 4, a, b, c; p. 25, 3.

4. The Waw Conjunctive.

The conjunction "and" was originally written וַ but now is written:

a. Ordinarily with simple Sheʷa .... וְ. E. g. וְאוֹר,(and light).

b. Before בּ, מ, and פ and consonants with simple Sheʷa ... וּ. E. g. וּמַיִם,(and water)וּלְמַיִם(and to waters).

c. Before gutturals having compound Sheʷa with corresponding short vowels .... ־ַ, ־ֶ, ־ָ. E. g. וַאֲנִי,(and I).

d. Before a tone or accented syllable, sometimes with tone-long .... ־ָ. E. g. וָבֹהוּ,(and waste).

e. Before יְהִי, it becomes וַיְהִי.

III. Vocabulary

87. קָוָה he collected, waited

88. יִקָּוֶה he will be collected

89. יִקָּווּ they will be collected

90. מִקְוֶה collection, hope (m)

91. קוּם to rise, stand

92. יְקוּם whatever exists or lives, a being (m)

93. קוֹמָה stature, height (f)

94. מָקוֹם place (m)

95. יָבֵשׁ it was dry

96. יַבָּשָׁה dry land (f)

97. יָם sea, west (m)

98. נָתַן he gave

99. יִתֵּן he will give

100. וַיִּתֵּן and he gave

PART ONE — LESSON TWELVE

I. Be prepared to write from memory the vocabulary lists Nos. 1–78.

II. Sentences to be translated into Hebrew and written in exercise book:

1. The man saw the heavens which God had made.
2. The heavens are above the waters.
3. The place was between the evening and the morning.
4. God sent the light from the heaven to earth.
5. He will be seen above the place.
6. The heavens will be collected in the expanse above the earth.
7. He created the waters which will be seen in the seas.
8. He called the dry land earth and the waters seas.
9. And the waters were collected in the seas under the heavens.
10. And the man will be seen between the waste and the abyss.
11. God dwelt in the heavens above the earth and the seas.
12. The dry land is beneath the heavens.

PART ONE — LESSON THIRTEEN

I. Reading Lesson — Gen. 1:11–13.

62.   תַּ דְ שֵׁ א

SH DH T
ē   ă
(she) shall cause to spring forth.

This is the causative feminine imperfect, the תּ indicating feminine as in No. 56. The —ַ in the preformative syllable (the syllable containing the consonant and vowel indicating stem and gender) indicates this stem. This stem is called the Hifil. Cf. No. 25.

63.   דֶּ֫שֶׁא
    ' SH D
    ĕ é
    grass

This noun is from the root דשא as is the above verb form. The ⸺ is the same as in מְרַחֶפֶת, אֶרֶץ, and עֶרֶב. ⸺ in the ultimate syllable is used to aid pronunciation.

64.   עֵ֫שֶׂב
    V S '
    ĕ ē
    herb

A noun similar in form to above also using ⸺ in the ultimate syllable to aid pronunciation.

65.   מַזְרִיעַ
    ' R Z M
    (ă) î ă
    causing to seed

This is the Hifil (causative) participle, the same as מַבְדִּיל (No. 41). Note the use of pathach furtive under final ע. The use of ⸺ is as in No. 62 to indicate causative stem. The '⸺ is also used in the perfect, imperfect, infinitive construct and participle as the *stem vowel*.

66.   זֶ֫רַע
    ' R Z
    ă é
    seed

This noun is from the root זרע as is the above participle. Note the use of ⸺ as in No. 63, but ⸺ instead of ⸺ under ר because gutturals prefer "a" class vowels. See p. 39, II, 3, a.

67.   עֵץ
    TS '
    ē
    tree of

This noun is in the construct state used with the following noun.

68. פְּרִי
R P
î ⓔ
fruit

This noun is in the absolute state used with the preceding noun. See p. 10, II, 3.

69. עֹשֶׂה פְּרִי
R P P H S '
î ⓔ ě ō
fruit making

This verb is the Kal (simple active) participle of the verb עָשָׂה ("to do or make.") The daghes-forte in the פ of the following noun is called daghes̆-forte conjunctive. (See p. 39, II, 2.)

70. לְמִינוֹ
N M L
ô î ⓔ
his kind to

The final וֹ is the short form of the pronominal suffix, third, masculine singular.

71. זַרְעוֹ־בוֹ
V –' R Z
ô ô ǎ
him in his seed

Both usages of וֹ are as in above noun. It is the third masculine singular suffix meaning *his* or *him*.

בוֹ = בְּ (in) + וֹ (him).

72. וַתּוֹצֵא
' TS T T W
ē ô ǎ
she caused to and come forth

This is a Hifil (causative) imperfect as תַּדְשֵׁא. The ־ has contracted with וֹ making וֹ, hence it is תוֹצֵא instead of תַּוְצֵא.

73. לְמִינֵהוּ
H N M L
û ē î ⓔ
his kind to

This is the same as No. 70 only the long form of the third masculine singular pronominal suffix הוּ is used. ־ֵ is used as a connecting vowel.

74. שְׁלִישִׁי
SH L SH
î î ⓔ
third

The ordinals from 2–10 use ־ִי thus differing from the cardinals. Cf. No. 52. (See p. 174, II, 1, d.)

II. Grammar

1. The daghes-forte in spirant consonants always doubles the hard
    sound. E. g. הַפָּנִים,(the faces).

2. When the daghes-forte is used in the initial letter of a word, the
    initial letter is joined to the final vowel of the preceding word
    and is called "dagheš-forte conjunctive." E. g. עֹשֶׂה פְּרִי,
    (making fruit). This occurs only after ־ַ, ה־ַ, or ה־ֶ.

3. The guttural consonants have three peculiarities, namely:

    a. They prefer "A" class vowels.

    b. They will not be doubled, i. e. take the dagheš-forte.

    c. They take compound Sheᵉwa, except ר.

4. Comparison of conjunction וְ and inseparable prepositions.

    a. Likeness — they are the same as to:

        (1) their original vowel . . . . כַּ לַ בַּ וַ
        (2) their resultant form . . . . כְּ לְ בְּ וְ
        (3) the change of Sheᵉwa to Hirek . . בִּרְקִיעַ וַיְהִי, לְ, כִּ
        (4) the change to corresponding
             short vowel . . . . לַעֲשׂוֹת וַאֲנִי, כַּ, בַּ
        (5) the change to tone-long Kamets . לָבְהוּ וָבְהוּ, בָּ, כָ

    b. Differences:

        (1) Waw Conjunctive does not take the vowel of the article,
             but the inseparable prepositions do.

        (2) Waw Conjunctive becomes וּ before labials and before
             consonants with simple Sheᵉwa, except before יְ. This
             does not apply to inseparable prepositions.

(3) Waw Conjunctive is sometimes used as a conversive with the Perfect of the verb. This does not apply to inseparable prepositions.

III. Vocabulary:

101. דָּשָׁא it sprouted

102. דֶּשֶׁא grass (m)

103. עֵשֶׂב herb (m)

104. זָרַע he sowed

105. מַזְרִיעַ causing to sow or seed (causative participle)

106. זֶרַע seed (m)

107. זְרֹעַ arm, strength, might (c)

108. פָּרָה it bore, brought forth

109. פְּרִי fruit (m)

110. עֵץ tree, wood (m)

111. מִין kind, species (m)

112. יָצָא he went out or forth

113. שְׁלִישִׁי third

114. שָׁלַח he sent

PART ONE — LESSON FOURTEEN

I. Reading Lesson — Gen. 1:14, 15.

75. מְאֹרֹת
     TH R ' M
     ô ô ⓔ
     luminaries

וֹ is written defectively in both instances, but they should be fully written as מְאוֹרֹת. This is the plural of מָאוֹר, the ־ָ reducing to ־ְ being antepretonic. (See p. 42, II, 1.)

76. בִּרְקִיעַ
     ' Q R B
     (ă) ĭ ⓔ ĭ
     expanse of (the) in

Construct form of רָקִיעַ, the ־ָ reducing to ־ְ as in above noun (No. 75). ־ְ under בְּ becomes ־ִ when standing before another ־ְ, (See p. 24, II, 1, b.)

Since ⸺ under ר is vocal it is called a medial Sheʷwa. (See p. 42, II, 2.)

77. לְהַבְדִּיל
L D V H L
î   ă ⓔ
cause a division   to

This is the Hifil (causative) infinitive construct since to it may be added prepositions and pronominal suffixes. Cf. with מַבְדִּיל (No. 41).

78. וְהָיוּ
Y H W
û ā ⓔ
they shall be   and

This is the Kal (simple active), perfect with the waw conversive which when used with the perfect is וְ. (See p. 43, II, 3.)

79. לְאֹתֹת
TH TH ' L
ô ô ⓔ
signs   for

Plural of אוֹת the feminine plural ending וֹת having been added. The vowels are defectively written but should be written fully as: אוֹתוֹת.

80. וּלְמוֹעֲדִים
M DH ' M L
î Ⓐ ô ⓔ û
seasons for and

Plural of מוֹעֵד, the masculine plural ending ים־ having been added. The ⸺ is reduced to ⸺ under the guttural. (See p. 39, II, 3, c.) The conjunction וְ becomes וּ before לְ. — Why? (See p. 35, II, 4, b.)

81. וּלְיָמִים
M M Y L
î ā ⓔ û
days for and

Plural of יוֹם though irregular as to the word itself, its masculine ending ים־ is regular.

82. וְשָׁנִים
M N SH W
î ā ⓔ
years and

Plural of שָׁנָה, a masculine noun which in the singular has a feminine ending.

83.   לִמְאוֹרֹת   Feminine ending should be written וֹת.

TH R ' M L   Why the — under ל and vocal Sh°wa

ô ô ⓔ ǐ

luminaries   for   — under מ? (See p. 42, II, 1, 2.)

84.   לְהָאִיר   Like No. 77 this is the Hifil infinitive

R ' H L   construct. It is from the verb אוֹר and

î ā ⓔ

cause to shine   to   the — under ה has become —. Why?

           (See p. 15, II, 4, a.)

II. Grammar

1. The reduction of a full vowel to Sh°wa.

Reduction is the process by which a vowel is minimized to the shortest pronunciation possible, a short grunt. This occurs in verbs when the final short vowel loses its accent, or tone, as in adding personal terminations, or pronominal suffixes (e. g. תִּקְטְלִי becomes תִּקְטְלִי); and in nouns when the penultimate vowel in an open syllable is two or more places from the tone, due to formation of the construct state or adding of personal terminations, or pronominal suffixes. E. g. דְּבָרִי becomes דְּבָרִי (my word).

2. The so-called "medial Sh°wa".

Sometimes Sh°wa reduced from a full vowel seems to waver between two syllables. It cannot be ignored and treated as silent because it is reduced from a full vowel. It seems to close one syllable and open the following one. E. g. בְּרָקִיעַ in the construct state becomes בִּרְקִיעַ, the Sh°wa under ב becoming — since there cannot be two consecutive vocal Sh°was.

3 The Waw Conversive with the Perfect.

Begin in

←——————————

the Imperfect, and to continue in the Imperfect with the conjunction, use the Perfect form with וְ, or imperfect with וַ.

E. g. וְהָיוּ —"and they will be."

וַיְהִיוּ —"and they will be."

See page 16 for use of the Waw Conversive with the
Imperfect.

4. Review constantly all rules and illustrations of grammar.

III. Vocabulary.

115. מָאוֹר luminary (m)

116. הָאִיר cause to shine
(causative in-
finitive of אוֹר
[No. 35] used
with לְ)

117. הַבְדִּיל cause to divide
(same as above
from בָּדַל
[No. 43])

118. מוֹעֵד season (m)

119. מוֹעָדָה appointed place
refuge (f)

120. שָׁנָה he repeated,
changed

121. שָׁנָה year (f)

122. אוֹת sign (f)

PART ONE — Lesson Fifteen

I. Be prepared to write from memory all rules of grammar and illustrations to date.

II. Sentences to be translated into Hebrew and written in exercise book:

1. The herb (is) making seed according to his kind.

2. And he divided the dry land from the sea in which (was) water.

3. The man saw the fruit tree which (was) in the midst of the place.

4. The earth will cause to go forth grass for the man.

5. He saw the light in the expanse of the waters.

6. God created the luminaries to cause to divide between the night and the day.

7. And he made the sun and it will be a sign of the day.

8. The man saw the sign of the night which is the moon.

9. God created the sign of the day and called it the sun.

10. In seasons the earth will spring forth the fruit tree which makes fruit according to his kind.

11. The man saw the grass, the herb, the tree, the sun, the moon, and the stars in place.

12. God ruled the stars in the expanse of the heavens.

PART ONE — LESSON SIXTEEN

I. Reading Lesson — Gen. 1:16, 17.

85.　　וַיַּעַשׂ
　　S ' Y Y W
　　ă ă　　ă
　　he made　and

This is a shortened form of the Kal imperfect used with the waw conversive as וַיִּרְא (No. 22).

86.　　שְׁנֵי
　　N SH
　　ê ⓔ
　　two of

The construct form of the numeral שְׁנַיִם.

87.　　הַגְּדֹלִים
　　M L DH G G H
　　î ô ⓔ　　ă
　　great　the

An adjective with the masculine plural ending ‍ים‍ָ. Note the regular use of the article and that ô is written defectively. The singular masculine form is גָּדֹל. When the plural ending was added the ‍ָ under ג being an open antepretonic syllable reduced to ‍ְ. See p. 46, I I, 1, as to rule for adjectives.

88.　　לְמֶמְשֶׁלֶת
　　TH L SH M M L
　　ĕ é　　ĕ ⓔ
　　ruling of　for

Construct form of the feminine singular noun מֶמְשָׁלָה and used with the preposition לְ.

89.　　הַקָּטֹן
　　N T Q Q H
　　ō ā　　ă
　　small　the

Masculine singular adjective used in agreement with its noun.

90.　　הַכּוֹכָבִים
　　M V K K K H
　　î ā ô　　ă
　　stars　the

Masculine noun with the regular plural ending ‍ים‍ָ.

91.   וַיִּתֶּן

   N T T Y Y W
   ē   ĭ   ă
   he gave and

The Kal imperfect of נָתַן used with the waw conversive. The נ being weak as in יִקְּוּ, has been assimilated which is shown by the daghes̆-forte in ת. Cf. Nos. 47 and 53.

92.   אֹתָם

   M TH ʼ
   ā   ô
   them

The short form of the 3rd plural masculine pronominal suffix uses אֹת which is a form of אֵת (the sign of the definite and direct object) which is used with pronominal suffixes. See chart on p. 54 especially as to the use of the pronominal suffix with אֵת.

II. Grammar

1. Rule for adjectives.

Adjectives follow the nouns they modify and agree in gender, number, and definiteness. E. g. הָאִישׁ הַטּוֹב (the good man).

הָאִשָּׁה הַטּוֹבָה (the good woman).

2. Conjugation of verbs.

The treatment of verbs is similar to other Semitic languages. The verb stems are formed on the verb root and by reduplicating or repeating one or more of its radicals and by use of prefixes. Action, mood, person, number, and gender are expressed by addition of prefixes and suffixes. Pronominal suffixes as objects are attached directly to the verb with resultant vowel changes. There are no tenses in the sense of making *time* primal; each stem with its Perfect, Imperfect, Infinitives, Imperatives, and

Participles expresses *action* of every necessary kind. The time element is expressed by the context as to past, present or future.

III. Vocabulary

123. גָּדַל he was great, mighty

124. גָּדוֹל great, mighty

125. קָטֹן small, little, young

126. מֶמְשָׁלָה dominion, rule (f)

127. מֶמְשֶׁלֶת (const.) dominion or rule of

128. שְׁנַיִם two (const. שְׁנֵי)

129. שֶׁמֶשׁ sun (m) and (f)

130. יָרֵחַ moon (m)

131. כּוֹכָב star (m)

PART ONE — Lesson Seventeen

I. Reading Lesson — Gen. 1:18–20.

93.   וְלִמְשֹׁל
   L SH M L W
   ō ⓔ ĭ ⓔ
   rule to and

Kal infinitive construct of מָשַׁל (he ruled). Both Sh°was are vocal, the ⟙ under מ being a medial Sh°wa. Why? (See p. 42, II, 2, and p. 24, II, 1, b).

94.   וּלְהַבְדִּיל
   L D V H L
   î   ă ⓔ û
  cause to divide to and

Hifil (causative) infinitive construct of בָּדַל (he divided). The ⟙ under an inseparable preposition must be preceded by conjunction וּ.

95.   רְבִיעִי
   ‘ V R
   î î ⓔ
   fourth

A numeral. Cf. No. 74.

96.   **יִשְׁרְצוּ**
TS R SH Y
û ⓔ   ĭ
Let (they shall) swarm

Kal imperfect 3rd masculine plural of **שָׁרַץ** (he swarmed). — under **שׁ** is a syllable divider. Why?

97.   **שֶׁרֶץ**
TS R SH
ĕ é
swarm

This noun is from the root **שׁרץ** as is the above verb (No. 96). The — is the tone long "a" class vowel as used in **דֶּשֶׁא, אֶרֶץ**. Cf. No. 63. The — is a short ĕ used to facilitate pronunciation and because of its usage this class of nouns is called Segholates. See II, 1 of this lesson.

98.   **נֶפֶשׁ**
SH PH N
ĕ é
soul of

This noun is from the root **נפשׁ** meaning "to breathe, to live." It is another Segholate noun as above, No. 97. It is in the construct state used with the following noun. The absolute and construct form of Segholate masculine singular are the same.

99.   **חַיָּה**
H Y Y CH
ā ă
life

A feminine noun from the root **חיי** meaning "to live." The feminine ending is **הָ**.

100.   **וְעוֹף**
PH ' W
ô ⓔ
fowl and

A masculine noun from the root **עוף** meaning "to fly." **ף** is the final form of **פ**.

101.   **יְעוֹפֵף**
PH PH ' Y
ē ô ⓔ
let fly

This is an intensive imperfect masculine singular from the above verb root. Cf. No. 100. This intensive is not the usual regular form and found only in two types of irregular verbs.

II. Grammar

1. Nouns called Segholates.

These are nouns originating from one original short vowel, and a Seghol has been added to form an ultmate closed syllable in order to facilitate pronunciation. The noun received its name from the use of this helping vowel. The original short vowel receiving the tone becomes tone-long, as — becoming —; and — becoming —; and — becoming —. E. g. אֶרֶץ became אֶרֶץ, עֹשֶׁב became עֵשֶׂב.

Note the many nouns of this class that have been used in the reading.

2. Personal Pronouns.

He	הוּא	They (m)	הֵמָּה, הֵם
She	הִיא	They (f)	הֵנָּה, הֵן
Thou (m)	אַתָּה	Ye (m)	אַתֶּם
Thou (f)	אַתְּ	Ye (f)	אַתֵּנָה, אַתֵּן
I	אֲנִי, אָנֹכִי	We	נַחְנוּ, אֲנַחְנוּ

Practice to pronounce as well as to write the above pronouns. The knowledge of pronouns is basic.

III. Vocabulary

132.	שָׁרַץ he swarmed	137.	חַיָּה life, beast (f)
133.	שֶׁרֶץ swarm (m)	138.	עוּף to fly
134.	נָפַשׁ he breathed	139.	עוֹף fowl (m)
135.	נֶפֶשׁ soul, breath (f)	140.	רְבִיעִי fourth
136.	חָיָה he lived		

PART ONE — LESSON EIGHTEEN

I. Be prepared to write from memory the personal pronouns.

II. Review reading and grammar of past two lessons.

III. Sentences to be translated into Hebrew and written in exercise book:

1. God made the small luminary for the ruling of the night.
2. The great luminary gave light for the earth.
3. The moon and the stars will be seen in the heavens above the earth.
4. I (am) on the dry land and thou (art) in the heavens.
5. The earth will cause to sprout forth grass and herbs for life upon the place.
6. The man saw the fowls which will fly upon the faces of the expanse of the earth.
7. God gave them to rule in the night and in the day.
8. In good seasons the fruit tree will give great fruit.
9. The good man saw the light of the stars above the earth.
10. God made the good man for ruling of the earth and seas.
11. The swarm swarmed beneath the waters of the seas.
12. The great man saw the earth which God created.

PART ONE — LESSON NINETEEN

I. Reading Lesson — Gen. 1:21–24.

102.   וַיִּבְרָא   Kal imperfect 3rd masculine singular
     ' R V Y Y W   with waw conversive from בָּרָא (he cre-
      ā   ĭ   ă   ated) cf. וַיִּקְרָא (No. 29).
   created he and

103. הַתַּנִּינִם
M N N N T T H
î î ă ă
sea-monsters the

A plural masculine noun from the root תנן meaning "to stretch." Both hireks are unchangeably long though the last one is defectively written.

104. כָּל
L K
ŏ
every

The ⸗ (ō) is shortened to ⸗ (ŏ) because by use of the makkef the syllable is unaccented. Note this first use of Kamets-hatuf.

105. הָרֹמֶשֶׂת
TH S M R H
ĕ é ô ā
creeping the

The feminine form of the Kal participle, the ⸗ (ô) is nearly always written defectively. Note the use of ⸗ (é) and the use of the article before weak gutterals. (See p. 19, II, 3, c.)

106. שָׁרְצוּ
TS R SH
û ⓔ ā
(they) swarmed

Kal perfect plural common of שָׁרַץ. (See No. 96.)

107. לְמִינֵהֶם
M H N M L
ĕ ê î ⓔ
their kinds to

The 3rd per. mas. plural pronominal suffix הֶם is used with its connecting vowel ⸗ (ê) which is defectively written. It should be ־ֵי. Cf. No. 73.

108. כָּנָף
PH N K
ā ā
wing

A feminine noun singular absolute. Both vowels are tone long hence the construct form is כְּנַף.

109. וַיְבָרֶךְ
K R V Y Y W
ĕ ā ⓔ ă
he blessed and

The Piel (intensive) active 3rd person mas. singular imperfect with the waw conversive. ⸗ (ⓔ) is a medial Shᵉwa due to ' as in וַיְהִי not being doubled since only a Sheʷa supports it. The ⸯ in final ךְ is always a syllable divider. The final ⸯ is due to shifting of Tone (accent) to the penult. Why?

110. לֶאמֹר
R M ' L
ō ê
say to

אֱמֹר is the Kal infinitive construct and is used with לְ. Before ⸯ לְ becomes לֶ (See p. 24, II, 1, c) becoming לֶאמֹר. The ⸯ and ⸯ contract making ⸯ (ê) unchangeably long though always defectively written.

111. פְּרוּ
R P
û ⓔ
be ye fruitful

Kal imperative masculine plural of פָּרָה.

112. וּרְבוּ
V R
û ⓔ û
multiply ye and

A plural form as No. 111 and from the verb רָבָה (he multiplied). Note use of וּ before רְ. Why?

113. וּמִלְאוּ
' L M
û ĭ û
fill ye and

A plural form as No. 111 and from מָלֵא (he was full). Note use of וּ before מִ. Why?

114. יֶרֶב
V R Y
ĕ ĭ
let multiply

Kal imperfect (short form) masculine, singular 3rd person from same verb as No. 112.

115. חֲמִישִׁי
SH M CH
î î Ⓐ
fifth

A numeral. Cf. No. 74.

116. לְמִינָהּ
H N M L
â î ⓔ
her kind to

The 3rd feminine singular pronominal suffix הָ— is used having its vowel —ָ (ā) contracted with its connecting vowel —ָ (ā) making הָ— (â). The הּ retains its consonantal form by the use of the Mappik, as הּ.

117. בְּהֵמָה
H M H B
ā ē ⓔ
cattle

A feminine singular noun in the absolute state.

118. וָרֶמֶשׂ
S M R W
ĕ é ā
creeper and

A masculine singular Segholate noun. Why called Segholate? See No. 97. —ָ under וֹ is due to standing before a tone (accented) syllable.

119. וְחַיְתוֹ
TH Y CH W
ô ⓒ ă ⓔ
beast of and

An archaic construct form of חַיָּה. The usual construct form is חַיַּת. The —ְ under יּ is medial Sheʷa, hence no daghes-lene in ת.

II. Grammar

1. Note the first use of Kamets-hatuf (—ָ, ŏ) in כָּל. It is recognized by being in an unaccented closed syllable.

2. The intensive stem of the verb.

וַיְבָרֶךְ, meaning "and to be blessed" is built on the intensive active stem of the verb, called Piel. This stem is used to express the intensifying or repetition of an action, and the simple producing or causing of an action. Note carefully and record when this stem is used in connection with God or Jehovah.

3. The pronominal suffixes.

	Separate forms	With אֵת	With בְּ and לְ	With כְּ	With מִן
Sg. 3 m	הוּ, וֹ	אֹתוֹ	בּוֹ	כָּמֹהוּ	מִמֶּנּוּ
3 f	הָ	אֹתָהּ	בָּהּ	כָּמֹוֹהָ	מִמֶּנָּה
2 m	ךָ	אֹתְךָ, אֹתָךְ	בֶּךָ, בְּךָ	כָּמֹוֹךָ	מִמְּךָ
					מִמְּךָ
2 f	ךְ	אֹתָךְ	בָּךְ	—	מִמֵּךְ
1 c	נִי, ־ִי	אֹתִי	בִּי	כָּמֹונִי	מִמֶּנִּי
Pl.					
3 m	ם, הֶם	אֹתָם, אֶתְהֶם	בָּם, בָּהֶם	כְּמֹוֹהֶם, כָּהֶם	מֵהֶם
3 f	ן, הֶן	אֹתָן, אֶתְהֶן	בָּהֶן	כָּהֵנָּה	מֵהֶן
					מֵהֵנָּה
2 m	כֶם	אֶתְכֶם	בָּכֶם	כְּמֹוֹכֶם, כָּכֶם	מִכֶּם
2 f	כֶן	—	בָּכֶן	—	מִכֶּן
1 c	נוּ	אֹתָנוּ	בָּנוּ	כָּמֹונוּ	מִמֶּנּוּ

a. כֶם, כֵן, הֶם, and הֶן always receive the accent and are called "grave" or "heavy"; all the others are called "light."

b. ־ִי is used with nouns and נִי with verbs.

c. הֶם and הֶן are used with nouns, chiefly plural; ם and ן are used with verbs and singular nouns.

III. Vocabulary

141. תָּנַן he stretched

142. תַּנִּין sea monster, serpent, great fish (m)

143. רָמַשׂ he crept

144. רֶמֶשׂ creeper (m) (only collective)

145. כֹּל all, every

146. כָּנָף wing (f)

147. רָבָה he multiplied
148. מָלֵא he was full
   (adj. same in
   form)

149. מְלֹא fullness (m)
150. חֲמִישִׁי fifth
151. בְּהֵמָה cattle (f) (Const.
   בֶּהֱמַת)

PART ONE — LESSON TWENTY

I. Reading Lesson — Gen. 1:25–27.

120.   הָאֲדָמָה
    H M DH ' H
    ā   ā⊕ ā
    ground the

A feminine noun as seen from feminine ending, ָה. Note that א uses ־ֲ. Why?

121.   נַעֲשֶׂה
    H S ' N
    ĕ ⊕ ă
    Let us make

Kal 1st person plural imperfect from עָשָׂה (he made).

122.   אָדָם
    M DH '
    ā   ā
    man

A masculine singular noun. Always note quantity of nouns. Both vowels are tone long.

123.   בְּצַלְמֵנוּ
    N M L TS B
    û   ē   ă ⊕
    our image in

The accent mark ־ used is disjunctive and therefore the צ in following word must have a daghes̆-lene. The absolute singular form is צֶלֶם (image).

124.   כִּדְמוּתֵנוּ
    N TH M DH K
    û   ē û   ⊕ ĭ
    our according to likeness

The ־ under ד is a medial Shᵉwa. נו also used in No. 123 is the first person plural pronominal suffix.

125.   וְיִרְדּוּ   Kal 3rd person masculine imperfect with
     D R Y W   conjunction וְ from רָדָה (he ruled).
     û   ĭ ⓔ
     they shall rule and

126.   בִּדְגַת   Construct form of the feminine noun
     TH GH DH V   דָּגָה (fish). Note that — under ד is
     ă   ⓔ ĭ   a medial Sheʷa. Why? Note the four
     fish of in   spirant letters have no daghes̆-lene.

127.   הָרֹמֵשׂ   Kal participle from רָמַשׂ (he crept)
     S M R H   used as an adjective. — is וֹ but written
     ē ô ā   defectively.
     creeping the

128.   בְּצַלְמוֹ   The same noun as No. 123 used the
     M L TS B   short form of the 3rd per. masculine
     ô   ă ⓔ   pronominal suffix.
     his image in

129.   אֹתוֹ   The short form of the 3rd person singular
     TH ’   masculine pronominal suffix used with
     ô   ô   אֵת as No. 92.
     him

130.   זָכָר   A masculine singular noun. Cf. אָדָם
     R K Z   as to form.
     ā ā
     male

131.   וּנְקֵבָה   A feminine singular noun as noted from
     H V Q N   the feminine ending הָ. Note that
     ā ē ⓔ û   the conjunction is written as וּ. Why?
     female and

II. Grammar

1. Disjunctive accents.

There are eighteen disjunctive accents, which when used disjoin the sentence so that an initial spirant letter must have a Dagheš-lene. The accents can be noted in this way. This is sufficient for the beginner to know.

2. The demonstrative pronouns.

a. זֶה, this (m); זֹאת, this (f); אֵלֶּה, these (m and f).

b. The third person singular and plural personal pronouns are used to represent "that" and "those" respectively.

c. Rules for usage

The demonstrative pronouns "this" and "that" may be pronouns or adjectives. When pronouns, they do not take the article and the order is as in English. When they are adjectives, their noun is definite, and they stand after the noun they modify. When used with another adjective, the demonstrative stands last.

E. g.

זֶה הָאִישׁ׃ — This (is) the man.
זֶה הָאִישׁ הַטּוֹב׃ — This (is) the good man.
הָאִישׁ הַזֶּה׃ — This man.
הָאִישׁ הַטּוֹב הַזֶּה׃ — This good man.

III. Vocabulary

152. אָדָם man (m)

153. אֲדָמָה ground (f)

154. צֶלֶם image (m)

155. דָּמָה he was like, similar

156. דְּמוּת likeness (f)

157. רָדָה he tread down, ruled

158. דָּגָה fish (f)

159. זָכָר male (m)

160. נְקֵבָה female (f)

PART ONE — Lesson Twenty-One

I. Review reading to date.

II. Review the personal and demonstrative pronouns and pronominal suffixes.

III. Sentences to be translated into Hebrew and written in exercise book:

1. God gave every beast of the ground food according to its kind.

2. The fish will be collected in the great seas.

3. These are the sea monsters which the man saw in the sea.

4. God created man and woman and said to them, Have dominion in all the fowl and beasts of the earth.

5. God gave the fruit, the grass, and the herb to the cattle for food.

6. The man saw every creeping creeper upon the ground.

7. He made the male and the female according to His likeness and in His image.

8. All which God had done was exceedingly good.

9. God created every beast of the earth according to its kind.

10. God said to the man upon the sixth day to rule in the earth and in the seas.

11. The man will cause to go forth the cattle and the creeper and the beast of the earth and the fowl of the heavens.

12. Those are the cattle which the man gave to God.

PART ONE — LESSON TWENTY-TWO

I. Reading Lesson — Gen.1:28–31.

132. וְכִבְשֻׁהָ
H SH V KH W
ā û   ĭ ⓔ
it subdue ye and

The Kal 2nd person plural masculine imperative form, from כָּבַשׁ (he subdued). —ֻ is a defective writing of וּ (û) which is the plural sign.

133. וּרְדוּ
DH R
û ⓔ û
rule ye and

The accent mark ″ indicates a disjunctive accent and hence the following בּ has a daghes̆-lene.

134. הִנֵּה
H N H
ē ĭ
behold

An interjection.

135. נָתַתִּי
T T TH N
î   ă ā
I have given

The Kal first person singular perfect from נָתַן (he gave). נ is a weak consonant and will not close a syllable unless doubled or final in a word. Hence it is assimilated and shown by the daghes̆-forte in תּ.

136. לָכֶם
M K L
ĕ ā
you to

The 2nd per. mas. plural pronominal suffix כֶם used with לְ. Due to these second person plural suffix having always the accent it is to be noticed that the inseparable prepositions בְּ, לְ always use —ָ.

137.　זֹרֵעַ
'　R Z
(ă)　ē ô
seeding

Kal participle of זָרַע (he sowed or seeded). Note use of pathach furtive. Why?

138.　לְאָכְלָה
H L KH ' L
ā　ŏ ⓔ
food for

This noun is from the root אכל (eat). The ⟍ is not ā, but ŏ. Why?

139.　רוֹמֵשׂ
S M R
ē ô
creeping

Kal participle of רָמַשׂ (he crept). Note that ô is fully written which is unusual in these participles. It is more often written defectively.

140.　יֶרֶק
K R Y
ĕ é
greeness of

The masculine segholate noun used in the construct state. Why?

141.　מְאֹד
DH ' M
ô ⓔ
exceedingly (or) very

A noun meaning "force or might" used as an adverb. ⟍ is ô but is written in this word defectively.

142.　הַשִּׁשִּׁי
SH SH SH SH H
î　ĭ　ă
sixth the

A numeral used with the article. Cf. No. 74.

II.　Grammar

1. The weakness of נ.

נ when closing a syllable, will be assimilated and shown by a Daghes̆-forte in the following consonant. If following consonant is a guttural, rules for weak and strong gutturals apply.

E. g. נָתַתִּי for נָתַנְתִּי.

2. The article and the construct state.

A noun in the construct state *never* takes the article, its definiteness depending upon the following noun in the absolute. E. g. אוֹר הַשָּׁמַיִם *the* light of *the* heavens.

3. The interrogative pronouns.

a. מִי, who; מָה, what.

b. They always introduce a sentence.

c. מִי is indeclinable and introduces a sentence without the use of Makkef. Note לְמִי, to whom.

d. Rules for מָה

    (1) Before non-gutturals   — מַה־זֶּה What (is) this?

    (2) Before weak gutturals   — מָה־אֵלֶּה What (are) these?

    (3) Before strong gutturals — מַה־הִיא What (is) it?

    (4) Before gutturals with ָ — מֶה־עָשָׂה What has he done?

III. Vocabulary Lesson

161.	כָּבַשׁ he subdued	167.	מַאֲכֶלֶת knife (f)
162.	הִנֵּה behold	168.	יֶרֶק greenness (m)
163.	אָכַל he ate	169.	יָרָק greens, herbs (m)
164.	אֹכֵל eating (m)	170.	מְאֹד very, exceed-
165.	אָכְלָה food (f)		ingly
166.	מַאֲכָל food (m)	171.	שִׁשִּׁי sixth

PART ONE — LESSON TWENTY-THREE

Review Lesson:

1. Review Gen. 1:1–25 for examination.

2. Review all grammar as given in this syllabus.

3. Final word test will be taken from words Nos. 123–171.

PART TWO — LESSON ONE

I. Reading Lesson — Gen. 2:1–3.

143. וַיְכֻלּוּ

(they) were and completed

Intensive passive called Pual, imperfect third masculine plural with waw conversive from כָּלָה (he ended or finished). The Pual form here means "it was completed or thoroughly finished."

144. צְבָאָם

their host

צָבָא is a masculine noun meaning "host" used with the pronominal suffix ם. It uses the connecting vowel ◌ָ and has the accent hence ◌ָ under צ reduced to ◌ְ.

145. וַיְכַל

he finished and

Piel imperfect third masculine singular used with waw conversive, from the root כלה (to end or finish). This form is a short form regular imperfect of יְכַלֶּה. Cf. No. 143.

146. הַשְּׁבִיעִי

seventh the

An ordinal used as an adjective modifying בַּיּוֹם. Note rule for adjective, p. 46, II, 1.

147. מְלַאכְתּוֹ

his work

Construct form of מְלָאכָה. A feminine singular noun and used with the masculine singular pronominal suffix וֹ.

148. וַיִּשְׁבֹּת
he rested   and

Kal impf. 3rd masculine singular used with waw conversive from שָׁבַת (he ceased, rested).

149. וַיְקַדֵּשׁ
he sanctified   and

Piel impf. 3rd masculine singular used with waw conversive from קָדַשׁ (he separated). In Piel this verb means "he sanctified." The daghes-forte in the middle radical is the sign of the intensives. Cf. Nos. 109 and 145.

150. לַעֲשׂוֹת
make   to

Kal inf. const. of verb root עשׂה (do or make). Note use of ◌ֲ which is used with gutturals. Why is ◌ַ used under לְ? See p. 24, II, 1. c.

II. Grammar

1. Hebrew verbs.

Review p. 25, sec. II, 2; and p. 46, sec. II, 2 for conjugation of verbs.

There are seven stems which show type of action:

(1) Kal — simple active — קָטַל — he killed

(2) Nifal — simple passive — נִקְטַל — he was killed
and middle

(3) Piel — intensive active — קִטֵּל — he massacred

(4) Pual — intensive passive — קֻטַל — he was massacred

(5) Hithpael — intensive middle — הִתְקַטֵּל — he committed
and reciprocal   suicide

(6) Hifil — causative active — הִקְטִיל — he caused to kill

(7) Hofal — causative passive — הָקְטַל — he was caused to kill

The above names, except Kal, are the 3d. sing. masc. Perfects of the former paradigm verb פָּעַל,(to do).

2. The regular verb (Strong).

A verb is called strong when none of its three root letters is a guttural or a weak consonant, as ו, י initial נ; or when the second and third root letters are not the same.

3. Conjugation of Kal Perfect of קָטַל. The Perfect in any stem expresses complete action.

(1) he killed — קָטַל.

(2) she killed — קָטְלָה — קָטַל+ה֥ regular feminine sign, formerly ת.

(3) thou (m) killedst — קָטַלְתָּ — קָטַל+תָּ from pronoun אַתָּה.

(4) thou (f) killedst — קָטַלְתְּ — קָטַל+תְּ from pronoun אַתְּ.

(5) I killed — קָטַלְתִּי — קָטַל+תִּי regular affix, 1st person in all perfects.

(6) they killed — קָטְלוּ, קָטַל plus ו regular plural sign.

(7) ye (m) killed — קְטַלְתֶּם, קָטַל plus תֶּם from pronoun אַתֶּם.

(8) ye (f) killed — קְטַלְתֶּן, קָטַל plus תֶּן from pronoun אַתֶּן.

(9) we killed — קָטַלְנוּ, קָטַל plus נו from pronoun נַחְנוּ.

Before vowel affixes, the stem vowel (בֶ) is reduced to Sh⁰wa (בְ). See rule for reduction, p. 42, sec. II, 1. תֶּם and תֶּן being heavy affixes (from pronominal suffix), always have the tone; therefore the pretonic vowel בָ, ante-pretonic, is reduced to Shᵉwa.

The term "affix" is used for additions for gender and number, and "suffix" for regular pronominal suffixes.

4. The stative verb which indicates a state or a condition, uses
בֵ, בֻ, or בֹ. The conjugation is the same as the regular perfect, only the stem vowel remains constant as found subject to reduction before vowel affixes.

E. g.   כָּבֵד —(be heavy)

              כָּבְדָה

              כָּבַדְתָּ   etc.

5. Learn thoroughly the affixes for gender and number, for those are the same in all Perfects in all classes of verbs.

III. Vocabulary Lesson

172.	כָּלָה he ended, finished	177.	שֶׁבֶת rest, quietness (f)
173.	מַלְאָךְ messenger, angel (m)	178.	שַׁבָּת rest, Sabbath (c)
174.	מְלָאכָה work, service, mission (f)	179.	קָדַשׁ he separated
		180.	קֹדֶשׁ holiness (m)
175.	צָבָא host, army (m)	181.	קָדֵשׁ consecrated,
176.	שָׁבַת he ceased, rested		devoted
		182.	שְׁבִיעִי seventh

PART TWO — LESSON TWO

I. Reading Lesson — Gen. 2:4–6.

151.   אֵ לֶּ ה
these

Common gender, in usage the plural of זֶה and זֹאת. Cf. p. 57, II, 2.

152.   תּוֹלְדוֹת
generations of

Absolute and construct form (cf. vocabulary list No. 185). The latter is the usage here. Why is daghes-lene missing in דֹ? See p. 15, II, 3.

153.   בְּהִבָּרְאָם
their being   in created

Nifal (passive) inf. const. to which prepositions and suffixes may be added. The small הֹ is a traditional form kept by the Massoretic scholars.

154.   יְהוָֹה
Jehovah

See p. 67, II, 1.

155.   שִׂיחַ
shrub of

Singular masculine noun used in the construct state. Cf. 152.

156.   הַשָּׂדֶה
field   the

Masculine singular noun used with the article.

157.   טֶרֶם
not yet

An adverb.

158.   יִצְמָח
(it) will sprout forth

Kal impft. masc. singular of verb root צמח (sprout forth). The ־ַ became ־ָ because of the pausal accent.

159.   לֹא
not

A negative. The vowel is וֹ (ô) but here defectively written.

160. הִמְטִיר   Hifil (causative active) 3rd masc. singu-
(*he*) *had caused to*   lar perf. of verb root מטר (rain). Note
rain   that the perfect uses ⁻ under preformative Consonant while the impf.
infin. const. and participle have ⁻.

161. אַיִן   A noun but often used as a predicate.
nothing   "There is or was not."

162. לַעֲבֹד   Kal infinitive construct, verb root of
serve to   עבד. Cf. No. 150.

163. וְאֵד   Masculine singular noun.
mist and

164. יַעֲלֶה   Kal impf. 3rd masc. singular of verb
(*he*) *used to go up*   root עלה. The imperfect here is used
to express customary action. The tense
or time element is dependent upon the
context.

165. מִן   The full writing *should be* used only
from   before the article.

166. וְהִשְׁקָה   Hifil perf. 3rd masc. singular used with
used to cause and   the waw conversive וְ and expressing
to drink   therefore customary action as No. 164.
It is from verb root שקה (drink).

II. The First Use of the Name of Jehovah

This is the personal name of God. The original voweling of
this name has been lost but is thought to have been יַהְוֶה.
The later Jews in their reverence for this name never pro-

nounce it and substitute the word אֲדֹנָי, Lord. The present voweling comes from this word, Lord, and was thus written by the Jews to remind them to pronounce אֲדֹנָי instead. It is translated "LORD" in the King James Version and in the Revised Standard Version.

III. Grammar

1. Conjugation of the simple passive and middle stem, Nifal.

This stem is indicated by a נ prefixed and given vowel ◌ָ. This vowel standing in a closed and unaccented performative syllable becomes ◌ִ. E. g. נָקְטַל becoming נִקְטַל. This thinning of ◌ָ to ◌ִ is called attenuation and occurs in closed preformative syllables with ◌ָ except the Hifil impft., imper., infs. and participle as well as with gutturals. It follows the order of the Kal, having נִק for ק.

IV. Vocabulary Lesson

183. יָלַד he brought forth
184. יֶלֶד lad, boy (m)
185. תּוֹלְדוֹת generations (f)
       (never found
       in the sing.)
186. יְהֹוָה Jehovah
       (see p. 67)
187. אַיִן there is not,
       nothing
188. טֶרֶם not yet
189. לֹא not
190. אֵד mist (m)

191. שָׂדֶה field (m)
192. שִׂיחַ shrub (m)
193. צָמַח it sprouted
194. צֶמַח sprout (m)
195. שָׁקָה he drank
196. שִׁקּוּ drink (m)
197. מָטַר it rained
198. מָטָר rain (m)
199. עָלָה he went up,
       ascended
200. עֹלָה burnt offering
       (f)

PART TWO — Lesson Three

I. Review thoroughly the Kal and Nifal stems of קָטַל.

II. There will be a weekly vocabulary review either oral or
    written of words assigned in previous two lessons. Review
    words No. 172–200.

III. Sentences to be translated into Hebrew and written in exercise
     book:

1. And the cattle and the fowl and all which God made
    were collected in one place.
2. There was no man on the dry land to serve the ground.
3. God caused it to rain from the heavens on the sixth day.
4. Yet this man and that soul will not be seen in this earth.
5. And the beast and the creeper saw the stars from that
    place in which they were.
6. He will bless the day because he rested from his great
    work.
7. God sanctified the great luminaries and their host which
    are in the midst of the heavens.
8. And the earth and the stars and all which God had
    created were completed.
9. God saw all which he had created and he said that it
    was very good.
10. God rested on that day, the seventh, which he sanctified.
11. The mist used to go up and water all the dry ground.
12. The shrub had not yet sprouted in the field because
    Jehovah had not caused to rain.

PART TWO — Lesson Four

I. Reading Lesson — Gen. 2:7–9.

167.   וַיִּיצֶר
he formed and

Kal imperfect 3rd masculine singular with waw conversive from verb root יצר. Note — under צ due to waw conversive drawing accent because pre-formative syllable is open. Cf. וַיֹּאמֶר and וַיַּעַשׂ.

168.   עָפָר
dust

This form is the absolute. The construct is עֲפַר. Why?

169.   וַיִּפַּח
he breathed and

Kal imperfect 3rd masculine singular from verb root נפח (breathe). The daghešׁ-forte in פ is to show the assimilation of נ.

170   בְּאַפָּיו
his nostrils in

Construct plural of אַף used with pronominal suffix וֹ which has contracted with construct ending making יו—. The daghešׁ-forte in פ is to show assimilation of נ which is part of the original form.

171.   נִשְׁמַת
breath of

Construct feminine singular of נְשָׁמָה. See p. 32, II, 3, c.

172.   חַיִּים
lives

Plural absolute of חַי (life), a masculine noun.

173. וַיִּטַּע
(he) planted   and

Kal imperfect 3rd masculine singular from verb root נטע (plant). Cf. No. 169.

174. גָּן
garden

Common singular noun in absolute state. Cf. with הַגָּן in verse 9. ָ indicates a pausal form, secondary.

175. מִקֶּדֶם
east   from

Regular use of מִן, when the noun with which it is used has not the article.

176. וַיָּשֶׂם
he placed   and

Kal imperfect 3rd masculine singular from verb root שִׂים (place, put) used with waw conversive. Why ֶ under שׂ? See No. 167.

177. שָׁם
there

An adverb.

178. יָצָר
he formed

Kal perfect 3rd masculine singular. Cf. No. 167. This is a pausal form hence ַ under צ became ָ.

179. וַיַּצְמַח
(he) caused to and
sprout

Hifil imperfect 3rd masculine singular with waw conversive. Cf. No. 158 and 25. Note use of ַ in preformative syllable as sign of Hifil except in perfect.

180. נֶחְמָד
desired

Nifal participle from the verb root חמד (desire). The נ is the sign of the Nifal. The stem vowel of a participle is always long.

181. לְמַרְאֶה
sight or ap-   for
pearance

Masculine noun from verb root ראה (see).

182.   לְ מַ אֲ כָ ל   Masculine noun from verb root אכל
      food for   (eat).

183.   הַ דַ עַ ת   Kal infinitive construct used as a noun.
     knowing the   It is from the verb root ידע (know).

184.   וָ רָ ע   A masculine noun from verb root רעע
      evil and   (be evil). Why are both Kamets tone
                    long?

II. Grammar

1. The conjugation of the intensive stems.

    a. The intensive active stem, Piel.

       This stem is indicated by a daghes̆-forte in the middle radical
       of the root. In the original form קַטֵל, both vowels attenu-
       ated to –̣– but stem vowel became –̤– under tone, hence קְטֵל.
       Observe the vowel –̤– in first form only, and the –̣– constant
       in a closed syllable. It follows the order of the Kal.

    b. The intensive passive stem, Pual.

       This stem is also indicated by a daghes̆-forte in the middle
       radical and has –̣– which is commonly used to characterize
       the passive, קֻטַל. Observe the –̣– in the first syllable and
       the doubling of middle radical. It follows the order of the Kal.

    c. The intensive middle and reciprocal stem, Hithpael.

       This stem is also indicated by a daghes̆-forte in the middle
       radical and is similar to the Piel stem except it has a pre-
       formative syllable הִת, which is commonly used in Semitic
       languages to characterize the middle, reciprocal and passive,
       הִתְקַטֵל. Observe the preformative syllable הִת which is

constant and the penultimate ‒ृ, which does not attenuate to ‒ृ. It follows the order of the Piel.

2. The conjugation of the causative stems.

a. The causative active stem, Hifil.

This stem is indicated by a prefixed הַ, forming a preformative syllable with ‒ַ as original vowel. The stem vowel originally was ‒ַ but attenuated to ‒ִ, הַקְטַל. The stem vowel was lengthened to ‒ִי anomalously instead of tone long ‒ֵ, and the ‒ַ in a closed preformative syllable attenuated to ‒ִ, hence הִקְטִיל. This stem follows the order of the Kal, except observing the closed preformative syllable, הִק, and the ‒ִי remaining long before vowel affixes.

b. The causative passive stem, Hofal.

This stem is indicated by a prefixed הַ, forming a preformative syllable with ‒ֻ as original passive vowel (cf. Pual). This vowel was deflected to ‒ָ (short o) but sometimes the ‒ֻ is found; as הֻקְטַל becoming הָקְטַל. Observe the preformative syllable הָק, which is constant. It follows the order of the Kal.

3. Master the Kal Perfect and the characteristics of each stem, then the entire conjugation of the Perfects will be more easily understood.

III. Vocabulary

201.	יָצַר he formed	204.	נָפַח he breathed, blew
202.	יֵצֶר thought, image (m)	205.	אָנַף he breathed, was angry
203.	עָפָר dust (m)	206.	אַף nose, nostril (m)

207.	נְשָׁמָה breath (f)	214.	חֶמֶד attractiveness (m)
208.	נָטַע he planted	215.	חֶמְדָּה desire, longing (f)
209.	נֶ טַ ע planting (m)	216.	יָדַע he knew
210.	גַּן garden (c)	217.	דַּעַת to know, knowl-
211.	שִׂים to place or put		edge (f)
212.	מַרְאֶה appearance,	218.	רָעַע he broke in
	sight (m)		pieces, was evil
213.	חָמַד he desired	219.	רַע evil, injury (m)

PART TWO — LESSON FIVE

I. Reading Lesson — Gen. 2:10–14.

185.   וְ נָ הָ ר   Noun masculine singular absolute from
river   and   verb root נהר (flow).

186.   יֹצֵא   Kal participle from verb root יצא (go
going out   out).

187.   מֵעֵדֶן   Proper name literally meaning "delight
Eden from   or pleasure". It is used with contracted
     form of preposition מִן. Why so used
     and vowel change?

188.   וּמִשָּׁם   וְ+מִן+שָׁם. Why is such contraction
there from and   possible?

189.   יִפָּרֵד   Nifal imperfect 3rd masculine singular
it divides itself   from verb root פרד (divide). The Nifal
     form is the same for the simple passive
     and middle.

190.   לְאַרְבָּעָה
four   for

Numeral used as adjective, feminine singular. Note that feminine form of numeral is used to modify *masculine* nouns. See p. 174, II, 1, b, (2).

191.   רָאשִׁים
heads

Irregular plural of רֹאשׁ.

192.   פִּישׁוֹן

"Pishon." It is from a verb meaning "to flow over, spread, leap."

193.   הַסֹּבֵב
surrounding   the

Kal participle from verb root סבב (surround). It is here used as an adjective.

194.   חֲוִילָה

"Havilah." It is from two words: חוֹל, "sand," and חֶבֶל, "region."

195.   אֲשֶׁר־שָׁם

"which there" = "where."

196.   הַזָּהָב
gold   the

Noun, masculine singular absolute used with the article הַ.

197.   וּזֲהַב
gold of   and

Noun, masculine singular construct used with conjunctive וּ. The ֲ used under ו because it preceeds a guttural. Why have both tone long vowels of absolute form changed in the construct?

198.   הַהִוא
that   the

Archaic form of 3rd per. fem. singular pronoun used as a remote demonstrative and adjective.

199.   הַבְּדֹלַח
bedellium   the

Noun masculine singular absolute used with article.

200.   אֶבֶן
stone of

Noun masculine singular construct. Why? Both masculine singular absolute and construct have same form in this class of nouns.

201.   הַשֹּׁהַם
onyx the

Noun, masculine singular absolute with the article ־הַ.

202.   גִּיחוֹן
Gihon

Proper name from verb root גּוּחַ (gush forth).

203.   כּוּשׁ
Cush

Cush is better known as Ethiopia. Name is derived probably from a verb root meaning "to burn, be sunburnt." The verb form is not used in any extant Hebrew. Ethiopia, the Greek equivalent, means "burnt faces."

204.   חִדֶּקֶל
Tigris

This was not known definitely until equivalent was found in the Assyrian inscriptions namely: "I-dig-lat."

205.   קִדְמַת
eastward of

Noun, feminine singular, construct of קִדְמָה.

206.   אַשּׁוּר
Assyria

Name of ancient Semitic empire of which English equivalent is Assyria.

207.   פְּרָת
Euphrates

The Euphrates which is derived from "Frat," broad stream, and "Eu," good. The latter is a Greek word which was added later.

II. Grammar

1. The use of the pronoun.

   a. As a personal pronoun: הוּא הַסוֹבֵב, "it the surrounding."
   b. As a remote demonstrative: הָאָרֶץ הַהִיא "that land."
   c. As a copula: וְהַנָּהָר הָרְבִיעִי הוּא פְרָת,"and the fourth river is (it) Euphrates."

2. The copula.

   This is expressed in three ways:

   a. By forms of the verb הָיָה, the regular copulative verb. E. g. הַבָּקָר הָיוּ חֹרְשׁוֹת,"the oxen were ploughing"(Job 1:14).
   b. By use of the personal pronoun. It has often the force of a copula. (See II, 1, c above.)
   c. By use of no definite term.

   More often the relation of subject and predicate is sufficiently suggested by simply placing them together. E. g. הָעֵץ טוֹב,"The tree (is) good"(Gen. 3:6).

3. Review conjugation of the Perfect of קָטַל. Knowledge of the strong verb is basic for study of other classes of verbs and of nouns. Now is the time to master the perfects.

III. Vocabulary

220. קָדַם he went before, preceded
221. קֶדֶם east (m)
222. קִדְמָה eastward (f)

223. נָהָר river (m)
224. פָרַד he divided, separated
225. סָבַב he surrounded

226. סָבִיב circuit (m)

227. יֵלֵךְ
הָלַךְ } he went

228. אֶבֶן stone (f)

229. זָהָב gold (m)

230. בְּדֹלַח bedellium (pearl) (m)

231. שֹׁהַם onyx (m)

PART TWO — Lesson Six

I. Review and drill orally and by writing, the seven stems of the perfect of קָטַל.

II. Weekly written or oral review of words 201–231.

III. Sentences to be translated into Hebrew and written in exercise book:

1. Jehovah God gave fruit from the tree of lives to the man.
2. The man went into the garden which he called Eden.
3. The river which goes eastward of the Havilah is Tigris.
4. The tree of the knowledge of that good and this evil was not for food.
5. God breathed in the nostrils of the man and gave the spirit of life to all the beasts of the earth.
6. There was dust in the field because it had not rained.
7. He saw the river which surrounds the land in which is gold.
8. The great God made the man for a living soul.
9. The name of that great river is Euphrates.
10. The second river going eastward divided itself.
11. The man went to the land of the Havilah and dwelt there.
12. The third river watered all the dry land for the man.

PART TWO — Lesson Seven

I. Reading Lesson — Gen. 2:15, 16.

208.   וַיִּקַּח
he took and

Kal imperfect 3rd person masculine singular with waw conversive from verb root לָקַח (take). The ל in this irregular verb is here treated as נ in נָטַע. יִלְקַח becomes יִקַּח similar to יִנְטַע becoming יִטַּע.

209.   וַיַּנִּחֵהוּ
he caused to rest and
him

Hifil imperfect 3rd person masculine singular with waw conversive from verb root נוח (rest). The masculine singular 3rd person pronominal suffix הוּ uses its regular connecting vowel ֵ with the imperfect since the verb closes with a consonant.

210.   לְעָבְדָהּ
her serve to

Kal infinitive construct from verb root עבד (serve). The feminine singular 3rd person pronominal suffix הָ has contracted with its connecting vowel ָ making הָ. See No. 116.

211.   וּלְשָׁמְרָהּ
her keep to and

Kal infinitive construct from verb root שמר (keep) used with 3rd per. fem. pronominal suffix as in above verb.

212.   וַיְצַו
(he) commanded and

Piel imperfect 3rd masculine singular with waw conversive from צוה (command). This is the **short or Jussive** form, the regular form being יְצַוֶּה.

213. אָכֹל
eating

Kal infinitive absolute from verb root אכל (eat). The ‾ is וֹ (ô) and should be fully written. See p. 80, II, 1 as to its usage.

214. תֹאכֵל
thou shalt eat

Kal imperfect 2nd masculine singular from the same verb root as above verb. Cf. וַיֹּאמֶר. This is the pausal form in this class of verbs.

II. Grammar

1. The use of the infinitive absolute.

Whenever an Infinitive Absolute precedes a finite verb, it intensifies the meaning, or marks the absolute certainty of the idea or fact to be conveyed, or both. When it follows the finite verb, its action is like a Participle.

2. The conjugation of the Kal Imperfect.

The Imperfect as to Forms

Energetic	Subjunctive	Jussive	Regular
Uses גַּ— with regular form before 3rd person pronominal suffixes.	Same as regular, and also uses הַ— added to 1st person, sing. and plural making a cohortative.	Same as regular except in Hifil, — for יִ—, e. g. יַקְטֵל. The waw conversive is used only with the jussive.	יִקְטֹל etc.

It is to be noted that only remnants of these forms remain in the jussive, subjunctive and energetic, but they still function as such. The Arabic still retains in full these distinct forms.

The Imperfect, in any stem, expresses repeated or unfinished action. The original stem vowel is $-$ which is lengthened because of its tone to $-$; and the preformative vowel $-$ attenuates to $-$ because in a closed, unaccented, preformative syllable.

(1) he   will kill — יִקְטֹל from   — יַקְטֻל   י used to in-
                                                                  dicate mas-
                                                                  culine sing.

(2) she   will kill — תִּקְטֹל from   — תַּקְטֻל   תַּ the usual
                                                                  sign of femi-
                                                                  nine pre-
                                                                  fixed.

(3) thou (m) wilt kill — תִּקְטֹל from   — תַּקְטֻל   תַּ from אַתָּה
                                                                  (thou, m).

(4) thou (f) wilt kill — תִּקְטְלִי from   — תַּקְטְלִי   תּ from אַתְּ
                                                                  (thou, f.)
                                                                  and י$-$ from
                                                                  old form of
                                                                  pronoun. Cf.
                                                                  Arabic
                                                                  "anti."

(5) I   shall kill — אֶקְטֹל from   — אַקְטֻל   א from אֲנִי
                                                                  (I).

(6) they (m) will kill — יִקְטְלוּ from ‏יַקְטְלוּ‎ — plural of ‏יַקְטֵל‎ with וּ the usual plural ending of verbs.

(7) they (f) will kill תִּקְטֹלְנָה from תִּקְטֹלְנָה plural of ‏תִּקְטֵל‎ with ‏נָה‎ from ‏הֵנָּה‎ (they, f).

(8) ye (m) will kill תִּקְטְלוּ from תִּקְטְלוּ plural of ‏תִּקְטֵל‎ with וּ the usual plural ending.

(9) ye (f) will kill תִּקְטֹלְנָה from תִּקְטֹלְנָה plural of ‏תִּקְטְלִי‎ with ‏נָה‎ from ‏אַתֵּנָה‎ (ye, f).

(10) we shall kill — נִקְטֹל from נַקְטֵל — plural with נ from ‏נַחְנוּ‎ (we).

3. The prefixes and affixes of the Imperfect for all Imperfects of every stem in all classes of verbs are:

a. Prefixes: ‏יְ, תְּ, תְּ, תְּ, אְ, יְ, תְּ, תְּ, תְּ, נְ‎.

b. Affixes: ‏—, —, —, ִי, —, וּ, נָה, וּ, נָה, —‎.

4. Sometimes יִּ‎ְ‎ for יֶ‎ְ‎ and וֹּ‎ for וֹ‎ is used. This is a relic of ancient forms and is used in the Aramaic.

5. Note that the radicals of the root remain constant as well as affixes and preformative prefixes in all stems.

III. Vocabulary

232.	לָקַח‎ he took	238.	עֲבֹדָה‎ work, labor (f)
233.	מַלְקוֹחַ‎ spoil, booty	239.	צָוָה‎ he commanded
234.	נוּחַ‎ to rest	240.	צַו‎ command (m)
235.	נוֹחַ‎ rest, quiet (m)	241.	מִצְוָה‎ commandment
236.	עָבַד‎ he served		(f)
237.	עֶבֶד‎ servant, slave		
	(m)		

PART TWO — Lesson Eight

I. Reading Lesson — Gen. 2:17, 18.

215.	וּמֵעֵץ‎	.וְ‎+מִן‎+עֵץ‎. עֵץ‎ is here used in the
	tree of from (the) and	construct state. Why are these words united and two vowels changed?
216.	תֹּאכֵל‎	Same as No. 214 but not pausal in form.
	you shall eat	
217.	מִמֶּנּוּ‎	When מִן‎ is used with pronominal suf-
	it from	fixes (except 3rd person plural forms) it is reduplicated. The ‎ְ‎ under מ‎ is deflected to ‎ֶ‎ for differentiation. The ה‎ of the suffix הוּ‎ is assimilated back-

ward and is indicated by daghes̆-forte in בּ. See p. 54, II, 3.

218.   אֲכָלְךָ
thy eating

Kal infinitive construct used with 2nd masculine singular suffix ךָ. The stem vowel ֹ (ō) is shortened to ָ (ŏ) in adding ךָ or כֶּם.

219.   מוֹת
dying

Kal infinitive absolute from verb root מוּת (die). See p. 80, II, 1 as to its usage.

220.   תָּמוּת
thou shalt die

Kal imperfect 2nd person masculine singular of same verb root as above form (No. 219).

221.   הֱיוֹת
(the) being of

Kal infinitive construct from verb root היה (to be). It is here used as a verbal noun in the construct state. Cf. עֲשׂוֹת (No. 150).

222.   לְבַדּוֹ
his-separation   to

לְ+בַּד+וֹ. The daghes̆-forte in ד indicates the contraction with a second ד as the noun is from the verb root בדד (separate).

223.   אֶעֱשֶׂה־לּוֹ
him   for   I will make

Kal imperfect 1st person singular form from verb root עשׂה (make). The daghes̆-forte in ל is conjunctive. Why? See p. 39, II, 2.

224.   עֵזֶר
helper

Masculine singular noun from verb root עזר (help).

225.   כְּ נֶ גְ דּ וֹ   כְּ+נֶגֶד+וֹ. The original form נֶגֶד is
   him against as   used with pronominal suffixes.

II. Grammar

1. The Daghes̆-forte Conjunctive.

When the initial letter of a word is connected to the final vowel
of a preceding word by a point, this point is called the daghes̆-
forte conjunctive.

E. g. אֶעֱשֶׂה־לּוֹ — I will make for him. See p. 39, II, 2.

2. The use of sibilants with the Hithpael.

When the syllable הִתְ precedes ס, שׂ or שׁ, the תּ changes position
with the sibilants as הִשְׁתַּמֵּר for הִתְשַׁמֵּר. With צ the תּ further
becomes ט as in הִצְטַדֵּק for הִתְצַדֵּק. With תּ, ט, ד the תּ is
assimilated as הִטַּהֵר for הִתְטַהֵר. Cf. Isa. 52:5.— Note מִנֹּאַץ
for מִתְנֹאַץ.

3. The conjugation of the Nifal and Intensive Imperfect stems.

a. The Nifal Imperfect.

The original form is הִנְקָטֵל (cf. Arabic, אִנ) to which prefixes
and affixes indicating the Imperfect are added, the הֹ giving
place to the necessary prefixes of gender and number, becoming יִנְקָטֵל. The נ being weak is assimilated and shown by
daghes̆-forte in the first radical; — is lengthened to —ָ,
being in an open unaccented syllable; and — is lengthened to
— under the tone; hence יִקָּטֵל.
The vowels remain constant, except stem vowel, and the
conjugation follows then the order of the Kal; as יִקָּטֵל,
תִּקָּטֵל etc.

b. The Piel Imperfect.

The original Perfect קָטַל became קִטֵּל but in the Imperfect, the pretonic ◌ַ remained when prefixes were added and the vowel of the prefix, being ante-pretonic, was reduced to Sheʷa: יְקַטֵּל.

Observe the characteristic daghes̆-forte in second radical, and the vowels remaining constant. It follows the order of the Kal.

c. The Pual Imperfect.

The Pual Perfect is קֻטַּל, and to this root and vowels were added the affixes and prefixes. The vowel of the preformative consonant, being antepretonic, is reduced to Sheʷa: יְקֻטַּל.

Observe the characteristic daghes̆-forte in second radical, and the vowels remaining constant. It follows the order of the Kal.

d. The Hithpael Imperfect.

The Hithpael Perfect is הִתְקַטֵּל. To this root and vowels were added the affixes and prefixes, the ה giving way to the prefixed consonants of gender and number: יִתְקַטֵּל.

Observe the characteristic daghes̆-forte in the second radical, the preformative syllable and all vowels remaining constant. It follows the order of the Kal.

III. Vocabulary

242. מוּת to die

243. מָוֶת death (m)

244. בַּד separation (m)

245. עָזַר he helped, assisted

246. עֵזֶר helper (m)

247. נָגַד he declared, told, showed (only used in causative stems)

248. נֶגֶד before, over against, opposite to

249. נָגִיד leader, prince (m)

PART TWO — LESSON NINE

I. Review and practice oral reading. This is necessary.

II. Weekly oral or written review of words 232–249.

III. Sentences to be translated into Hebrew and written in exercise book.

1. God will give the good garden to the man to keep it and serve it.

2. What will the cattle see upon the water?

3. The small bird rested upon the great tree in the good field.

4. The man will surely eat from the tree of life.

5. God commanded them that they should not eat the fruit of that tree.

6. The man who eats from this tree will surely die.

7. God created a helper for the man as his counterpart.

8. The beast which went to the river was killed.

9. In his separation he rested from his work which he had done.

10. And God caused to rest him in the garden of Eden.

11. He dwelt in the garden and God commanded that he shall not eat of the fruit of the tree.

12. The man saw no animal to be his counterpart.

PART TWO — Lesson Ten

I. Reading Lesson — Gen. 2:19–21.

226.   וַיָּבֵא א
he caused to and come

Hifil jussive imperfect 3rd masculine singular with waw conversive from verb root בּוֹא (come).

227.   לִרְאוֹת
see   to

Kal infinitive construct from verb root ראה (see). Why does ⟨ ָ ⟩ under ל change to ⟨ ִ ⟩? See p. 24, II, 1, b.

228.   שְׁמוֹ
his name

Noun שֵׁם used with pronominal suffix וֹ. The ⟨ ֵ ⟩ has reduced to ⟨ ְ ⟩ in adding light suffixes but is retained in adding affix for gender and number as שֵׁמוֹת in next verse.

229.   מָצָא
he found

Kal perfect 3rd masculine singular from verb root מצא (find).

230.   וַיַּפֵּל
(he) caused to and fall

Hifil jussive imperfect 3rd masculine singular with waw conversive from verb נפל (fall). The assimilation of nun is shown by daghes̆-forte in פ.

231.   תַּרְדֵּמָה
deep sleep

Feminine noun from verb root רדם (to sleep heavily).

232.   וַיִּישָׁן
he slept   and

Kal jussive imperfect 3rd masculine singular with waw conversive from verb root ישן (sleep). This is a pausal form hence stem vowel ⟨ ֵ ⟩ became ⟨ ָ ⟩.

233.   אַחַת
      one

Feminine of אֶחָד, — is short because of implied doubling of ח.

234.   מִצַּלְעֹתָיו
      his ribs from

Plural construct of feminine noun צֵלָע used with 3rd person singular masculine suffix וֹ and preposition מִן. Cf. בְּאַפִּיו (No. 170).

235.   וַיִּסְגֹּר
      he closed and

Kal jussive imperfect 3rd masculine singular from verb root סגר (close). Cf. יִקְטֹל (he will kill), as found in paradigm of strong verb.

236.   בָּשָׂר
      flesh

Masculine singular absolute noun. Both vowels are tone long. Cf. כָּנָף (No. 108), אָדָם (No. 122), זָכָר (No. 130).

237.   תַּחְתֶּנָּה
      her (it) instead of

Preposition תַּחַת plus syllable called the "nun emphatic" to express emphasis נָּ֫ plus the feminine singular pronominal suffix הָ whose consonant ה has been assimilated backward as shown by dagheš-forte in נ, and a protective ה (a vowel letter) added.

II. Grammar

1. The conjugation of the causative Imperfects.

   a. The Hifil Imperfect.

The original form is based on the Perfect, the root and stem vowels being constant. The original — of the preformative syllable remains unattenuated, and ה gives way to the prefixes of the Imperfect: יַקְטִיל.

Observe that the vowels remain constant except in 2d and 3d. fem. plu. where יִ֫ gives way to ◌ֵ֫. It follows the order of the Kal.

b. The Hofal Imperfect.

The original form is based on the Perfect, the root and stem vowels being constant. The ה gives way to the prefixes of the Imperfect: יָקְטַל.

Observe that the vowels remain constant. It follows the order of the Kal.

2. The Jussive Imperfect.

As the Imperative does not take a negative, it was necessary that there be a form to express a negative command, hence the Jussive. Its use, however, is not confined to negative commands, but it is used as a regular Imperfect, being the form used with the Waw Conversive. It differs in form from the regular Imperfect only in the Hifil, where ◌ֵ֫ is retained for the יִ֫ of regular Imperfect. E. g. וַיַּבְדֵּל. The Jussive forms of ל"ה and ע"ו will be discussed when these classes are studied.

3. The conjugation of the Imperatives.

There are Imperatives only in the active and middle stems, and hence none in the Pual and Hofal, which are strictly passive.

The Imperative is based on the 2d. person forms of the Imperfects, the prefixes of the Imperfect being dropped and original preformative consonants, if any as ה in Nifal, Hifil, and Hithpael returning. E. g. Kal תְּקְטֹל with תְּ dropped — קְטֹל

               תְּקְטְלִי with תְּ dropped — קְטְלִי etc.

III. Vocabulary Lesson

250.	בּוֹא to go in	257.	יָשֵׁן he slept	
251.	מָבוֹא entrance (m)	258.	שֵׁנָה sleep, dream (f)	
252.	שֵׁמוֹת names (m)	259.	אַחַת one (f)	
253.	מָצָא he found	260.	צֵלָע rib, side (f)	
254.	נָפַל he fell	261.	בָּשָׂר flesh (m)	
255.	מַפֶּלֶת fall, ruin (f)	262.	סָגַר he shut	
256.	תַּרְדֵּמָה deep sleep (f)	263.	סְגוֹר enclosure (m)	

PART TWO — Lesson Eleven

I. Reading Lesson — Gen. 2:22, 23.

238. וַיִּבֶן
he built   and

Kal jussive imperfect 3rd masculine singular with waw conversive from the verb
root בנה (build). The regular imperfect form is יִבְנֶה which is shortened by
dropping הֶ— in the jussive. The —ֶ
under בּ was added to aid pronunciation.
Cf. וַיַּעַשׂ, וַיַּרְא, וַיְהִי.

239. לְאִשָּׁה
woman   for

Feminine noun, absolute state. The
masculine form is אִישׁ (man).

240. וַיְבִאֶהָ
he caused to go in   and
her

Hifil imperfect 3rd person masculine
with waw conversive, from verb root
בוֹא (go in) and 3rd person feminine
pronominal suffix. —ֶ is a connecting
vowel used with the imperfect and receives the tone (accent). Hence —ָ

in preformative syllable is reduced
to ⸺.

241.   זֹאת
      this

Feminine singular form of demonstrative pronoun. See p. 57, II, 2, a, c.

242.   הַפָּעַם
    stroke the

The article is here used as a demonstrative — "this" with the noun "stroke." This is the idiom for "now."

243.   מֵעֲצָמַי
   my bones from

The plural construct of עֶצֶם used with the 1st person singular pronominal suffix ַי‑ and the preposition מִן. The original plural masculine construct ending ֵי‑ and ַי‑ have contracted making ַי‑.

244.   מִבְּשָׂרִי
   my flesh from

The singular construct of בָּשָׂר used with 1st person singular pronominal suffix ִי‑ and the preposition מִן.

245.   יִקָּרֵא
  it shall be called

Nifal imperfect 3rd person masculine singular from verb root קרא (call). Why is there a dagheš-forte in ק?

246.   לֻקֳחָה־זֹאת
   this was taken

Pual perfect 3rd person feminine singular from verb root לקח (take). Dagheš-forte is sometimes omitted when only supported by Shᵉwa, hence the omission in לֻקֳ, which is indicated by a short line above the consonant called "rafe." See p. 15, II, 2, b. (2). The dagheš-forte in ־ז is conjunctive. Why?

II. Grammar

1. The conjugation of the Infinitives.

There are two Infinitives to each stem though all forms have not as yet been found due to the small amount of extant Hebrew literature. The author holds to the above statement as a logical deduction.

a. The Infinitive Absolute is a verbal noun as well as a verb, and is called "absolute" because no suffixes, prefixes, or prepositions can be added to it. It is not based on either the Perfect or Imperfect stem, though it shows relation to them as seen in the Nifal forms. For example see paradigms.

b. The Infinitive Construct is based upon the 3d per. masculine sing. Imperfect with the prefix of the Imperfect omitted and characteristic prefixed consonant if any returned as in Hifil, הַקְטִיל.

It is called "Construct" because to it may be added suffixes, prefixes, or prepositions. Its use is as in English.

2. The conjugation of the Participles.

a. The action implied is that of continuous action.

b. Apart from the Kal and Nifal, the Participles are based on the 3d masc. sing. Imperfect, the prefix of the Imperfect giving way to the characteristic sign מ of the Participle, as מְקַטֵּל. The stem vowel is always long.

c. The Kal has two Participles.

(1) the "Active" Participle.

The original form was קָטִל (kātĭl) the same as now in Arabic. The ָ lengthened to ֵ under the tone, and

the ⟘ was deflected to וֹ, no doubt due to similarity in
pronunciation. The וֹ is always fully written in Isaiah I
Manuscript of Dead Sea Scrolls.

(2) The Gerundive.

The original form was קָטוֹל and the ⟍ lengthened to
⟘ due to being in an open pretonic syllable. This is
called a "passive" Participle by grammarians, but this
term is paradoxical for it is in an active stem.

Its function is that of the gerundive. In its use, it is
about the same as the Latin gerundive, and indicates
or denotes a condition that produces a necessity, "ought
to be," or obligation; for example, "ought to be loved,
hated, killed, etc."

This verbal form suggests a permanent quality as the
ground of the action, as not only "to be feared," but
"worthy to be feared," hence, "ought to be feared."
E. g. Gen. 3:14 אָרוּר אַתָּה, cursed art thou. Cf. verse 17.

d. The Nifal Participle.

The Nifal Participle is the same in form as the 3d masc.
sing. of the perfect except that the stem vowel is long.

3. The Cohortative.

a. The Cohortative Imperfect.

This is indicated by adding הָ⟘ to the Imperfect form of
the first persons, singular and plural, though there are a
few examples in third person in poetry. It signifies in the
singular, desire and determination, and in the plural, ex-
hortation. Compare with the hortatory subjunctive of Greek.
E. g. אַגְדְּלָה, I will make great; נִלְבְּנָה, let us make brick.

b. The Cohortative Imperative.

As with the Imperfect, this is indicated by the addition of
הָ‑. It is used to soften the command into an earnest
entreaty or expression of strong desire. E. g. שִׁמְעָה,"O hear,"
תְּנָה,"give."

III. Vocabulary

264.	בָּנָה he built		article used adverb-
265.	בֵּן son (m)		ially, meaning
266.	בַּת daughter (f)		"now, this time")
267.	אֱנוֹשׁ man, common	271.	פַּעֲמוֹן bell (m)
	people (m)	272.	עָצַם he closed (as the
268.	אִשָּׁה woman (f)		eyes), became
269	פָּעַם he impelled,		strong or mighty.
	urged	273.	עֶצֶם bone (f)
270.	פַּעַם stroke, anvil,	274.	עֹצֶם strength (m)
	step (f) (With	275.	עָצוּם strong, mighty

PART TWO — LESSON TWELVE

I. Review thoroughly the paradigm of the strong verb so that
it is fully mastered.

II. Select one of the following verbs and work out in full.

1. דָּבַר — speak   6. מָשַׁל — rule

2. גָּדַל — be great   7. שָׁפַט — judge

3. דָּבַק — cleave   8. פָּקַד — visit

4. שָׁבַת — rest   9. לָבַשׁ — put on

5. קָדַשׁ — separate   10. כָּתַב — write

III. Weekly oral or written review of words, Nos. 250–275.

IV. Sentences to be translated into Hebrew and written in exercise book:

1. That is the bone from which God created the woman.

2. He will close his flesh because the man will sleep.

3. Who caused a deep sleep to fall upon that little man?

4. What did the woman kill in the garden?

5. This now is from my flesh and from my bones.

6. Who was taken from the man?

7. Ye (f.) are upon the dry land, and I am on the water.

8. The man gave names to the herbs of the field and to the beasts of the garden.

9. The man called the animal to see what he will call to it.

10. God gave names to the man and the woman in the good garden.

11. And God closed his flesh and made the woman.

12. He created the woman from the rib of the man and caused her to come to him.

PART TWO — Lesson Thirteen

I. Reading Lesson — Gen. 2:24, 25.

247.   עַל ־ כֵּן   An idiom meaning "therefore."
        so upon

248.   יַעֲזָב ־   Kal imperfect 3rd person   masculine
    (he) will forsake   singular from verb root עזב (forsake).
                  Note use of ָ (ŏ). Why? Cf. יִקְטֹל
                  he will kill.

249. אָבִיו

his father

אָב is an irregular noun in the singular form using ִי‎ֲ before adding pronominal suffixes and here contracting with ו making יו‎ֲ.

250. אִמּוֹ

his mother

אֵם is an "Ayin Doubled" noun hence the dagheš-forte shown when adding suffixes or affixes.

251. וְדָבַק

(he) shall cleave and

Kal perfect 3rd masculine singular with waw conversive from verb root דבק (cleave). Cf. קָטַל.

252. בְּאִשְׁתּוֹ

his wife in

Irregular construct form of אִשָּׁה used with 3rd masculine singular pronominal suffix וֹ and preposition בְּ.

253. וַיִּהְיוּ

they were and

Kal jussive imperfect 3rd person masculine plural with waw conversive from verb root היה (be or become). Cf. וְהָיוּ (and they shall be) in vs. 24.

254. עֲרוּמִּים

naked

Masculine plural form of adjective עָרֹם. Why does ‎ָ become ‎ֲ? ‎ו is an incorrect writing of ‎ֻ. Why?

255. יִתְבֹּשָׁשׁוּ

they will be ashamed of themselves

Pausal form of Hithpael imperfect 3rd person masculine plural from verb root בוש (to be ashamed). In pause the stem vowel having been reduced to ‎ְ becomes here ‎ָ.

II. Grammar

1. The pronominal suffixes with the Perfect stem of the strong verb.

a. There are three general rules to be noted in adding pronominal suffixes:

(1) There may be a change in some form of the stem.

(2) There may be a change of vowels inside of the stem.

(3) There may be the use of a connecting vowel, as:

(a) with the Perfect, generally ָ◌,

(b) with the Imperfect, generally ֶ◌.

b. The pronominal suffixes with the Perfect.

Suffix		Singular	Kal, Perfect
1. c.	נִי◌ = me		קָטַל — 3 m.
2. m.	ךָ◌ = thee[3]	(change הָ◌ back to ◌תָ)	קָטְלָת — 3 f.
2. f.	ךְ◌ = thee[3]	תָּ or	קָטַלְתָּ — 2 m.
3. m.	וֹ or הוּ◌ = him	(change תָּ to תִּי)	קָטַלְתְּ — 2 f.
3. f.	הָ or הָ◌ = her[2]		קָטַלְתִּי — 1 c.

Plural

1. c.	נוּ◌ = us		קָטְלוּ — 3 c.
2. m.	כֶם◌ = you[3]	(change כֶם תֶּם and תֶּן תֵּן to תוּ)	קְטַלְתּוּ — 2 m.
2. f.	כֶן◌ = you[3]		קְטַלְתּוּ — 2 f.
3. m.	ם◌ = them		קְטַלְנוּ — 1 c.
3. f.	ן◌ = them		

(1) The third feminine singular attaches suffixes forming a syllable *without* a connecting vowel, except ֶ◌ before ךְ, and ◌ַ before ם and ן, the penultimate ◌ַ becoming ◌ָ.

The tone remains always upon the penultimate syllable
(תֶ֫) or (תָ֫). No extant use with כֶּם or כֶּן.

(2) הָֽיָ is contracted to הָ in 3d sing. fem. suffixes. The
final ָ is omitted to prevent recurrence of the same
sound.

(3) The basis of ךְ, ךָ, כֶּם and כֶּן seems to be a lost form
of the regular pronoun which was employed so as to
distinguish the pronominal suffixes from the afformatives of the perfect. This last form is seen in the Ethiopic
— katal*ka* (2d per. mas.).

(4) In the Piel, the ֵ is sometimes shortened to ֶ or ִ.

(5) In the Hifil יִ does not change.

III. Vocabulary

276.	אָב	father (m)	282.	עָרַם he made bare, he
277.	אֵם	mother (f)		was cunning
278.	בּוֹשׁ	to be ashamed	283.	עָרֹם naked (adj.)
279.	דָּבַק	he clave	284.	עָרוֹם naked (adj.)
280.	דָּבֵק	cleaving (adj.)	285.	עָרוּם crafty, cunning
281.	עָזַב	he forsook		(adj.)

PART TWO — Lesson Fourteen

I. Reading Lesson — Gen. 3:1, 2.

256.   וְהַנָּחָשׁ   Masculine noun in Absolute state. Note
     serpent the and   regular use of article and conjunction.

257.   עָרוּם   The Kal Gerundive used as an adjective.
     crafty

258.   אַ ף   A conjunctive particle.

   surely

259.   וַ תֹּ א מֶ ר   Kal jussive imperfect 3rd person femi-

   she said   and   nine singular used with waw conversive,

                       from verb root אמר (say). Cf. mas-

                       culine singular 3rd person form וַיֹּאמֶר

                       (and he said). Cf. תִּקְטֹל.

II. Grammar

1. How to classify verbs as to their different classes.

ל (3rd radical)	ע (2nd radical)	פ (1st radical)
י (ה)	י	א
ו	ו	נ
ה } vowel א } letters	All gutturals	י
		ו
Gutturals	Note that י is usually	Gutturals
(ר, ע, ח, ה)	found instead of ו	(except א)
	though verb is ע״ו.	
Second and third radical same called ע״ע (Doubled Ayin verb).		

Instead of classifying verbs when one of the root radicals is
not strong by numerals, the letters of the former paradigm verb
are used.

   הָיָה — פ guttural, ע״ו and ל״ה.

   אָכַל — פ״א.

   הָלַל — פ guttural and ע״ע.

ו ב ב ב ₃

2. Comparison.

Comparison is expressed by the use of the preposition מִן. E. g.
"The woman is better than the man" is literally "The woman is
good from the man." — הָאִשָׁה טוֹבָה מִן הָאִישׁ׃

3. The pronominal suffixes with the Imperfect and Imperative.
Note that the stem vowel reduces to ־ְ.

SINGULAR

Suffix		Kal Imperfect	
1 c.	נִי־ = me	יִקְטֹל	— 3 m.
2 m.	ךָ־ = thee[1]	תִּקְטֹל	— 3 f.
2 f.	ךְ־ = thee	תִּקְטֹל	— 2 m.
3 m.	הוּ־ = him	תִּקְטְלִי	— 2 f.
3 f.	הָ־ = her	אֶקְטֹל	— 1 c.

PLURAL

Suffix			Kal Imperfect	
1 c.	נוּ־ = us		יִקְטְלוּ	— 3 m.
2 m.	כֶם־ = you[1]	(ו for נָה)	תִּקְטְלוּ	— 3 f.
2 f.	כֶן־ = you[1]		תִּקְטְלוּ	— 2 m.
3 m.	ם־ = them	(ו for נָה)	תִּקְטְלוּ	— 2 f.
3 f.	ן־ = them		נִקְטֹל	— 1 c.

Kal Imperative

קְטֹל[2],[3]	— 2 m. sing.
קִטְלִי	— 2 f. sing.
קִטְלוּ	— 2 m. plu.
קִטְלוּ (נָה for ו)	— 2 f. plu.

(1) The stem vowel becomes short (־ֹ to ־ְ) because two
vocal Shᵉwa's cannot stand together.

(2) Kamets-hatuf (‑̣) is used as the pretonic vowel when the pronominal suffix with connecting vowel ‑̣ is used.

(3) Infinitive Construct follows analogy of the 2nd masculine, singular, Imperative with כֹּם and כֹּן the ‑̣ (ŏ) may be used with either 1st or 2nd radical of verb.

III. Vocabulary

286. נָחַשׁ (only used in Piel in O. T.) he used enchantment
287. נַ חַ שׁ enchantment (m)
288. נָחָשׁ serpent (m)
289. אַף surely, also, indeed, yea

PART TWO — Lesson Fifteen

I. Be able to attach pronominal suffixes to the verb quickly. This takes much practice. The same principles are applicable to each stem of the verb keeping in mind the type of vowel used. Changes do not occur in vowels if the vowels are unchangeable or are in a closed syllable.

II. Written word review of words Nos. 276–289.

III. Sentences to be translated into Hebrew and written in exercise book:

1. The man forsook his good father and clave unto his wife.
2. They will not be ashamed to go before the face of God.
3. Both of them went into the field to see the beasts and the cattle.
4. The woman which God gave is from the side of man.

5. The star of the night is smaller than the sun of the day.

6. What did God make for himself from the dust of the ground?

7. Is the man better than the woman? (Use He-interrogative).

8. The man forsook his father and mother and clave to his wife.

9. The serpent said that we may eat of every tree in the garden.

10. They were not ashamed of themselves when the man and his wife were both naked.

11. When the deep sleep fell upon the good man, God took from his side a rib which became a woman.

12. The woman told the crafty serpent that she could not eat from the fruit of the tree of knowledge of good and evil.

PART TWO — Lesson Sixteen

I. Reading Lesson — Gen. 3:3–5.

260. תִּגְּעוּ
      ye shall touch

Kal imperfect 2nd person masculine plural form from verb root נגע (touch). Following chart as to the classification of verbs on p. 100, this is a פ״ן and ל guttural verb. Cf. תִּקְטְלוּ.

261. פֶּן
      lest

An adverb.

262. תְּמֻתוּן
      ye shall die

Kal imperfect 2nd person masculine plural form verb מות (die). ן is an

archaic ending which was later shortened
to וֹ. ‎ ֻ ‎ is a defective writing of וֹ
(û). This is an ע״וּ verb. Cf. תִּקְטְלוּ.

263.   יֹ דֵ עַ
        knowing

Kal participle masculine singular from
verb root יֹדֵע (know). Note use of
pathach furtive under עַ. This is a
פ״וּ and ל guttural verb. Cf. קֹטֵל.
Note plural construct form יֹדְעֵי used
in verse 5.

264.   אֲ כָ לְ כֶ ם
        your eating

Kal infinitive construct from verb root
אכל (eat) and used with 2nd person
masculine plural pronominal suffix כֶם.
See p. 102, II, 3, (3). This is a פ״א
verb.   Cf. קְטָלְכֶם or קָטָלְכֶם.

265.   וְ נִ פְ קְ חוּ
        will be opened and

Nifal perfect 3rd common plural from
verb root פקח (open) used with waw
conversive. This is a ל guttural verb.
Cf. נִקְטְלוּ.

266.   עֵ י נֵ י כֶ ם
        your eyes

Plural masculine or dual construct of
עַיִן used with 2nd person masculine
plural pronominal suffix כֶם.

267.   וִ הְ יִי תֶ ם
        ye shall be and

Kal perfect 2nd masculine plural from
verb root היה (be) used with waw
conversive. This is a פ guttural,
ע״וּ and ל״ה verb. Why is ‎ ֻ ‎ used
with וֹ?

268.   כֵּא ל ׄה י ם   This is the contracted form of כֶּאֱלֹהִים
       God as   ֱ and ֶ contracted making ֵ (ê).
       Cf. לֵאמֹר (No. 110).

II. Grammar

1. How to parse a verb.

Parsing a verb is describing it as to its class, stem, action, gender, number and person. E. g. רָאָה is in ל״ה, ע and פ guttural class, Kal stem, perfect action, masculine gender, singular number, and third person.

2. The Guttural verbs.

These verbs are treated separately from the so-called weak verbs, and by some grammarians are called strong verbs, פָּעַל being used as the paradigm verb for the strong verb. The basis of those verbs is the strong verb and they are subject to the three general rules for gutturals besides a few special rules in each class. See page 39 for the three general rules for gutturals.

3. The Pe-Guttural verb. (See paradigm on pp. 124–125.)

a. The basis is the strong verb.

b. Remember the three general rules for gutturals.

    (1) They prefer "a" class vowels. Hence the ִ in the preformative of the Kal Imperfect remains ַ instead of thinning out to ִ, as יַעֲטֹל; cf. יִקְטֹל.

    (2) They prefer compound Sheᵉwa. E. g. עֲטֹל for עְטֹל in Kal Infinitive construct.

(3) They cannot be doubled. E. g. יֵעָטֵל for יֵעַטֵּל in Nifal.

c. The special rules.

(1) ה is treated in the Nifal Imperfect, Imperative, and Infinitive construct as a *weak* guttural. E. g. יֵחָשֵׁב.

(2) The "a" and "o" class Kal Imperfects.

This verb has two forms in the Kal Imperfect: one using ־ֹ as the stem vowel, and the other using ־ַ. This latter is undoubtedly due to the influence of the guttural. E. g. יַעֲטֹל and יֶעֱטַל.

(3) The use of the "e" class vowels in the "a" class Kal Imperfect, Nifal Perfect and Participle, and Hifil Perfect, for the sake of euphony. E. g. יֶעֱטַל.

(4) The use of compound Sheʷa to aid in pronunciation. E. g. יַעֲטֹל becoming יֶעֱטַל. Note that the compound Sheʷa is sometimes omitted, as נֶחְמָד in Gen. 3:6.

(5) The compound Sheʷa is changed to its corresponding short vowel when it would stand before simple Sheʷa. E. g. תַּעַטְלִי for תַּעֲטְלִי.

III. Vocabulary

290.	נָגַע he touched	292.	מוֹדָע friend (m)
291.	נֶגַע stroke, blow, plague (m)	293.	פָּקַח he opened
		294.	עַיִן eye, fountain (f)

PART TWO — LESSON SEVENTEEN

I. Reading Lesson — Gen. 3:6–9.

269.   וַתֵּרֶא

(she) saw and

Kal jussive imperfect 3rd person feminine singular with waw conversive from verb root רָאה (see). This is a פ and ע guttural, and ל"ה verb.

270.   תַאֲוָה

delight

Feminine noun, absolute singular.

271.   לָעֵינַיִם

both eyes to

Dual absolute form of עַיִן. Used with preposition לְ (to).

272.   לְהַשְׂכִּיל

cause to make to
wise

Hifil Inf. Construct from verb root שׂכל (to be wise). This is a strong or regular verb. Cf. הַקְטִיל.

273.   וַתִּתֵּן

she gave and

Kal jussive Imperfect 3rd person feminine singular from verb root נתן (give). This is a פ"ן verb. Cf. וַיִּתֵּן, mas. singular form (No. 91).

274.   עִמָּה

her with

Preposition עִם+הָ֫ (הָ֫).

275.   וַתִּפָּקַחְנָה

were opened and

Nifal jussive imperfect 3rd person feminine plural with waw conversive from verb root פקח (open). This is a ל guttural verb. Cf. תִּקָּטֵלְנָה.

276.   וַיֵּדְעוּ

they knew and

Kal jussive imperfect 3rd person masculine plural with waw conversive from

verb root יָדַע (know). This is a פ"ו
and ל guttural verb. Cf. יִקְטְלוּ.

277.   וַיִּתְפְּרוּ
        they sewed   and

Kal jussive imperfect 3rd person masculine plural with waw conversive from
verb root תָּפַר (sew). This is a ל
guttural verb but since ר is a very weak
guttural this verb is treated as a strong
verb. Cf. יִקְטְלוּ.

278.   עֲלֵה
        leaf of

Singular construct form of עָלֶה, a masculine noun.

279.   תְּאֵנָה
        fig tree

Feminine noun singular absolute.

280.   וַיִּשְׁמְעוּ
        they heard   and

Kal jussive imperfect 3rd person masculine plural, with waw conversive from
verb root שָׁמַע (hear). This is a ל
guttural verb. Cf. יִקְטְלוּ.

281.   קוֹל
        voice

Masculine noun singular absolute.

282.   מִתְהַלֵּךְ
        walking

Hithpael participle from verb root הָלַךְ
(walk, go). This is a פ guttural verb.
Cf. מִתְקַטֵּל.

283.   וַיִּתְחַבֵּא
        (he) hid himself   and

Hithpael jussive imperfect 3rd masculine
singular with waw conversive from verb
root חָבָא (hide). This is a פ guttural
and ל"א verb. Cf. יִתְקַטֵּל.

284.　אַיֶּ֫כָּה   אַיֵּ (where)+נֶ־ (nun epenthetic)+ךָ
　　　　thou where   (thou). The ה is a protective ending.
　　　　　　　　　　　　See p. 109, II, 1, as to use of the nun
　　　　　　　　　　　　epenthetic.

II. Grammar

1. The Nun Epenthetic (Energetic).

The Nun Epenthetic with its vowel ־ֶ is used before pronominal suffixes when attached to verbs and adverbs to prevent a
strained pronunciation especially in pausal and emphatic forms.
E. g. (1) אַיֶּ֫כָּה — "Where (art) thou?" — vs. 9.   אַיֵּ (where),
　　　plus נֶ־ (nun assimilated), plus ךָ (protective ה
　　　added).

　　(2) תֹּאכֲלֶ֫נָּה (3:17).
　　　　תֹּאכַל, plus נֶ־, plus הָ (the ה assimilated backwards
　　　and protective ה added).

2. The parsing of verbs.

Write out in full the parsing of every verb and check same during
class recitation. Seek accuracy.

3. The Pe-Guttural verb (continued).

a. Review and practise application of rules.

b. Select one of the following verbs and work out in full:

1. חָמַד — desire   5. עָבַד — serve
2. עָזַב — forsake   6. חָזַק — be strong
3. עָלַם — conceal   7. חָבַשׁ — bind
4. הָפַךְ — turn   8. חָדַל — cease

9. חָכַם — be wise
10. עָשַׁק — oppress
11. עָמַד — stand
12. חָשַׂךְ — withhold
13. חָשַׁב — impute

14. חָצַב — dig
15. חָלַק — distribute
16. חָלַץ — draw out
17. חָמַל — pity

III.   Vocabulary

295.   עָלֶה   leaf (m) from עָלָה
296.   אֵי   where
297.   גַּם   also
298.   עִם   with
299.   חָבָא   he hid
300.   חָגַר   he girded
301. חֲגוֹרָה   girdle (f)
302.   קוֹל   voice, thunder (m)

303.   שָׁמַע   he heard
304.   שָׂכַל   he was wise
305.   שֵׂכֶל   regard, under-
          standing (m)
306.   תַּאֲוָה   delight (f)
307.   תְּאֵנָה   fig tree
308.   תָּפַר   he sewed

PART TWO — Lesson Eighteen

I. What to prepare for examination

1. Verses 1–17 of chapter III are to be prepared for literal translation; and all verbs for parsing as to class, stem, and action.

2. Sentences will be selected from those assigned for written exercises.

3. All principles of syntax studied must be learned and illustrated.

4. The strong and guttural verbs, and all necessary rules.

II. Written or oral review of words, Nos. 290–308.

III. Grammar — the **Ayin Guttural verb.** (See paradigm on pp. 126, 127.)

1. The basis is the strong verb.

2. Remember the three general rules for gutturals.

  a. They prefer "a" class vowels. E. g. יִקְאַל for יִקְאֵל.

  b. They prefer compound Sheʷa. E. g. קָאֲלָה for קָאְלָה.

  c. They cannot be doubled. E. g. קָאֵל for קָאֵל.

3. Special rules.

  There is one special thing to note: ע is considered strong, as seen in intensive stems, קֵעֵל.

PART TWO — Lesson Nineteen

I. Reading Lesson — Gen. 3:10–13.

285. שָׁמַעְתִּי   Kal perfect 1st person singular. Cf. No.
      I heard   280.

286. וָאִירָא   Kal jussive imperfect 1st person singular
      I was afraid and   with waw conversive from verb root ירא
                     (fear). This is a פ"ו, ע guttural and
                     ל"א verb. Cf. אֶקְטֹל.

287. וָאֵחָבֵא   Nifal jussive imperfect 1st person singu-
      I hid myself and   lar. Cf. No. 283.

288. הִגִּיד   Hifil perfect 3rd masculine singular from
      (He) caused to tell   verb root נגד (tell). This is a פ"ן verb.

Cf. הִקְטִיל. Note the assimilation of נ as shown by daghes̆-forte in גּ.

289. הֲ מִן
from?

הֲ is called the He interrogative and introduces a question. See p. 113, II, 2.

290. צִוִּיתִיךָ
thee I commanded

Piel perfect 1st person singular from verb root צוה (command). Used with 2nd masculine singular pronominal suffix ךָ. This is a ע״ו and ל״ה verb. Cf. קְטַלְתִּי. This verb is always used in the intensive stem.

291. לְבִלְתִּי
not to

בִּלְתִּי is the negative used with the infinitive construct standing between the preposition and infinitive.

292. אֲכָל־
eat

Kal infinitive construct from verb root אכל (eat). The stem vowel ō is shortened to ŏ because of use of makkef. This is a פ״א verb. Cf. קְטֹל.

293. נָתַתָּה
thou gavest

Kal perfect 2nd person masculine singular from verb root נתן (give). This is a פ״נ verb. Cf. קָטַלְתָּ. Note the daghes̆-forte in תָּ shows the assimilation of נ since here it will not remain to close the syllable, there being a following consonant in the word. The final ה is a protective ה, seldom used.

294. עִמָּדִי
me with

Preposition עִמָּד 1st person singular pronominal suffix ־ִי.

295. הִוא   The pronoun used here as subject is
       she   emphatic.

296. לִי   The daghes-forte in לְ is a daghes-forte
      me to   conjunctive. See p. 39, 2.

297. הִשִּׁיאַנִי   Hifil perfect 3rd person masculine singu-
     (*he*) *caused to deceive*   lar from verb root נשא (deceive) used
           me   with 1st common singular pronominal
                      suffix נִי. This is a פ"ן and ל"א verb.
                      Cf. הִקְטִיל.

298. וָאֹכֵל   Kal jussive imperfect 1st person singu-
     I ate   and   lar. This is a shortened form for אֹאכֵל,
                      the second א being omitted since it is
                      silent. The ֵ of the waw conversive is
                      ָ (â) because א rejects the daghes-
                      forte and hence the lengthening is
                      compensative.

II. Grammar

1. The use of the negative, בִּלְתִּי.

This negative is most frequently used with the infinitive construct, and the inseparable preposition is joined to it.

E. g. לְבִלְתִּי אֲכָל־ "to not eat."

It is used sometimes with a finite verb.

2. The use of the He-interrogative.

The simple question whether direct or indirect most commonly
begins with the particle הֲ, called the He-interrogative.

a. It is regularly written . . . . הַ

E. g. הַמִּן־הָעֵץ.

b. Before gutturals or consonants with simple Shᵉwa . . הַ

E. g. הֶחָפֵץ, הַכְּתֹנֶת.

c. Before gutturals with — for dissimilarity . . . . הֶ

E. g. הֶאָמַר.

d. Sometimes with Daghes̆-forte separative . . . . . הַ

E. g. הַלְּבֶן.

3. The Ayin Guttural verb (continued).

a. Review and practice application of rules.

b. Select one of the following verbs and work out in full:

1. גָּאַל — redeem
2. שָׁאַל — ask
3. בָּהַל — confound
4. קָהַל — congregate
5. כָּחַד — hide
6. לָחַם — fight
7. פָּחַד — tremble
8. שָׁרַת — minister
9. שָׂרַף — burn
10. קָרַב — draw near

11. צָרַף — refine
12. פָּרַשׂ — spread out
13. פָּעַל — do
14. צָעַק — cry
15. בָּרַךְ — bless
16. הָרַג — kill
17. חָרַב — be dried up
18. עָרַךְ — arrange
19. רָעַשׁ — shake

III. Vocabulary

309. יָרֵא he feared
310. יִרְאָה fear, (no plural) (f)
311. מוֹרָא fear, reverence (m)

312. בִּלְתִּי not (used with infinitive)
313. נָשָׁא he deceived

PART TWO — LESSON TWENTY

I. Reading Lesson — Gen. 3:14–17.

299.	וֹאֹת *this*	The daghes in זֹ is daghes̆ forte. Why? See p. 85, II, 1. Note the use of the pausal accent ⸱⸱ (segholta).
300.	אָרוּר *cursed*	Kal gerundive from verb root ארר (curse). This is a פ guttural and ע״ע guttural verb. Cf. קָטוֹל.
301.	גְחֹנְךָ *thy stomach*	Construct from of גָחוֹן with 2nd masculine singular pronominal suffix ךָ (thee).
302.	תֵלֵךְ *thou shalt go*	Kal imperfect 2nd person masculine singular from verb root ילך (go). This is a פ״ו verb. Cf. תִּקְטֹל.
303.	יְמֵי *days of*	Plural construct of the irregular noun יוֹם.
304.	וְאֵיבָה *hatred and*	Singular absolute form with conjunction.
305.	אָשִׁית *I will put*	Kal imperfect 1st person singular from verb root שׁית (put). This is an ע״י verb. Cf. אֶקְטֹל.
306.	יְשׁוּפְךָ *thee he shall bruise*	Kal imperfect 3rd person masculine singular from verb root שׁוף (bruise). This is an ע״ו verb, used with the 2nd

person masculine singular pronominal
suffix ךָ. Cf. יָקְטֹל.

307. תְּשׁוּפֶנּוּ
him thou shalt bruise

2nd person masculine singular of same
stem of verb as No. 306. It is used with
the nun epenthetic and 3rd person masculine singular pronominal suffix וּ.
See p. 109, II, 1.

308. הַרְבָּה
causing to multiply

Hifil inf. absolute, irregular for הַרְבֵּה,
from verb root רבה (multiply). This is
a פ guttural and ל"ה verb. Cf. הַקְטֵל.
What is the force of the Infinitive Absolute?

309. אַרְבֶּה
I will cause to multiply

1st person singular impft. of same stem
as No. 308.

310. עִצְּבוֹנֵךְ
thy travail

Singular construct form with 2nd feminine singular pronominal suffix (ךְ).

311. וְהֵרֹנֵךְ
thy conception

Singular construct form with 2nd feminine singular pronominal suffix (ךְ) and
waw conjunctive.

312. עֶצֶב
travail

Singular Absolute form from same original root as No. 310. This is a Segholate
noun. Cf. אֶרֶץ. It is used with the
preposition בְּ.

313. תֵּלְדִי
*thou shalt bring
forth*

Kal imperfect, 2nd feminine singular
from verb root ילד (bring forth). This
is a פ"ו verb. Cf. תִּקְטְלִי.

314.	בָּנִים *sons*	Irregular plural absolute of בֵּן.
315.	תְּשׁוּקָתֵךְ *thy desire*	Singular construct form of תְּשׁוּקָה with 2nd feminine singular pronominal suffix (ךְ).
316.	אִשְׁתֶּךָ *thy wife*	Pausal form used with 2nd masculine singular pronominal suffix (ךָ). The accent is on the penult and thus another segholta should be used to indicate it.
317.	אֲרוּרָה *cursed*	Feminine form of the Kal gerundive. Cf. No. 300.
318.	בַּעֲבוּרֶךָ *thee on account of*	Preposition בַּעֲבוּר used with 2nd masculine singular pronominal suffix (ךָ). The daghes-lene in בּ is due to preceding disjunctive accent.
319.	תֹּאכְלֶנָּה *it thou shalt eat*	Kal imperfect 2nd masculine singular from verb root אכל (eat). This is a פ"א verb. Cf. תִּקְטֹל. Note the use of the nun epenthetic (energetic) and contracted form of 3rd feminine singular pronominal suffix הָ.

II. Grammar

1. The Lamed-Guttural verb. (See paradigm on pp. 128, 129.)

   a. The basis is the strong verb.

   b. Remember the three general rules for gutturals.

     (1) They prefer "a" class vowels. E. g. יִקְטַח for יִקְטֹח.

(2) They prefer compound Shᵉwa. This is only found before pronominal suffixes. E. g. שְׁלָחֲךָ.

(3) They cannot be doubled. This rule does not apply in the regular conjugation of this class of verbs.

c. Special rules.

(1) The retention of the original ◌ָ where in the strong verb it became ◌ֻ or ◌ֹ except in Participles, Infinitive Absolutes and Kal Infinitive Construct. E. g. קָטַח for קְטַח.

(2) The use of the Pathach-furtive after all long vowels except "a" class. E. g. קְטֵחַ.

(3) The use of a helping vowel in the second person feminine singular Perfect. The vowel used is ◌ַ. E. g. קָטַחַתְּ for קְטַחְתְּ.

III. Vocabulary

314.	אָרַר	he cursed	322.	עָקֵב	heel (m)
315.	אָיֵב	he hated	323.	עָקֹב	crooked, fraud-
316.	אֵיבָה	enmity, hatred (f)			ulent (adj.)
317.	גָּחוֹן	belly, stomach (m)	324.	עָצַב	he suffered pain
318.	חַי	life (m)	325.	עֶצֶב	pain, travail (m)
319.	הֵרוֹן	conception (m)	326.	עִצָּבוֹן	pain, travail (m)
320.	יָלִיד	born (adj.)	327.	שׁוּף	to bruise, wound
321.	עָקַב	he took by the heel, supplanted, defrauded	328.	תְּשׁוּקָה	desire, longing (f)
			329.	בַּעֲבוּר	on account of, for the sake of

PART TWO — Lesson Twenty-One

I. Written word review of words 309–329.

II. Grammar — the Lamed-Guttural verb (continued).

1. Review and practice application of rules.

2. Select one of the following verbs and work out in full.

1.	גָּבַהּ — be high		12.	בָּקַע — cleave
2.	בָּטַח — trust		13.	כָּנַע — be humbled
3.	בָּרַח — flee		14.	כָּרַע — bend the knee
4.	זָרַע — sow		15.	פָּגַע — meet, touch
5.	זָבַח — sacrifice		16.	פָּשַׁע — transgress
6.	מָשַׁח — anoint		17.	קָרַע — rend
7.	פָּרַח — flourish		18.	רָשַׁע — be wicked
8.	רָצַח — slay		19.	שָׁבַע — swear
9.	שָׁלַח — send		20.	שָׁמַע — hear
10.	שָׂמַח — rejoice		21.	תָּקַע — strike
11.	בָּלַע — swallow			

III. Sentences to be translated into Hebrew and written in exercise book: (These sentences will be due at the time of Lesson Three, Part Three).

1. Blessing God blessed the good man and his wife.

2. Their eyes will be opened because they had eaten from this tree.

3. The woman ate from the fruit of that tree which was desirable to make her wise.

4. The woman and her husband sewed for themselves girdles.

5. The serpent came into the garden and told her that she would not die.

6. The man said to the woman, Thou didst give to me the fruit which I ate.

7. Upon that day God spoke to both of them in the midst of the field.

8. Because the serpent told them to eat from the tree of the knowledge of good and evil, God said, Cursed art thou.

9. God put enmity between the seed of the serpent and the woman.

10. The man heard God's voice and said, I was afraid and I hid myself in the trees of the garden.

11. Jehovah cursed the serpent from all the cattle and beasts of the ground because he had done this.

12. The man harkened to the voice of his wife and ate from the fruit of that tree.

PARADIGMS

Kal Middle O	Kal Middle E	Hofal	Hifil	Hithpael
קָטֹל	קָטֵל	הָקְטַל	הִקְטִיל	הִתְקַטֵּל
קָטְלָה	קָטְלָה	הָקְטְלָה	הִקְטִילָה	הִתְקַטְּלָה
קָטֹלְתָּ	קָטֵלְתָּ	הָקְטַלְתָּ	הִקְטַלְתָּ	הִתְקַטַּלְתָּ
קָטֹלְתְּ	etc.	הָקְטַלְתְּ	הִקְטַלְתְּ	הִתְקַטַּלְתְּ
קָטֹלְתִּי		הָקְטַלְתִּי	הִקְטַלְתִּי	הִתְקַטַּלְתִּי
קָטְלוּ		הָקְטְלוּ	הִקְטִילוּ	הִתְקַטְּלוּ
קְטַלְתֶּם		הָקְטַלְתֶּם	הִקְטַלְתֶּם	הִתְקַטַּלְתֶּם
קְטַלְתֶּן		הָקְטַלְתֶּן	הִקְטַלְתֶּן	הִתְקַטַּלְתֶּן
קָטֹלְנוּ		הָקְטַלְנוּ	הִקְטַלְנוּ	הִתְקַטַּלְנוּ
יָקְטֹל	יָקְטֹל	יָקְטַל	יַקְטִיל	יִתְקַטֵּל
	תָּקְטֹל	תָּקְטַל	תַּקְטִיל	תִּתְקַטֵּל
	תָּקְטֹל	תָּקְטַל	תַּקְטִיל	תִּתְקַטֵּל
	תָּקְטְלִי	תָּקְטְלִי	תַּקְטִילִי	תִּתְקַטְּלִי
	אָקְטֹל	אָקְטַל	אַקְטִיל	אֶתְקַטֵּל
	יָקְטְלוּ	יָקְטְלוּ	יַקְטִילוּ	יִתְקַטְּלוּ
	תָּקְטֹלְנָה	תָּקְטַלְנָה	תַּקְטֵלְנָה	תִּתְקַטֵּלְנָה
	תָּקְטְלוּ	תָּקְטְלוּ	תַּקְטִילוּ	תִּתְקַטְּלוּ
	תָּקְטֹלְנָה	תָּקְטַלְנָה	תַּקְטֵלְנָה	תִּתְקַטֵּלְנָה
	נָקְטֹל	נָקְטַל	נַקְטִיל	נִתְקַטֵּל
	קְטֹל		הַקְטֵל	הִתְקַטֵּל
	קִטְלִי	Wanting	הַקְטִילִי	הִתְקַטְּלִי
	קִטְלוּ		הַקְטִילוּ	הִתְקַטְּלוּ
	קְטֹלְנָה		הַקְטֵלְנָה	הִתְקַטֵּלְנָה
	קָטוֹל	הָקְטֵל	הַקְטֵל	הִתְקַטֹל
	קְטֹל (קְטָל)		הַקְטִיל	הִתְקַטֵּל
	קֹטֵל	מָקְטָל	מַקְטִיל	מִתְקַטֵּל

STRONG VERB

Pual	Piel	Nifal	Kal		
קֻטַּל	קִטֵּל	נִקְטַל	קָטַל	Sg. 3 m.	
קֻטְּלָה	קִטְּלָה	נִקְטְלָה	קָטְלָה	3 f.	
קֻטַּלְתָּ	קִטַּלְתָּ	נִקְטַלְתָּ	קָטַלְתָּ	2 m.	
קֻטַּלְתְּ	קִטַּלְתְּ	נִקְטַלְתְּ	קָטַלְתְּ	2 f.	Perfect
קֻטַּלְתִּי	קִטַּלְתִּי	נִקְטַלְתִּי	קָטַלְתִּי	1 c.	
קֻטְּלוּ	קִטְּלוּ	נִקְטְלוּ	קָטְלוּ	Pl. 3 c.	
קֻטַּלְתֶּם	קִטַּלְתֶּם	נִקְטַלְתֶּם	קְטַלְתֶּם	2 m.	
קֻטַּלְתֶּן	קִטַּלְתֶּן	נִקְטַלְתֶּן	קְטַלְתֶּן	2 f.	
קֻטַּלְנוּ	קִטַּלְנוּ	נִקְטַלְנוּ	קָטַלְנוּ	1 c.	
יְקֻטַּל	יְקַטֵּל	יִקָּטֵל	יִקְטֹל	Sg. 3 m.	
תְּקֻטַּל	תְּקַטֵּל	תִּקָּטֵל	תִּקְטֹל	3 f.	
תְּקֻטַּל	תְּקַטֵּל	תִּקָּטֵל	תִּקְטֹל	2 m.	
תְּקֻטְּלִי	תְּקַטְּלִי	תִּקָּטְלִי	תִּקְטְלִי	2 f.	
אֲקֻטַּל	אֲקַטֵּל	אֶקָּטֵל	אֶקְטֹל	1 c.	Imperfect
יְקֻטְּלוּ	יְקַטְּלוּ	יִקָּטְלוּ	יִקְטְלוּ	Pl. 3 m.	
תְּקֻטַּלְנָה	תְּקַטֵּלְנָה	תִּקָּטַלְנָה	תִּקְטֹלְנָה	3 f.	
תְּקֻטְּלוּ	תְּקַטְּלוּ	תִּקָּטְלוּ	תִּקְטְלוּ	2 m.	
תְּקֻטַּלְנָה	תְּקַטֵּלְנָה	תִּקָּטַלְנָה	תִּקְטֹלְנָה	2 f.	
נְקֻטַּל	נְקַטֵּל	נִקָּטֵל	נִקְטֹל	1 c.	
	קַטֵּל	הִקָּטֵל	קְטֹל	Sg. 2 m.	
	קַטְּלִי	הִקָּטְלִי	קִטְלִי	2 f.	Imperative
Wanting	קַטְּלוּ	הִקָּטְלוּ	קִטְלוּ	Pl. 2 m.	
	קַטֵּלְנָה	הִקָּטַלְנָה	קְטֹלְנָה	2 f.	
קֻטֹּל	קַטֹּל קַטֵּל	הִקָּטֹל נִקְטֹל	קָטוֹל	Absolute	Infin.
	קַטֵּל	הִקָּטֵל	קְטֹל	Construct	
מְקֻטָּל	מְקַטֵּל	נִקְטָל	קֹטֵל	Participle	
			קָטוּל	Gerundive	

Hofal	Hifil	Hithpael	Pual
הָעֳטַל	הֶעֱטִיל	הִתְעַטֵּל	עֻטַּל
הָעָטְלָה	הֶעֱטִילָה	Regular	Regular
הָעֳטַלְתָּ	הֶעֱטַלְתָּ	as	as
הָעֳטַלְתְּ	הֶעֱטַלְתְּ	Strong	Strong
הָעֳטַלְתִּי	הֶעֱטַלְתִּי	Verb	Verb
הָעָטְלוּ	הֶעֱטִילוּ		
הָעֳטַלְתֶּם	הֶעֱטַלְתֶּם		
הָעֳטַלְתֶּן	הֶעֱטַלְתֶּן		
הָעֳטַלְנוּ	הֶעֱטַלְנוּ		
יָעֳטַל	יַעֲטִיל	יִתְעַטֵּל	יְעֻטַּל
תָּעֳטַל	תַּעֲטִיל	Regular	Regular
תָּעֳטַל	תַּעֲטִיל	as	as
תָּעָטְלִי	תַּעֲטִילִי	Strong	Strong
אָעֳטַל	אַעֲטִיל	Verb	Verb
יָעָטְלוּ	יַעֲטִילוּ		
תָּעֳטַלְנָה	תַּעֲטֵלְנָה		
תָּעָטְלוּ	תַּעֲטִילוּ		
תָּעֳטַלְנָה	תַּעֲטֵלְנָה		
נָעֳטַל	נַעֲטִיל		
	הַעֲטֵל	הִתְעַטֵּל	
Wanting	הַעֲטִילִי	Regular as	Wanting
	הַעֲטִילוּ	Strong Verb	
	הַעֲטֵלְנָה		
הָעֳטֵל	הַעֲטֵל	הִתְעַטֵּל	עֻטֹּל
	הַעֲטִיל		
מָעֳטָל	מַעֲטִיל	מִתְעַטֵּל	מְעֻטָּל

PE GUTTURAL VERB

Piel	Nifal	Kal			
עִטֵּל	נֶעֱטַל	עָטַל		Sg. 3 m.	Perfect
	נֶעֶטְלָה	עָטְלָה		3 f.	
Regular	נֶעֱטַלְתָּ	עָטַלְתָּ		2 m.	
as	נֶעֱטַלְתְּ	עָטַלְתְּ		2 f.	
Strong	נֶעֱטַלְתִּי	עָטַלְתִּי		1 c.	
Verb	נֶעֶטְלוּ	עָטְלוּ		Pl. 3 c.	
	נֶעֱטַלְתֶּם	עֲטַלְתֶּם		2 m.	
	נֶעֱטַלְתֶּן	עֲטַלְתֶּן		2 f.	
	נֶעֱטַלְנוּ	עָטַלְנוּ		1 c.	
יְעַטֵּל	יֵעָטֵל	יֶעֱטַל	יַעֲטֹל	Sg. 3 m.	Imperfect
	תֵּעָטֵל	תֶּעֱטַל	תַּעֲטֹל	3 f.	
Regular	תֵּעָטֵל	תֶּעֱטַל	תַּעֲטֹל	2 m	
as	תֵּעָטְלִי	תֶּעֶטְלִי	תַּעַטְלִי	2 f.	
Strong	אֵעָטֵל	אֶעֱטַל	אֶעֱטֹל	1 c.	
Verb	יֵעָטְלוּ	יֶעֶטְלוּ	יַעַטְלוּ	Pl. 3 m.	
	תֵּעָטַלְנָה	תֶּעֱטַלְנָה	תַּעֲטֹלְנָה	3 f.	
	תֵּעָטְלוּ	תֶּעֶטְלוּ	תַּעַטְלוּ	2 m	
	תֵּעָטַלְנָה	תֶּעֱטַלְנָה	תַּעֲטֹלְנָה	2 f.	
	נֵעָטֵל	נֶעֱטַל	נַעֲטֹל	1 c.	
עַטֵּל	הֵעָטֵל	עֲטַל	עֲטֹל	Sg. 2 m.	Imperative
Regular	הֵעָטְלִי	עִטְלִי	עִטְלִי	2 f.	
as Strong	הֵעָטְלוּ	עִטְלוּ	עִטְלוּ	Pl. 2 m.	
Verb	הֵעָטַלְנָה	עֲטַלְנָה	עֲטֹלְנָה	2 f.	
עַטֹּל, עַטֵּל	נַעֲטוֹל, הֵעָטֹל	עָטוֹל		Absolute	Infin.
עַטֵּל	הֵעָטֵל	עֲטֹל		Construct	
מְעַטֵּל	נֶעֱטָל	עֹטֵל		Participle	
		עָטוּל		Gerundive	

Paradigm C — THE

Hofal	Hifil	Hithpael	Pual
הָקְאַל	הִקְאִיל	הִתְקָאֵל	קֻאַל
Regular	Regular	הִתְקָאֲלָה	קֻאֲלָה
as	as	הִתְקָאַלְתָּ	קֻאַלְתָּ
Kal	Strong	הִתְקָאַלְתְּ	קֻאַלְתְּ
	Verb	הִתְקָאַלְתִּי	קֻאַלְתִּי
		הִתְקָאֲלוּ	קֻאֲלוּ
		הִתְקָאַלְתֶּם	קֻאַלְתֶּם
		הִתְקָאַלְתֶּן	קֻאַלְתֶּן
		הִתְקָאַלְנוּ	קֻאַלְנוּ
יָקְאַל	יַקְאִיל	יִתְקָאֵל	יְקֻאַל
Regular	Regular	תִּתְקָאֵל	תְּקֻאַל
as	as	תִּתְקָאֵל	תְּקֻאַל
Kal	Strong	תִּתְקָאֲלִי	תְּקֻאֲלִי
	Verb	אֶתְקָאֵל	אֲקֻאַל
		יִתְקָאֲלוּ	יְקֻאֲלוּ
		תִּתְקָאַלְנָה	תְּקֻאַלְנָה
		תִּתְקָאֲלוּ	תְּקֻאֲלוּ
		תִּתְקָאַלְנָה	תְּקֻאַלְנָה
		נִתְקָאֵל	נְקֻאַל
	הַקְאֵל	הִתְקָאֵל	
Wanting	Regular as	הִתְקָאֲלִי	Wanting
	Strong Verb	הִתְקָאֲלוּ	
		הִתְקָאַלְנָה	
הָקְאֵל	הַקְאֵל		
	הַקְאִיל	הִתְקָאֵל	
מָקְאָל	מַקְאִיל	מִתְקָאֵל	מְקֻאָל

AYIN GUTTURAL VERB

Piel	Nifal	Kal		
קָאֵל, קָאַל	נִקְאַל	קָאַל	Sg. 3 m.	
קֵאֲלָה	נִקְאֲלָה	קָאֲלָה	3 f.	
קֵאַלְתָּ	נִקְאַלְתָּ	קָאַלְתָּ	2 m.	
קֵאַלְתְּ	נִקְאַלְתְּ	קָאַלְתְּ	2 f.	Perfect
קֵאַלְתִּי	נִקְאַלְתִּי	קָאַלְתִּי	1 c.	
קֵאֲלוּ	נִקְאֲלוּ	קָאֲלוּ	Pl. 3 c.	
קֵאַלְתֶּם	נִקְאַלְתֶּם	קְאַלְתֶּם	2 m.	
קֵאַלְתֶּן	נִקְאַלְתֶּן	קְאַלְתֶּן	2 f.	
קֵאַלְנוּ	נִקְאַלְנוּ	קָאַלְנוּ	1 c.	
יְקָאֵל	יִקָּאֵל	יִקְאַל	Sg. 3 m.	
תְּקָאֵל	תִּקָּאֵל	תִּקְאַל	3 f.	
תְּקָאֵל	תִּקָּאֵל	תִּקְאַל	2 m.	
תְּקָאֲלִי	תִּקָּאֲלִי	תִּקְאֲלִי	2 f.	
אֲקָאֵל	אֶקָּאֵל	אֶקְאַל	1 c.	
יְקָאֲלוּ	יִקָּאֲלוּ	יִקְאֲלוּ	Pl. 3 m.	Imperfect
תְּקָאֵלְנָה	תִּקָּאַלְנָה	תִּקְאַלְנָה	3 f.	
תְּקָאֲלוּ	תִּקָּאֲלוּ	תִּקְאֲלוּ	2 m.	
תְּקָאֵלְנָה	תִּקָּאַלְנָה	תִּקְאַלְנָה	2 f.	
נְקָאֵל	נִקָּאֵל	נִקְאַל	1 c.	
קָאֵל	הִקָּאֵל	קְאַל	Sg. 2 m.	
קָאֲלִי	הִקָּאֲלִי	קַאֲלִי	2 f.	Imperative
קָאֲלוּ	הִקָּאֲלוּ	קַאֲלוּ	Pl. 2 m.	
קָאֵלְנָה	הִקָּאַלְנָה	קְאַלְנָה	2 f.	
קָאֵל	נִקְאוֹל	קָאוֹל	Absolute	Infin.
קָאֵל	הִקָּאֵל	קְאֹל	Construct	
מְקָאֵל	נִקְאָל	קֹאֵל	Participle	
		קָאוּל	Gerundive	

Hofal	Hifil	Hithpael	Pual
הָקְטַח	הִקְטִיח	הִתְקַטַּח	קֻטַּח
Regular	הִקְטִיחָה	הִתְקַטְּחָה	Regular
as	הִקְטַחְתָּ	הִתְקַטַּחְתָּ	as
Kal	הִקְטַחַתְּ	הִתְקַטַּחַתְּ	Kal
	הִקְטַחְתִּי	הִתְקַטַּחְתִּי	
	הִקְטִיחוּ	הִתְקַטְּחוּ	
	הִקְטַחְתֶּם	הִתְקַטַּחְתֶּם	
	הִקְטַחְתֶּן	הִתְקַטַּחְתֶּן	
	הִקְטַחְנוּ	הִתְקַטַּחְנוּ	
יָקְטַח	יַקְטִיח	יִתְקַטַּח	יְקֻטַּח
Regular	תַּקְטִיח	תִּתְקַטַּח	Regular
as	תַּקְטִיח	תִּתְקַטַּח	as
Kal	תַּקְטִיחִי	תִּתְקַטְּחִי	Kal
	אַקְטִיח	אֶתְקַטַּח	
	יַקְטִיחוּ	יִתְקַטְּחוּ	
	תַּקְטֵחְנָה	תִּתְקַטַּחְנָה	
	תַּקְטִיחוּ	תִּתְקַטְּחוּ	
	תַּקְטֵחְנָה	תִּתְקַטַּחְנָה	
	נַקְטִיח	נִתְקַטַּח	
Wanting	הַקְטַח	הִתְקַטַּח	Wanting
	הַקְטִיחִי	הִתְקַטְּחִי	
	הַקְטִיחוּ	הִתְקַטְּחוּ	
	הַקְטֵחְנָה	הִתְקַטַּחְנָה	
הָקְטֵם	הַקְטֵם		קֻטֹּם
	הַקְטִיח	הִתְקַטֵּח	
מָקְטָח	מַקְטִיח	מִתְקַטֵּח	מְקֻטָּח

LAMED GUTTURAL VERB

Piel	Nifal	Kal		
קִטַּח	נִקְטַח	קָטַח	Sg. 3 m.	
קִטְּחָה	נִקְטְחָה	קָטְחָה	3 f.	
קִטַּחְתָּ	נִקְטַחְתָּ	קָטַחְתָּ	2 m.	
קִטַּחַתְּ	נִקְטַחַתְּ	קָטַחַתְּ	2 f.	Perfect
קִטַּחְתִּי	נִקְטַחְתִּי	קָטַחְתִּי	1 c.	
קִטְּחוּ	נִקְטְחוּ	קָטְחוּ	Pl. 3 c.	
קִטַּחְתֶּם	נִקְטַחְתֶּם	קְטַחְתֶּם	2 m.	
קִטַּחְתֶּן	נִקְטַחְתֶּן	קְטַחְתֶּן	2 f.	
קִטַּחְנוּ	נִקְטַחְנוּ	קָטַחְנוּ	1 c.	
יְקַטַּח	יִקָּטַח	יִקְטַח	Sg. 3 m.	
תְּקַטַּח	תִּקָּטַח	תִּקְטַח	3 f.	
תְּקַטַּח	תִּקָּטַח	תִּקְטַח	2 m.	
תְּקַטְּחִי	תִּקָּטְחִי	תִּקְטְחִי	2 f.	
אֲקַטַּח	אֶקָּטַח	אֶקְטַח	1 c.	Imperfect
יְקַטְּחוּ	יִקָּטְחוּ	יִקְטְחוּ	Pl. 3 m.	
תְּקַטֵּחְנָה	תִּקָּטַחְנָה	תִּקְטַחְנָה	3 f.	
תְּקַטְּחוּ	תִּקָּטְחוּ	תִּקְטְחוּ	2 m.	
תְּקַטֵּחְנָה	תִּקָּטַחְנָה	תִּקְטַחְנָה	2 f.	
נְקַטַּח	נִקָּטַח	נִקְטַח	1 c.	
קַטַּח	הִקָּטַח	קְטַח	Sg. 2 m.	
קַטְּחִי	הִקָּטְחִי	קִטְחִי	2 f.	Imperative
קַטְּחוּ	הִקָּטְחוּ	קִטְחוּ	Pl. 2 m.	
קַטֵּחְנָה	הִקָּטַחְנָה	קְטַחְנָה	2 f.	
קַטֹּח	נִקְטֹחַ	קָטוֹחַ	Absolute	Infin.
קַטַּח	הִקָּטַח	קְטֹחַ	Construct	
מְקַטֵּחַ	נִקְטָח	קֹטֵחַ	Participle	
		קָטוּחַ	Gerundive	

Paradigm E — THE

Hofal	Hifil	Hithpael	Pual
הֻטַּל	הִטִּיל	הִתְנַטֵּל	נֻטַּל
הֻטְּלָה	הִטִּילָה	Regular	Regular
הֻטַּלְתָּ	הִטַּלְתָּ	as	as
הֻטַּלְתְּ	הִטַּלְתְּ	Strong	Strong
הֻטַּלְתִּי	הִטַּלְתִּי	Verb	Verb
הֻטְּלוּ	הִטִּילוּ		
הֻטַּלְתֶּם	הִטַּלְתֶּם		
הֻטַּלְתֶּן	הִטַּלְתֶּן		
הֻטַּלְנוּ	הִטַּלְנוּ		
יֻטַּל	יַטִּיל	יִתְנַטֵּל	יְנֻטַּל
תֻּטַּל	תַּטִּיל	Regular	Regular
תֻּטַּל	תַּטִּיל	as	as
תֻּטְּלִי	תַּטִּילִי	Strong	Strong
אֻטַּל	אַטִּיל	Verb	Verb
יֻטְּלוּ	יַטִּילוּ		
תֻּטַּלְנָה	תַּטֵּלְנָה		
תֻּטְּלוּ	תַּטִּילוּ		
תֻּטַּלְנָה	תַּטֵּלְנָה		
נֻטַּל	נַטִּיל		
	הַטֵּל	הִתְנַטֵּל	
Wanting	הַטִּילִי	Regular as	Wanting
	הַטִּילוּ	Strong Verb	
	הַטֵּלְנָה		
הֻטֵּל	הַטֵּל	הִתְנַטֹּל	נֻטֹּל
הֻטֵּל	הַטִּיל	הִתְנַטֵּל	
מֻטָּל	מַטִּיל	מִתְנַטֵּל	מְנֻטָּל

PE NUN VERB

Piel	Nifal	Kal			
נָטֵל	נִטַּל	נָטַל		Sg. 3 m.	
Regular	נִטְלָה			3 f.	
as	נִטַּלְתָּ	Regular		2 m.	
Strong	נִטַּלְתְּ	as		2 f.	Perfect
Verb	נִטַּלְתִּי	Strong		1 c.	
	נִטְלוּ	Verb		Pl. 3 c.	
	נִטַּלְתֶּם			2 m.	
	נִטַּלְתֶּן			2 f.	
	נִטַּלְנוּ			1 c.	
יְנַטֵּל	יִנָּטֵל	יִטֹּל	יִטַּל	Sg. 3 m.	
Regular	Regular	תִּטֹּל	תִּטַּל	3 f.	
as	as	תִּטֹּל	תִּטַּל	2 m.	
Strong	Strong	תִּטְּלִי	תִּטְּלִי	2 f.	Imperfect
Verb	Verb	אֶטֹּל	אֶטַּל	1 c.	
		יִטְּלוּ	יִטְּלוּ	Pl. 3 m.	
		תִּטֹּלְנָה	תִּטַּלְנָה	3 f.	
		תִּטְּלוּ	תִּטְּלוּ	2 m.	
		תִּטֹּלְנָה	תִּטַּלְנָה	2 f.	
		נִטֹּל	נִטַּל	1 c.	
נַטֵּל	הִנָּטֵל	נְטֹל	טַל	Sg. 2 m.	
Regular	Regular	נִטְלִי	טְלִי	2 f.	
as	as	נִטְלוּ	טְלוּ	Pl. 2 m.	Imperative
Strong	Strong	נְטֹלְנָה	טַלְנָה	2 f.	
Verb	Verb				
נַטֹּל, נַטֵּל	הִנָּטֹל, נִטּוֹל	נָטוֹל		Absolute	Infin.
נַטֵּל	הִנָּטֵל	נְטֹל	טֶלֶת	Construct	
מְנַטֵּל	נִטָּל	נֹטֵל		Participle	
		נָטוּל		Gerundive	

Paradigm F — THE PE WAW (פ"ו)

Hofal	Hifil — פ"י	Hifil — פ"ו	Hithpael	Pual
הוּטַל	הֵיטִיל	הוֹטִיל	הִתְוַטֵּל	יֻטַּל
הוּטְלָה	הֵיטִילָה	הוֹטִילָה	Regular as Strong Verb	Regular as Strong Verb
הוּטַלְתָּ	הֵיטַלְתָּ	הוֹטַלְתָּ		
הוּטַלְתְּ	הֵיטַלְתְּ	הוֹטַלְתְּ		
הוּטַלְתִּי	הֵיטַלְתִּי	הוֹטַלְתִּי		
הוּטְלוּ	הֵיטִילוּ	הוֹטִילוּ		
הוּטַלְתֶּם	הֵיטַלְתֶּם	הוֹטַלְתֶּם		
הוּטַלְתֶּן	הֵיטַלְתֶּן	הוֹטַלְתֶּן		
הוּטַלְנוּ	הֵיטַלְנוּ	הוֹטַלְנוּ		
יוּטַל	יֵיטִיל	יוֹטִיל	יִתְוַטֵּל	יְטֻטַּל
תּוּטַל	תֵּיטִיל	תּוֹטִיל	Regular as Strong Verb	Regular as Strong Verb
תּוּטַל	תֵּיטִיל	תּוֹטִיל		
תּוּטְלִי	תֵּיטִילִי	תּוֹטִילִי		
אוּטַל	אֵיטִיל	אוֹטִיל		
יוּטְלוּ	יֵיטִילוּ	יוֹטִילוּ		
תּוּטַלְנָה	תֵּיטֵלְנָה	תּוֹטֵלְנָה		
תּוּטְלוּ	תֵּיטִילוּ	תּוֹטִילוּ		
תּוּטַלְנָה	תֵּיטֵלְנָה	תּוֹטֵלְנָה		
נוּטַל	נֵיטִיל	נוֹטִיל		
Wanting	הֵיטֵל	הוֹטֵל	הִתְוַטֵּל	Wanting
	הֵיטִילִי	הוֹטִילִי	Regular as Strong Verb	
	הֵיטִילוּ	הוֹטִילוּ		
	הֵיטֵלְנָה	הוֹטֵלְנָה		
	הֵיטֵל	הוֹטֵל	הִתְוַטֵּל	יֻטֹּל
	הֵיטִיל	הוֹטִיל	הִתְוַטֵּל	
מוּטָל	מֵיטִיל	מוֹטִיל	מִתְוַטֵּל	מְיֻטָּל

AND PE YODH (פ"י) VERBS

Piel	Nifal	Kal — פ"י	Kal — פ"ו		
יִטֵּל	נוֹטַל	יָטַל	יָטַל	Sg. 3 m.	Perfect
Regular	נוֹטְלָה	Regular	Regular	3 f.	
as	נוֹטַלְתָּ	as	as	2 m.	
Strong	נוֹטַלְתְּ	Strong	Strong	2 f.	
Verb	נוֹטַלְתִּי	Verb	Verb	1 c.	
	נוֹטְלוּ			Pl. 3 c.	
	נוֹטַלְתֶּם			2 m.	
	נוֹטַלְתֶּן			2 f.	
	נוֹטַלְנוּ			1 c.	
יְוַטֵּל	יִנָּטֵל	יִיטַל	יִיטַל	יֵטֵל	Sg. 3 m.	Imperfect
Regular	Regular	תִּיטַל	תִּיטַל	תֵּטֵל	3 f.	
as	as	תִּיטַל	תִּיטַל	תֵּטֵל	2 m.	
Strong	Strong	תִּיטְלִי	תִּיטְלִי	תֵּטְלִי	2 f.	
Verb	Verb	אִיטַל	אִיטַל	אֵטֵל	1 c.	
		יִיטְלוּ	יִיטְלוּ	יֵטְלוּ	Pl. 3 m.	
		תִּיטַלְנָה	תִּיטַלְנָה	תֵּטַלְנָה	3 f.	
		תִּיטְלוּ	תִּיטְלוּ	תֵּטְלוּ	2 m.	
		תִּיטַלְנָה	תִּיטַלְנָה	תֵּטַלְנָה	2 f.	
		נִיטַל	נִיטַל	נֵטֵל	1 c.	
יַטֵּל	הִנָּטֵל	יְטַל	טַל, טֵל	Sg. 2 m.	Imperative
Regular	Regular	יְטְלִי	טְלִי	2 f.	
as	as	יְטְלוּ	טְלוּ	Pl. 2 m.	
Strong	Strong	יְטַלְנָה	טַלְנָה	2 f.	
Verb	Verb				
יַטֵּל, יַטֵּל		יָטוֹל	יָטוֹל יָטוֹל	Absolute	Infin.
יַטֵּל	הִנָּטֵל	יְטֹל	טֶלֶת יְטֹל, טֶלֶת	Construct	
מְיַטֵּל	נוֹטָל	יֹטֵל	יֹטֵל	Participle	
		יָטוּל	יָטוּל	Gerundive	

Paradigm G —ʾTHE

Hofal	Hifil	Hithpael	Pual
הָקְטָה	הִקְטָה	הִתְקַטָּה	קֻטָּה
הָקְטְתָה	הִקְטְתָה	הִתְקַטְּתָה	קֻטְּתָה
הָקְטֵיתָ	הִקְטֵיתָ (־ֵתָ)	הִתְקַטֵּיתָ	קֻטֵּיתָ
הָקְטֵית	הִקְטִית (־ֵת)	הִתְקַטֵּית	קֻטֵּית
הָקְטֵיתִי	הִקְטֵיתִי (־ֵיתִי)	הִתְקַטֵּיתִי	קֻטֵּיתִי
הָקְטוּ	הִקְטוּ	הִתְקַטּוּ	קֻטּוּ
הָקְטֵיתֶם	הִקְטִיתֶם (־ֵתֶם)	הִתְקַטִּיתֶם	קֻטֵּיתֶם
הָקְטֵיתֶן	הִקְטִיתֶן	הִתְקַטִּיתֶן	קֻטֵּיתֶן
הָקְטֵינוּ	הִקְטֵינוּ	הִתְקַטֵּינוּ	קֻטֵּינוּ
יָקְטֶה	יַקְטֶה	יִתְקַטֶּה	יְקֻטֶּה
תָּקְטֶה	תַּקְטֶה	תִּתְקַטֶּה	תְּקֻטֶּה
תָּקְטֶה	תַּקְטֶה	תִּתְקַטֶּה	תְּקֻטֶּה
תָּקְטִי	תַּקְטִי	תִּתְקַטִּי	תְּקֻטִּי
אָקְטֶה	אַקְטֶה	אֶתְקַטֶּה	אֲקֻטֶּה
יָקְטוּ	יַקְטוּ	יִתְקַטּוּ	יְקֻטּוּ
תָּקְטֶינָה	תַּקְטֶינָה	תִּתְקַטֶּינָה	תְּקֻטֶּינָה
תָּקְטוּ	תַּקְטוּ	תִּתְקַטּוּ	תְּקֻטּוּ
תָּקְטֶינָה	תַּקְטֶינָה	תִּתְקַטֶּינָה	תְּקֻטֶּינָה
נָקְטֶה	נַקְטֶה	נִתְקַטֶּה	נְקֻטֶּה
	הַקְטֵה	הִתְקַטֵּה, הִתְקַט	
Wanting	הַקְטִי	הִתְקַטִּי	*Wanting*
	הַקְטוּ	הִתְקַטּוּ	
	הַקְטֶינָה	הִתְקַטֵּינָה	
הָקְטֵה	הַקְטֵה		
	הַקְטוֹת	הִתְקַטּוֹת	קֻטּוֹת
מָקְטֶה	מַקְטֶה	מִתְקַטֶּה	מְקֻטֶּה

LAMED HE (ל"ה) VERB

Piel	Nifal	Kal		
קָשָׂה	נִקְשָׂה	קָשָׂה	Sg. 3 m.	Perfect
קִשְּׂתָה	נִקְשְׂתָה	קָשְׂתָה	3 f.	
קִשִּׂיתָ	נִקְשֵׂיתָ (־יתָ)	קָשִׂיתָ	2 m.	
קִשִּׂית	נִקְשֵׂית	קָשִׂית	2 f.	
קִשִּׂיתִי, קִשֵּׂיתִי	נִקְשֵׂיתִי	קָשִׂיתִי	1 c.	
קִשּׂוּ	נִקְשׂוּ	קָשׂוּ	Pl. 3 c.	
קִשִּׂיתֶם	נִקְשֵׂיתֶם	קְשִׂיתֶם	2 m.	
קִשִּׂיתֶן	נִקְשֵׂיתֶן	קְשִׂיתֶן	2 f.	
קִשִּׂינוּ	נִקְשֵׂינוּ	קָשִׂינוּ	1 c.	
יְקַשֶּׂה	יִקָּשֶׂה	יִקְשֶׂה	Sg. 3 m.	Imperfect
תְּקַשֶּׂה	תִּקָּשֶׂה	תִּקְשֶׂה	3 f.	
תְּקַשֶּׂה	תִּקָּשֶׂה	תִּקְשֶׂה	2 m.	
תְּקַשִּׂי	תִּקָּשִׂי	תִּקְשִׂי	2 f.	
אֲקַשֶּׂה	אֶקָּשֶׂה	אֶקְשֶׂה	1 c.	
יְקַשּׂוּ	יִקָּשׂוּ	יִקְשׂוּ	Pl. 3 m.	
תְּקַשֶּׂינָה	תִּקָּשֶׂינָה	תִּקְשֶׂינָה	3 f.	
תְּקַשּׂוּ	תִּקָּשׂוּ	תִּקְשׂוּ	2 m.	
תְּקַשֶּׂינָה	תִּקָּשֶׂינָה	תִּקְשֶׂינָה	2 f.	
נְקַשֶּׂה	נִקָּשֶׂה	נִקְשֶׂה	1 c.	
קַשֵּׂה, קַשׂ	הִקָּשֵׂה	קְשֵׂה	Sg. 2 m.	Imperative
קַשִּׂי	הִקָּשִׂי	קְשִׂי	2 f.	
קַשּׂוּ	הִקָּשׂוּ	קְשׂוּ	Pl. 2 m.	
קַשֶּׂינָה	הִקָּשֶׂינָה	קְשֶׂינָה	2 f.	
קַשֹּׂה, קַשֵּׂה	נִקְשֹׂה, הִקָּשֵׂה	קָשֹׂה	Absolute	Infin.
קַשּׂוֹת	הִקָּשׂוֹת	קְשׂוֹת	Construct	
מְקַשֶּׂה	נִקְשֶׂה	קֹשֶׂה	Participle	
		קָשׂוּי	Gerundive	

Paradigm H — THE

Hofal	Hifil	Hithpael	Pual
הָקְטָא	הִקְטִיא	הִתְקַטֵּא	קֻטָּא
הָקְטָאָה	הִקְטִיאָה	הִתְקַטְּאָה	קֻטְּאָה
הָקְטֵאתָ	הִקְטֵאתָ	הִתְקַטֵּאתָ	קֻטֵּאתָ
	הִקְטֵאת	הִתְקַטֵּאת	
etc.	הִקְטֵאתִי	הִתְקַטֵּאתִי	etc.
Regular	הִקְטִיאוּ	הִתְקַטְּאוּ	Regular
	הִקְטֵאתֶם	הִתְקַטֵּאתֶם	
	הִקְטֵאתֶן	הִתְקַטֵּאתֶן	
	הִקְטֵאנוּ	הִתְקַטֵּאנוּ	
יָקְטָא	יַקְטִיא	יִתְקַטֵּא	יְקֻטָּא
	תַּקְטִיא	תִּתְקַטֵּא	
Regular	תַּקְטִיא	תִּתְקַטֵּא	Regular
as	תַּקְטִיאִי	תִּתְקַטְּאִי	as
Kal	אַקְטִיא	אֶתְקַטֵּא	Kal
	יַקְטִיאוּ	יִתְקַטְּאוּ	
	תַּקְטֶאנָה	תִּתְקַטֵּאנָה	
	תַּקְטִיאוּ	תִּתְקַטְּאוּ	
	תַּקְטֶאנָה	תִּתְקַטֵּאנָה	
	נַקְטִיא	נִתְקַטֵּא	
	הַקְטֵא	הִתְקַטֵּא	
	הַקְטִיאִי	הִתְקַטְּאִי	
Wanting	הַקְטִיאוּ	הִתְקַטְּאוּ	Wanting
	הַקְטֶאנָה	הִתְקַטֵּאנָה	
הָקְטֵא	הַקְטֵא	הִתְקַטֵּא	קֻטָּא
	הַקְטִיא	הִתְקַטֵּא	
מָקְטָא	מַקְטִיא	מִתְקַטֵּא	מְקֻטָּא

LAMED ALEF (ל"א) VERB

Piel	Nifal	Kal		
קִטֵּא, קִטָּא	נִקְטָא	קָטָא, קָטֵא	Sg. 3 m.	
קִטְּאָה	נִקְטְאָה	קָטְאָה	3 f.	
קִטֵּאתָ	נִקְטֵאתָ	קָטֵאתָ	2 m.	
קִטֵּאת	נִקְטֵאת	קָטֵאת	2 f.	Perfect
קִטֵּאתִי	נִקְטֵאתִי	קָטֵאתִי	1 c.	
קִטְּאוּ	נִקְטְאוּ	קָטְאוּ	Pl. 3 c.	
קִטֵּאתֶם	נִקְטֵאתֶם	קְטָאתֶם	2 m.	
קִטֵּאתֶן	נִקְטֵאתֶן	קְטָאתֶן	2 f.	
קִטֵּאנוּ	נִקְטֵאנוּ	קָטֵאנוּ	1 c.	
יְקַטֵּא	יִקָּטֵא	יִקְטָא	Sg. 3 m.	
תְּקַטֵּא	תִּקָּטֵא	תִּקְטָא	3 f.	
תְּקַטֵּא	תִּקָּטֵא	תִּקְטָא	2 m.	
תְּקַטְּאִי	תִּקָּטְאִי	תִּקְטְאִי	2 f.	
אֲקַטֵּא	אֶקָּטֵא	אֶקְטָא	1 c.	Imperfect
יְקַטְּאוּ	יִקָּטְאוּ	יִקְטְאוּ	Pl. 3 m.	
תְּקַטֵּאנָה	תִּקָּטֵאנָה	תִּקְטֶאנָה	3 f.	
תְּקַטְּאוּ	תִּקָּטְאוּ	תִּקְטְאוּ	2 m.	
תְּקַטֵּאנָה	תִּקָּטֵאנָה	תִּקְטֶאנָה	2 f.	
נְקַטֵּא	נִקָּטֵא	נִקְטָא	1 c.	
קַטֵּא	הִקָּטֵא	קְטָא	Sg. 2 m.	
קַטְּאִי	הִקָּטְאִי	קִטְאִי	2 f.	Imperative
קַטְּאוּ	הִקָּטְאוּ	קִטְאוּ	Pl. 2 m.	
קַטֵּאנָה	הִקָּטֵאנָה	קְטֶאנָה	2 f.	
קַטֹּא	נִקְטֹא	קָטוֹא	Absolute	Infin.
קַטֵּא	הִקָּטֵא	קְטֹא	Construct	
מְקַטֵּא	נִקְטָא	קֹטֵא	Participle	
		קָטוֹא	Gerundive	

Paradigm I — THE AYIN

Hithpoel	Poal	Poel	Hofal
הִתְקוֹטֵט	קוֹטַט	קוֹטֵט	הוּקַט
הִתְקוֹטְטָה	קוֹטְטָה	קוֹטְטָה	ה ו ק ט ה
הִתְקוֹטַטְתָּ	קוֹטַטְתָּ	קוֹטַטְתָּ	הוּקַטּוֹתָ
הִתְקוֹטַטְתְּ	קוֹטַטְתְּ	קוֹטַטְתְּ	הוּקַטּוֹת
הִתְקוֹטַטְתִּי	קוֹטַטְתִּי	קוֹטַטְתִּי	הוּקַטּוֹתִי
הִתְקוֹטְטוּ	קוֹטְטוּ	קוֹטְטוּ	ה ו ק ט ו
הִתְקוֹטַטְתֶּם	קוֹטַטְתֶּם	קוֹטַטְתֶּם	הוּקַטּוֹתֶם
הִתְקוֹטַטְתֶּן	קוֹטַטְתֶּן	קוֹטַטְתֶּן	הוּקַטּוֹתֶן
הִתְקוֹטַטְנוּ	קוֹטַטְנוּ	קוֹטַטְנוּ	הוּקַטּוֹנוּ
יִתְקוֹטֵט	יְקוֹטַט	יְקוֹטֵט	יוּקַט, יָקַט
תִּתְקוֹטֵט	תְּקוֹטַט	תְּקוֹטֵט	תּוּקַט
תִּתְקוֹטֵט	תְּקוֹטַט	תְּקוֹטֵט	תּוּקַט
תִּתְקוֹטְטִי	תְּקוֹטְטִי	תְּקוֹטְטִי	ת ו ק ט י
אֶתְקוֹטֵט	אֲקוֹטַט	אֲקוֹטֵט	אוּקַט
יִתְקוֹטְטוּ	יְקוֹטְטוּ	יְקוֹטְטוּ	י ו ק ט ו
תִּתְקוֹטֵטְנָה	תְּקוֹטֵטְנָה	תְּקוֹטֵטְנָה	תּוּקַטֶּינָה
תִּתְקוֹטְטוּ	תְּקוֹטְטוּ	תְּקוֹטְטוּ	ת ו ק ט ו
תִּתְקוֹטֵטְנָה	תְּקוֹטֵטְנָה	תְּקוֹטֵטְנָה	תּוּקַטֶּינָה
נִתְקוֹטֵט	נְקוֹטַט	נְקוֹטֵט	נוּקַט
הִתְקוֹטֵט		קוֹטֵט	
הִתְקוֹטְטִי	Wanting	קוֹטְטִי	Wanting
הִתְקוֹטְטוּ		קוֹטְטוּ	
הִתְקוֹטֵטְנָה		קוֹטֵטְנָה	
הִתְקוֹטֵט		קוֹטֵט	
	קוֹטַט	קוֹטֵט	הוּקַט
מִתְקוֹטֵט	מְקוֹטָט	מְקוֹטֵט	מוּקָט

DOUBLED (ע״ע) VERB

Hifil	Nifal	Kal			
הֵקֵט, הֵקַט	נָקֹט, נָקַט	קַט, קָטַט		Sg. 3 m.	Perfect
הֵ קַ טָּ ה	נָ קַ טָּ ה	־קַטָּה, קָטְטָה		3 f.	
הֲקִטּוֹתָ	נְקֹטּוֹתָ	קַטּוֹתָ		2 m.	
הֲקִטּוֹת	נְקֹטּוֹת	קַטּוֹת		2 f.	
הֲקִטּוֹתִי	נְקֹטּוֹתִי	קַטּוֹתִי		1 c.	
הֵ קַ טּוּ, הֵ קַ טּוּ	נָ קַ טּ וּ	־קַטּוּ		Pl. 3 c.	
הֲקִטּוֹתֶם	נְקֹטּוֹתֶם	קַטּוֹתֶם		2 m.	
הֲקִטּוֹתֶן	נְקֹטּוֹתֶן	קַטּוֹתֶן		2 f.	
הֲקִטּוֹנוּ	נְקֹטּוֹנוּ	קַטּוֹנוּ		1 c.	
יָקֵט, יַקֵּט	יִקֵּט	יִקֹּט	יָקֹט	Sg. 3 m.	Imperfect
תָּקֵט	תִּקֵּט	תִּקֹּט	תָּקֹט	3 f.	
תָּקֵט	תִּקֵּט	תִּקֹּט	תָּקֹט	2 m.	
תָּ קֵ טִּ י	תִּ קֵּ טִּ י	תִּקְּטִי	תָּקֹטִּי	2 f.	
אָקֵט	אֶקֵּט	אֶקֹּט	אָקֹט	1 c.	
יָ קֵ טּ וּ	יִ קֵּ טּ וּ	יִקֹּטּוּ	יָקֹטּוּ	Pl. 3 m.	
תְּקַטֶּינָה	תִּקַּטֶּינָה	תִּקֹּטְנָה	תְּקֹטֶּינָה	3 f.	
תָּ קֵ טּ וּ	תִּ קֵּ טּ וּ	תִּקֹּטּוּ	תָּקֹטּוּ	2 m.	
תְּקַטֶּינָה	תִּקַּטֶּינָה	תִּקֹּטְנָה	תְּקֹטֶּינָה	2 f.	
נָקֵט	נִקֵּט	נִקֹּט	נָקֹט	1 c.	
הָקֵט	הִקֵּט	קֹט		Sg. 2 m.	Imperative
הָ קֵ טִּ י	הִ קֵּ טִּ י	קֹטִּי		2 f.	
הָ קֵ טּ וּ	הִ קֵּ טּ וּ	קֹטּוּ		Pl. 2 m.	
הַקְטֶּינָה	הִקַּטֶּינָה	קֹטֶּינָה		2 f.	
הָקֵט	הִקּוֹט, הִקֵּט	קָטוֹט		Absolute	Infin.
הָקֵט	הִקֵּט	קֹט		Construct	
מֵקֵט	נָקֹט	קֹטֵט		Participle	
		קָטוּט		Gerundive	

Paradigm J — THE AYIN WAW (ע״ו)

Hithpolel	Polal	Polel	Hofal	Hifil
הִתְקוֹלֵל	קוֹלַל	קוֹלֵל	הוּקַל	הֵקִיל
הִתְקוֹלְלָה	קוֹלְלָה	קוֹלְלָה	הוּקְלָה	הֵ ָק י ל ה
הִתְקוֹלַלְתָּ	קוֹלַלְתָּ	קוֹלַלְתָּ	ה וּ ַק ל תָּ	הֲקִילֹותָ
הִתְקוֹלַלְתְּ	קוֹלַלְתְּ	קוֹלַלְתְּ	הוּקַלְתְּ	הֲקִילֹות
הִתְקוֹלַלְתִּי	קוֹלַלְתִּי	קוֹלַלְתִּי	ה וּ ַק ל תּ י	הֲקִילֹותִי
הִתְקוֹלְלוּ	קוֹלְלוּ	קוֹלְלוּ	הוּקְלוּ	הֵ ָק י ל וּ
הִתְקוֹלַלְתֶּם	קוֹלַלְתֶּם	קוֹלַלְתֶּם	הוּקַלְתֶּם	הֲקִילוֹתָם
הִתְקוֹלַלְתֶּן	קוֹלַלְתֶּן	קוֹלַלְתֶּן	הוּקַלְתֶּן	הֲקִילוֹתֶן
הִתְקוֹלַלְנוּ	קוֹלַלְנוּ	קוֹלַלְנוּ	ה וּ ַק ל נ וּ	הֲקִילֹונוּ
יִתְקוֹלֵל	יְקוֹלַל	יְקוֹלֵל	יוּקַל	יָקִיל
תִּתְקוֹלֵל	תְּקוֹלַל	תְּקוֹלֵל	תּוּקַל	תָּקִיל
etc.	etc.	תְּקוֹלֵל	תּוּקַל	תָּקִיל
		תְּקוֹלְלִי	תּוּקְלִי	תָּ ָק י ל י
		אֲקוֹלֵל	אוּקַל	אָקִיל
		יְקוֹלְלוּ	יוּקְלוּ	יָ ָק י ל וּ
		תְּקוֹלַלְנָה	תּ וּ ַק ל נ ה	תָּ ָק ל נ ה, תָּקִילֶינָה
		תְּקוֹלְלוּ	תּוּקְלוּ	תָּ ָק י ל וּ
		תְּקוֹלַלְנָה	תּ וּ ַק ל נ ה	תָּ ָק ל נ ה
		נְקוֹלֵל	נוּקַל	נָקִיל
הִתְקוֹלֵל		קוֹלֵל		הָקֵל
	Wanting	קוֹלְלִי	Wanting	הָ ָק י ל י
		קוֹלְלוּ		הָ ָק י ל וּ
		קוֹלַלְנָה		הָ ָק ל נ ה
				הָקֵל
הִתְקוֹלֵל	קוֹלֵל	קוֹלֵל	הוּקַל	הָקִיל
מִתְקוֹלֵל	מְקוֹלָל	מְקוֹלֵל	מוּקַל	מֵקִיל

AND AYIN YODH (ע"י) VERBS

Nifal	Kal — ע"י	Kal — ע"ו			
נָקוֹל	קָל	קַל	קָל	Sg. 3 m.	
נָקוֹלָה	קָלָה	קָלָה	קָלָה	3 f.	
נְקוֹלוֹתָ	קַלְתָ	קַלְתָ	קַלְתָ	2 m.	
נְקוֹלוֹת	קַלְתְ	קַלְתְ	קַלְתְ	2 f.	
נְקוֹלוֹתִי	קַלְתִי	קַלְתִי	קַלְתִי	1 c.	Perfect
נָקוֹלוּ	קָלוּ	קָלוּ	קָלוּ	Pl. 3 c.	
נְקוֹלוֹתֶם	קַלְתֶם	קַלְתֶם	קַלְתֶם	2 m.	
נְקוֹלוֹתֶן	קַלְתֶן	קַלְתֶן	קַלְתֶן	2 f.	
נְקוֹלוֹנוּ	קַלְנוּ	קַלְנוּ	קַלְנוּ	1 c.	
יִקּוֹל	יָקִיל	יָקוּל, יָבוֹא		Sg. 3 m.	
תִּקּוֹל	תָּקִיל	תָּקוּל		3 f.	
תִּקּוֹל	תָּקִיל	תָּקוּל		2 m.	
תִּקּוֹלִי	תָּקִילִי	תָּקוּלִי		2 f.	
אֶקּוֹל	אָקִיל	אָקוּל		1 c.	Imperfect
יִקּוֹלוּ	יָקִילוּ	יָקוּלוּ		Pl. 3 m.	
—	תָּקִילֶנָה	תְּקוּלֶינָה, תָּקָלְנָה		3 f.	
תִּקּוֹלוּ	תָּקִילוּ	תָּקוּלוּ		2 m.	
—	תָּקִילֶנָה	תְּקוּלֶינָה		2 f.	
נִקּוֹל	נָקִיל	נָקוּל		1 c.	
הִקּוֹל	קִיל	קוּל		Sg. 2 m.	
הִקּוֹלִי	קִילִי	קוּלִי		2 f.	Imperative
הִקּוֹלוּ	קִילוּ	קוּלוּ		Pl. 2 m.	
—	—	קֹלְנָה		2 f.	
הִקּוֹל, נָקוֹל	קוֹל	קוֹל		Absolute	Infin.
הִקּוֹל	קִיל	קוּל		Construct.	
נָקוֹל	קָל	קָל		Participle	
	קוֹל, קִיל	קוּל		Gerundive	

PART THREE — Lesson One

I. Reading Lesson — Gen. 3:18–21.

320. וְקוֹץ "and thorn." Masculine singular noun in the absolute state.

321. וְדַרְדַּר "and thistle." Masculine singular noun in the absolute state.

322. תַצְמִיחַ "she will cause to spring forth." Hifil imperfect 3rd feminine singular from verb root צמח (spring forth). This is a ל guttural verb. Cf. תַקְטִיל.

323. וְאָכַלְתָּ "and thou shalt eat." Kal pft. 2nd masculine singular with waw conversive from verb root אכל (eat). This is a פ״א verb. Note that the accent is on the ultima because of the waw conversive. With the perfect whenever possible the accent is shifted from the penult to the ultima, when used with waw conversive. Cf. קָטַלְתָּ.

324. בְּזֵעַת "in (the) sweat of." The singular construct of זֵעָה, a feminine noun. Used with the preposition בְּ.

325. אַפֶּיךָ "thy nostrils." The plural construct of אַף, a masculine noun and used with

the pronominal suffix קָ (2nd masculine singular).

326. לֶ חֶ ם   "bread." A singular noun common gender in absolute state.

327. שׁ וּ בְ ךָ   "thy returning." Kal inf. const. from verb root שׁוּב (return) used with pronominal suffix ךָ which is its subject. This is an ע״ו verb.

328. לֻ קָּ חְ תָּ   "thou wast taken." Pual pft. 2nd person masc. singular from verb root לקח (take). This is a ל guttural verb. Stem vowel ◌ֻ has been lengthened ◌ָ because it is in pause. Cf. קָטַלְתָּ.

329. תָּ שׁ וּ ב   "thou shalt return." Kal impft. 2nd masculine singular of same verb root as No. 327. Cf. תִּקְטֹל.

330. חַ וָּ ה   "Eve." Feminine proper noun. Cf. חַיָּה.

331. הִ וא   "she." Archaic form of הִיא.

332. וַ יַּ לְ בִּ שֵׁ ם   "and he caused to put on them." Hifil impft. 3rd mas. singular from verb root לבשׁ (put on). It is used with the waw conversive and 3rd masculine plural pronominal suffix ם. ◌ֵ (î) is written defectively for יֵ◌ (î). This is a regular strong verb. Cf. יַקְטִיל.

II. Grammar.

1. The irregular or weak verbs.

Verbs that contain one or more weak consonants or vowel letters are described as weak or irregular verbs.

They are classified as follows:

a. When the first radical is **א**, **י**, **ו**, or **נ**, they are called **פ״א**, **פ״י**, **פ״ו** or **פ״ן** respectively.

b. When the second radical is **י** or **ו**, or the second and third radicals are the same, they are called **ע״י**, **ע״ו**, or **ע״ע** respectively.

c. When the third radical is **א** or **ה**, they are called **ל״א** or **ל״ה** respectively.

Note: The former paradigm verb used for study was **פָּעַל**, and instead of using numerals to designate the radicals, the consonants of this verb are used.

2. The Pe-Nun (**פ״ן**) verb. (See paradigm on pp. 130, 131).

This verb has for its initial root letter **נ** (nun). This consonant as in many other languages is weak and does not close a syllable if another consonant follows. It drops out and the following consonant is doubled in compensation. This occurs in the English language as seen in "inregular" becoming "irregular," and "inlogical" becoming "illogical."

This verb is similar to the strong verb except as the omission of **נ** occurs.

a. Medial Nun is assimilated when it closes a preformative

syllable. Compensation is made by the use of a daghes̆-forte in the following consonant. E. g. Kal Imperfect יִנְטַל (yintal) becomes יִטַּל (yittal).

The Ayin-guttural verb is the exception to the above rules, the נ being retained.

b. There are two Kal Imperfects and Imperatives. In addition to the regular imperfect with ־ַ, there is also one with ־ֵ as the stem vowel.

c. Initial נ with a vocal sheʷa is lost in the Kal Imperative and Infinitive Construct with ־ֵ as stem vowel. E. g. נְטֵל becoming טֵל.

d. The Kal Infinitive Construct with ־ֵ adds ת־ֶ in compensation, the stem vowel lengthening to ־ֶ, thus becoming a Segholate.

e. The Hofal retains the original ־ֻ.

Note: The verb לָקַח follows the analogy of the פ״נ verb except in the Nifal stem where ל is retained.

III. Vocabulary

330. דַּרְדַּר thistle (m)
331. קוֹץ thorn (m)
332. צָמַח it sprang forth
333. צֶמַח shoot, branch (m)
334. זֵעָה sweat (f)
335. לָחַם he ate, consumed, sought

336. לֶחֶם bread (c)
337. חַוָּה Eve, life (f)
338. לָבַשׁ he put on (clothed in Hifil)
339. כְּתֹנֶת tunic (f)
340. עוֹר skin (m)

PART THREE — Lesson Two

I. Reading Lesson — Gen. 3:22–24.

333.   הֵן   "behold." An interjection.

334.   כְּאַחַד   "as one of." Sing. construct of אֶחָד and used with the inseparable preposition כְּ.

335.   לָדַעַת   "to know." Kal inf. const. from verb root ידע (know). This is a פ"ו and ל guttural verb. The preposition לְ has become לָ before the tone or accented syllable.

336.   וָחַי   "and he shall live." Kal pft. 3rd masculine singular used with waw conversive from verb root חיי (live). This is a פ guttural and ע"ע verb. The ְ of the waw conversive has become ָ before the tone syllable as in No. 335. Cf. קָטַל.

337.   וַיְשַׁלְּחֵהוּ   "and he sent him." Piel jussive impft. 3rd masculine singular used with waw conversive from verb root שלח (send). This is a ל guttural verb and is used with the 3rd mas. singular pronominal suffix הוּ. Why is the daghesh-forte of the waw conversive omitted from יְ? Cf. יְקַטֵּל.

338.   אֲשֶׁר־מִשָּׁם   "which from there" — "whence."

339.   וַיְגָרֶשׁ   "and he drove out." Piel jussive impft. 3rd masculine singular used with waw

conversive from verb root גָרשׁ (drive out).
This is an ע guttural verb. The stem
vowel ⸺ was shortened to ⸺ because the
waw conversive draws the accent since
the penultimate syllable is open. Why
did the ⸻ under גּ become long ⸻? Cf.
יָקְטֵל.

340.   וַיַּשְׁכֵּן   "And he caused to dwell." Hifil jussive
impft. 3rd masculine singular used with
waw conversive from verb root שׁכן (dwell).
Cf. יָקְטֵל, וַיַּבְדֵּל.

341.   הַכְּרֻבִים   "The cherubim." Absolute plural of masculine of כְּרוּב used with the article. The
⸻ is a defective writing for וּ (û).

342.   הַמִּתְהַפֶּכֶת   "The turning itself." Hithpael participle,
fem. singular from verb root הפך (turn).
It is used as an adjective. This is פ guttural
verb. Cf. מִתְקַטֵּל.

343.   לִשְׁמֹר   "to keep." Kal inf. construct. from verb
שׁמר (keep). This is a ל guttural verb
but since ר is a very weak guttural it follows more closely the regular or strong
verb. Cf. קְטֹל.

II. Grammar.

1. The Waw Conversive, וְ, before a tone syllable often becomes
וָ. E. g. וָחַי in vs. 22.

2. The Pe Nun verb (continued).

   a. Review and practice application of rules.

   b. Select one of the following verbs and work out in full.

1.	נָבַט — look		14.	נָפַל — fall
2.	נָבֵל — wither		15.	נָצַב — stand
3.	נָגַד — make known		16.	נָצַל — deliver
4.	נָגַע — touch		17.	נָצַר — guard
5.	נָגַף — smite		18.	נָקַב — define
6.	נָגַשׁ — approach		19.	נָקַם — avenge
7.	נָדַח — drive		20.	נָשַׂג — reach
8.	נָדַר — vow		21.	נָשַׁךְ — lend
9.	נָטַע — plant		22.	נָשַׁק — kiss
10.	נָטַשׁ — spread out		23.	נָתַן — give
11.	נָכַר — know		24.	נָתַץ — break down
12.	נָסַךְ — pour out		25.	נָתַק — draw out
13.	נָסַע — depart			

3. The Pe-Alef (פ״א) verb.

There are only six known verbs of the Pe-guttural class that are subject to special treatment in Kal Imperfect, and are thus designated פ״א verbs.

These verbs are: אָבַד,(perish);אָבָה,(be willing);אָכַל,(eat);אָמַר, (say);אָפָה,(bake);and אָחַז,(seize).

   a. Because the א quiesces or loses its consonantal character, the vowels ֱ and ֲ contracted to ָ which is modified to וֹ but written defectively ֹ.

   E. g. יֹאכַל — יוֹאכַל — יָאכַל — יַאֲכַל.

b. In the Kal Imperfect singular 1st person, אָאְכַל becomes אֹכַל the quiescent first radical being omitted.

c. The stem vowel is regularly ־ַ, but it becomes ־ֵ in pause, and ־ְ when unaccented.

4. Paradigm of פ״א verb.

Nifal	Kal		Per-fect
Same as Pe-Guttural	Same as Pe-Guttural		
	יֹאטַל	3 m. sing.	Im-per-fect
	תֹּאטַל	3 f.	
	תֹּאטַל	2 m.	
	תֹּאטְלִי	2 f.	
	אֹטַל	1 c.	
	יֹאטְלוּ	3 m. plu.	
	תֹּאטַלְנָה	3 f.	
	תֹּאטְלוּ	2 m.	
	תֹּאטַלְנָה	2 f.	
	נֹאטַל	1 c.	
	Same as Pe-Guttural etc.		Im-pera-tive

III. Vocabulary

341. הֵן behold

342. עַתָּה now

343. פֶּן lest

344. יָד hand (c)

345. דָּרַךְ he trod

346. דֶּרֶךְ way (c)

347. גֵּרַשׁ he drove

348. מִגְרָשׁ pasture (m)

349. עֵדֶן Eden, delight (m)

350. שָׁכַן he dwelt

351. מִשְׁכָּן dwelling, taber-
              nacle, (m)

352. כְּרוּב cherub (m)

353. לָהַט he burned, inflamed

354. לַהַט flame, glittering
              blade (m)

355. חָרַב it was dry, deso-
              late, he destroyed

356. חָרֵב dry, desolate

357. חֶרֶב sword, dryness (m)

358. הָפַךְ he turned

359. עָלַם he hid

360. עוֹלָם age, eternity (lit.—
              hidden years) (m)

PART THREE — Lesson Three

I. Review thoroughly the פ״ן and פ״א verbs.

II. Weekly written or oral review of words, Nos. 332–360.

III. Sentences to be translated into Hebrew and written in exercise
book:

1. Eve was Adam's wife (const. אֵשֶׁת).

2. The ground caused to sprout forth thistles for that man
who lived eastward of Eden.

3. Man shall return to the earth because he was taken from
the dust.

4. God clothed Eve and Adam with (אֵת) tunics made from
skins of beasts.

5. Lest the man eat from the fruit of the tree of life, God
drove him from the garden.

6. He sent the man from the garden to till the ground from
whence he was taken.

7. The Cherubim kept the way of life with the sword that turns itself.

8. I will give the man and his wife food all the days of their life.

9. The cattle did not eat the thorn and the thistle from the ground which God cursed.

10. The man shall eat from the fruit of the ground and the bread in the sweat of his nostrils.

11. He called his wife Eve because she became the mother of all man.

12. God drove the man and his wife from the garden in which was the tree of life.

PART THREE — Lesson Four

I. Reading Lesson — Gen. 4:1–4.

344. וַ תַּ הַ ר "and she conceived." Kal jussive imperfect 3rd person feminine singular from verb root הרה (conceive) and used with the waw conversive. The jussive is a shortened form of the regular imperfect — תַּהֲרֶה. This is a פ and ע guttural and ל"ה verb.

345. וַ תֵּ לֶ ד "and she bore." Kal jussive imperfect 3rd person feminine singular from verb root ילד (bear) and used with the waw conversive. This is a פ"וּ verb. Cf. תִּקְטֹל.

346. קָ נִ י תִ י "I have gained." Kal perfect 1st person common gender singular from verb root

קָנָה (gain). This is a ל״ה verb. Cf. קָטַלְתִּי.

347.   אֶ ת ־   "with." A preposition similar in meaning to עִם.

348.   וַ תֹּ סֶ ף   "and she added." Hifil jussive imperfect. 3rd person feminine singular from verb root יסף (add), and used with the waw conversive. ‍־ is written defectively for וֹ (ô). This is a פ״ו verb. Cf. יַקְטֵל.

349.   לָ לֶ דֶ ת   "to bear." Kal infinitive construct from verb root ילד (bear). Before the tone syllable ‍ֶ under ל sometimes lengthens to ‍ָ from original ‍ֶ. Cf. 345.

350.   אָ חִ י ו   "his brother." Irregular masculine noun with 3rd person singular masculine pronominal suffix וֹ.

351.   רֹ עֵ ה   "feeder of." Masculine singular construct of רֹעֶה. Kal participle from verb root רעה (feed). This is a פ and ע guttural and ל״ה Verb. Cf. קֹטֵל.

352.   יָ מִ י ם   "days." Absolute plural form of irregular masculine noun יוֹם.

353.   וַ יָּ בֵ א   "and he caused to come in, i. e. brought." Hifil jussive imperfect 3rd masculine singular from verb root בוא (come or go in). This is an ע״ו and ל״א verb. Cf. יַקְטֵל.

354.   לַ יְ ה וָ ה   "to Jehovah." Contracted form of לַיְהוָֹה.

355.   הֵ ב ִ י א   "caused to come in, i. e. brought." Hifil
perfect 3rd masculine singular from בּוֹא.
See No. 353.

356.   מ ִ בְּ כֹ ר ו ֹ ת   "from firstlings of." Plural construct of feminine noun בְּכֹרָה used with preposition מִן.

357.   וּ מ ֵ חֶ לְ בֵ הֶ ן   "and from fats their." Plural construct of
masculine noun חֵלֶב used with 3rd feminine
plural pronominal suffix הֶן, preposition מִן
and conjunction וְ. The — of the construct
ending is written defectively for יֵ—. Note
changes in use of conjunction and preposition.

358.   וַ יִּ שַׁ ע   "and he looked with favor." Kal jussive
imperfect 3rd masculine singular from verb
root שׁעה (look with favor) and used
with the waw conversive. This is an ע
guttural and ל"ה verb. Cf. יִקְטֹל.

359.   מ ִ נְ חָ ת ֹ ו   "his offering." Singular construct of feminine noun מִנְחָה and used with 3rd mas-
culine singular pronominal suffix וֹ.

II.   Grammar — the Pe-Yodh (פ"י) and Pe-Waw (פ"ו) verbs.
(See paradigm pp. 132, 133.)

1. These two verbs are the same in their conjugation except in
the Kal Imperfect and throughout the Hifil stem. E. g. יֵיטַל,
הֵיטִיל.

2. The first radical **י** is initial for both verbs, as יָטַל. When medial in beginning a syllable, the original **י** or **ו** remains except in the hithpael where either may be used. E. g. יִתְיַטֵּל or יִתְוַטֵּל, יִתְיַטֵּל.

3. There are two forms of the Kal Imperfect.

   a. "e" class with the **ו** lost, preformative vowel being lengthened because it is pretonic, similar to the פ״ן. E. g. יֵטֵל. This is only for פ״ו verbs.

   b. "a" class with **י** combining with preformative vowel (◌ַ) making יַ and being regular in conjugation. This stem is for both פ״י and פ״ו verbs. E. g. יִיטַל.

4. When medial:

   a. The **י** and **ו** are consonants when doubled. E. g. יְנַטֵּל.

   b. They unite when closing the preformative syllable with the preformative vowel, making an unchangeable long vowel. E. g. יִיטַל (yĭytăl) becomes יִיטַל (yîtăl). הֻוְטַל (hŭwtăl) becomes הוּטַל (hûtăl).

III. Vocabulary

361.	אֶת	with	370. קֵץ	end (m)
362.	אָח	brother (m)	371. צֹאן	flock (c)
363.	בְּכוֹר	first born (m)	372. רָעָה	he fed
364.	בִּכּוּר	first fruit (m)	373. רֵעַ	friend, lover (m)
365.	הָרָה	it conceived	374. רֵעוּת	friendship (f)
366.	חֵלֶב	fat, fatness (m)	375. שָׁעָה	he looked with favor
367.	יָסַף	he added	376. קָנָה	he gained, acquired
368.	מִנְחָה	offering (f)	377. קַיִן	Cain
369.	קָצַץ	he cut off	378. הֶבֶל	Abel

PART THREE — Lesson Five

I. Reading Lesson — Gen. 4:5–8.

360. וַיִּחַר "it burned." Kal jussive imperfect 3rd masculine singular used with waw conversive
from verb root חרה (burn). This is a פ
and ע guttural and ל"ה verb. Regular
imperfect is יֶחֱרֶה. Cf. יִקְטֹל.

361. וַיִּפְּלוּ "and they fell." Kal jussive imperfect 3rd
masculine plural used with waw conversive
from verb root נפל (fall). This is a פ"ן
verb. Cf. יִקְטְלוּ.

362. פָּנָיו "his faces." Cf. אַפָּיו (No. 170).

363. לָמָּה "to what" i. e. "Why." Interrogative pronoun מָה and preposition לְ. The daghes̆
forte in מ is a daghes̆ forte firmative used
to give greater firmness to the preceding
vowel.

364. פָּנֶיךָ "thy faces." Plural const. of mas. plu.
noun פָּנִים and used with 2nd masc. sing.
pronominal suffix ךָ. Cf. No. 362.

365. הֲלוֹא "(Is there) not." The negative לוֹא used
with the He interrogative. See p. 83, Lesson 19, II, 2. This negative is used here to
introduce a question expecting an affirmative answer. Cf. nonne? in Latin.

366.   תֵּיטִיב   "thou causest to do good or the right thing." Hifil impft. 2nd. mas. sing. from verb root יטב (do good). This is a פ"י verb. Cf. תַּקְטִיל.

367.   שְׂאֵת   "a lifting up." Irregular Kal inf. const. from verb root נשׂא (lift up). This is a פ"ן and ל"א verb. Cf. תֵּלֶת of פ"ן verbs.

368.   תְּשׁוּקָתוֹ   "his desire." Sing. const. of fem. noun תְּשׁוּקָה (No. 328 of vocabulary) and used with 3rd mas. sing. pronominal suffix וֹ.

369.   בִּהְיוֹתָם   "In being them." Kal inf. const. from verb root היה (be). It is used with preposition בְּ and 3rd plu. mas. pronominal suffix ם.

370.   וַיָּקָם   "and he arose." Kal jussive impft. 3rd mas. sing. used with waw conversive from verb root קום (rise). The regular Kal impft. is יָקוּם. This is an ע"ו verb.

371.   וַיַּהַרְגֵהוּ   "and he killed him." Kal jussive impft. 3rd mas. sing. used with waw conversive from verb root הרג (kill). This is a פ and ע guttural verb used with the 3rd mas. sing. pronominal suffix הוּ. The ־ under ר is a medial Shᵉwa reduced from stem vowel ־.

II.   Grammar — the use of הֲלֹא.

When a question expects an affirmative answer, הֲלֹא is used.

III. The Pe-Yodh (פ״י) and Pe-Waw (פ״ו) verbs (continued).

1. Review and practice application of rules.

2. Select one of the following verbs and work out in full.

1. יָבֵשׁ — be dry		16. יָעַץ — give counsel
2. יָגַע — labor		17. יָצַג — place
3. יָהַב — give		18. יָצַע — spread down
4. יָדַע — know		19. יָצַק — pour out
5. יָחַר — join		20. יָצַר — form
6. יָחַל — wait		21. יָצַת — kindle
7. יָכַח — reprove		22. יָקַץ — awake
8. יָכֹל — be able		23. יָקַר — be precious
9. יָלַד — bring forth		24. יָקַשׁ — bind
10. יָסַד — found		25. יָרַד — go down
11. יָלַךְ — walk		26. יָרַשׁ — seize
12. יָסַף — add		27. יָשַׁב — dwell
13. יָסַר — chastise		28. יָשֵׁן — sleep
14. יָעַד — appoint		29. יָשַׁע — deliver
15. יָעֵף — be weary		30. יָתַר — be left over

IV. Vocabulary

379.	הָרַג he killed	382.	חָטָא he sinned, missed
380.	חָרָה it burned		the mark
381.	חָרוֹן heat, anger,	383.	חַטָּאת sin, sin offering
	wrath (m)	384.	יָטַב he did good, well

385. נָשָׂא he lifted up

386. מַשָּׂא burden, load,
          prophecy (m)

387. שְׂאֵת lifting up, to lift (f)

388. רָבַץ it crouched, laid
          down

389. רֵבֶץ resting place (m)

390. שׁוּק he desired

391. פָּתַח he opened

392. פֶּתַח opening, door
          (m)

393. לָמָה why?

PART THREE — Lesson Six

I. Weekly oral or written review of words, Nos. 361–393.

II. Written review of rules and paradigms of פ״ן, פ״ו or פ״י verbs.

III. Sentences to be translated into Hebrew and written in exercise book:

1. Eve called him Cain because God had given to her the good word.

2. Adam could not enter the garden again.

3. Cain, the farmer, brought to God an offering from the fruits of the soil.

4. God looked with favor upon Abel's offering from his flock.

5. Cain was very angry and his face fell.

6. Why did God tell Cain to do the right thing?

7. Sin as a great beast crouches at the door of man's heart.

8. He slew his brother while they were (use infinitive) in the field.

9. Abel saw the good fruit which Cain brought for an offering to Jehovah.

10. The shepherd and the farmer at the end of days came to the place of the offering.

11. Jehovah commanded that they bring an offering from the firstlings of the flock.

12. God did not look with favor upon Cain's offering which he had brought from the fruit of the tree and the herb.

PART THREE — LESSON SEVEN

I. Reading Lesson — Gen. 4:9–12.

372.   אָחִיךָ   "thy brother." Irregular masculine noun, construct form used with 2nd per. mas. sing. pronominal suffix ךָ.

373.   יָדַעְתִּי   "I know." Kal pft. 1st per. sing. from verb root ידע (know). This is a פ״ו and ל guttural verb. Cf. קָטַלְתִּי. The accent mark ⸰ is a special accent mark and placed on the accented syllable. While — is the usual mark for the accented penultimate syllable, it will be noted that other marks are used. Their significance will be treated in a later course. It is well just to note where these marks are found, that syllable is accented. If two should be used, the accent is on the penult.

374.   דְּמֵי   "bloods of." Construct plural of the masculine noun דָּם. It is to be noted that the plural is used for "shed blood."

375.   פִּיהָ   "her mouth." Sing. construct form of masculine noun פֶּה used with 3rd fem. sing. pronominal suffix הָ.

376.   לָקַחַת   "to receive." Kal inf. construct from verb root לקח (receive). This is a ל guttural verb and hence the original ‗ under ק remains. Its helping vowel is ‗ because gutturals prefer "a" class vowels. This inf. construct follows the analogy of the פ״ן verb. Cf. טֶלֶת.

377.   תֵּת   "(to) give." Kal inf. const. from verb root נתן (give). This form is peculiar to this verb since its first and third radicals are נ both of which are assimilated. Why are the daghes fortes missing? Cf. תֵּלֶת.

378.   נָע   "wanderer." Kal participle from verb root נוע "wander." This is an ע״ו and ל guttural verb.

379.   וָנָד   "and fugitive." Kal participle from verb root נוד (flee). This is an ע״ו verb.

II. Grammar

1. The use of the participle as an adjective.

In vs. 10 the Kal Participle is used as an adjective, agreeing

in gender, number and person with the noun it limits, as
צְעָקִים.

2. The Lamed-He (לֿ"ה) verb. (See paradigm pp. 134, 135).

(1) This is really a לֿ"י or לֿ"ו verb, but the י or ו never appears
final except in the Kal Gerundive. The ו seems to have
been superceded by the י except in the Kal Infinitive Construct. The stem vowel was lengthened to ◌ָ when the
final consonant was lost, and a final ה was added to protect
the syllable. Thus:

קָטַי (kātăy) became קָטַ (kātă) with י dropped. Then
final vowel under tone was lengthened, becoming קָטָ
(kātā), and with protective ה added its final form is
קָטָה (kātāh).

The stem vowel when final is ◌ָ in the perfect, ◌ֶ in the
Imperfect and Participle, ◌ֵ in the Imperative, וֹת in the
Infinitive Construct, and regular (i. e. same as strong verb)
in the Infinitive Absolute. (See paradigm).

(2) Before vowel additions the י is missing except for pause or
emphasis. Before consonant affixes in the perfect it unites
with the stem vowel ◌ֶ, attenuated from ◌ַ making יִ◌
(e. g. קָטִיתָ) in the active stems; becomes יִ◌, ◌ֵ having
been lengthened to ◌ֵ (e. g. נִקְטִיתָ) in the passive stems;
and יִ◌ in the Imperfects and Imperatives (e. g. תִּקְטַיְנָה).
In later Hebrew יִ◌ is sometimes found in the active stems
due to the influence of the Aramaic.

(3) The third feminine Perfect singular uses ת which is evi-
dently a remnant of the ancient Semitic parent language.

This is found in the Assyrian, Arabic, and Aramaic. E. g.
קָטְתָה.

III. Vocabulary

394. אֵי Where?
(const. of אָי)
395. אָדַם it was red
396. דָּם blood (m)
397. צָעַק he cried out
398. פֶּה mouth (m)
(const. פִּי)
399. יָד hand (c)

400. כֹּחַ strength, vigor (m)
401. נוּעַ to wander
402. נָע wanderer (Kal part.)
403. נוּד to move to and fro, flee
404. נָד fugitive (Kal part.)

PART THREE — Lesson Eight

I. Reading Lesson — Gen. 4:13–17.

380.   עֲוֹנִי   "my iniquity." Sing. const. of mas. noun עָוֹן used with 1st per. sing. pronominal suffix ִי.

381.   מִנְּשׂוֹא   "From (to) bear." Kal inf. const. from verb root נשׂא (bear or lift up). ֹ (ō) is written incorrectly as וֹ. This is a פ"ן and ל"א verb Cf. קָטֹל. מִן is used here to express comparison.

382.   גֵּרַשְׁתָּ   "Thou hast driven out." Piel pft. 2nd per. mas. sing. from verb root גרשׁ (drive out). Cf. No. 339.

383.   הַיּוֹם   "this day." The article here is used as a demonstrative which force it often has.

384.   אֶסָּתֵר   "I shall be hidden." Nifal impft. 1st per. sing. from verb root סתר (hide). Cf. אֶקְטֵל.

385.   יַהַרְגֵנִי   "(he) will kill me." Kal impft. 3rd per. mas. sing. from verb root הרג (kill). This is a פ & ע guttural verb. It is used with 1st per. sing. pronominal suffix נִי. Note vowel changes necessitated in adding suffix. יַהֲרֹג plus נִי=יַהַרְגֵנִי. Why? Cf. No. 371.

386.   יִקָּם   "he shall be avenged." Hofal impft. 3rd mas. sing. pausal form from verb root נקם (avenge). This is a פ״ן verb. Cf. יְקְטַל.

387.   וַיָּשֶׂם   "and he put." Kal jussive impft. 3rd mas. sing. used with waw conversive from verb root שִׂים (put). Why did ◌ֶ under שׂ become ◌ָ? This is an ע״י verb.

388.   הַכּוֹת   "(to) cause to smite." Hifil inf. const. from verb root נכה (smite). Note loss of נ and ה. Why? This is a פ״ן and ל״ה verb.

389.   בֹּנֶה   "building." Kal participle from verb root בנה (build). This is a ל״ה verb. Cf. קֹטֵל. The daghesh-lene in ב is because of a previous disjunctive accent. Why is the accent changed from ultima to the penult?

II. Note the use of the Kal infinitive construct נְשׂוֹא in vs. **13**. What is its use and interpretation?

III. Grammar — the Lamed-He (ל״ה) verb (continued).

1. Review and practice application of rules.

2. Select one of the following verbs and work out in full:

1. בָּזָה — despise	21. שָׁקָה — drink
2. בָּכָה — weep	22. שָׁתָה — drink
3. בָּלָה — decay	23. תָּלָה — hang
4. בָּנָה — build	24. אָבָה — be willing
5. גָּלָה — reveal	25. אָלָה — swear
6. דָּמָה — be like	26. הָגָה — meditate
7. כָּבָה — quench	27. הָרָה — conceive
8. כָּלָה — finish	28. חָרָה — be angry
9. כָּסָה — conceal	29. עָלָה — go up
10. מָרָה — rebel	30. הָמָה — make noise
11. נָטָה — stretch out	31. חָלָה — be sick
12. סָפָה — end	32. חָנָה — encamp
13. פָּדָה — redeem	33. מָחָה — wipe off
14. פָּנָה — turn about	34. עָנָה — answer
15. צָפָה — watch	35. עָשָׂה — make
16. קָנָה — obtain	36. פָּרָה — be fruitful
17. קָשָׂה — be sharp	37. רָאָה — see
18. רָדָה — rule	38. רָצָה — be pleased
19. שָׁבָה — capture	39. רָפָה — be feeble
20. שָׁחָה — do obeisance	40. רָעָה — feed

IV. Vocabulary

405. סָתַר he hid

406. סֵתֶר a hiding, secrecy
        (m)

407. נָכָה he smote

408. נָכֶה smitten (adj.)

409. מַכָּה smiting, blow,
        stroke (f)

410. נָקַם he avenged

411. נָקָם vengeance (m)

412. עוּר he watched,
        awaken, arouse

413. עִיר city (a fortified
        place and watched)

414. עָוָה he made crooked,
        sinned

415. עָוֹן iniquity, guilt (m)

PART THREE — Lesson Nine

I. Weekly oral or written review of words, Nos. 394–415.

II. Continue study and review of ל"ה verbs.

III. Sentences to be translated into Hebrew and written in exercise book:

1. Cain said to God, Am I the one keeping my brother?

2. The blood of his brother kept on crying unto God from the ground.

3. The dry ground opened its mouth to take the blood of the good man.

4. When Cain tilled the ground it did not give its strength to him.

5. Was his iniquity greater than could be forgiven?

6. When God drove him from before His face, Cain became a wanderer and fugitive.

7. Anyone finding Cain and killing him Jehovah will avenge him sevenfold.

8. Cain built a great city and called it according to the name of his son Enoch.

9. Jehovah placed a sign to Cain that anyone finding him should not smite him.

10. The man who killed his brother went out from before God to dwell in the land of Nod.

11. The eyes of Cain were opened and he knew that he could not walk with God.

12. God caused to tell Cain that he could not dwell in the presence of God.

PART THREE — Lesson Ten

I. Reading Lesson — Gen. 4:18–22.

390.   וַיִּוָּלֶד   "and there was born." Nifal jussive impft. 3rd mas. sing. from verb root ילד (bear) and used with the waw conversive. This is a פ"ו verb. Cf. יָקְטֵל.

391.   וַיִּקַּח   "and (he) took." Kal. jussive impft. 3rd mas. sing. from verb root לקח (take) and used with the waw conversive. This is a ל guttural verb.

392.   שְׁתֵּי   "two of." Fem. const. sing. of שְׁתַּיִם.

393.   נָשִׁים   "wives." An irregular feminine noun, plural of אִשָּׁה.

394.   הַשֵּׁנִית   "the second." An adjective and ordinal, fem. form of שֵׁנִי.

395.   וַתֵּלֶד   "and she bore." Kal jussive impft. 3rd fem. sing. of ילד. Cf. No. 390.

396.   אֹהֶל   "tents." Mas. sing. collective noun and a "u" class segholate as is בֹּקֶר (morning). The original ֻ has lengthened to ֹ.

397.   מִקְנֶה   "possessions." Mas. sing. collective noun from קָנָה (to purchase, acquire, get, obtain).

398.   תֹּפֵשׂ   Kal participle from verb root תפשׂ (perform). This is a strong verb.

399.   לֹטֵשׁ   Kal participle from verb root לטשׁ (sharpen, hammer). This is another strong verb.

400.   חֹרֵשׁ   Kal participle from verb root חרשׁ (to scratch, engrave, plow), hence participle as noun means a "tool, or cutting instrument." This is a פ & ע guttural verb.

401.   נְחֹשֶׁת   "copper, bronze." It is used of the brazen serpent. Cf. נָחָשׁ("a serpent.")

402.   וַאֲחוֹת   "and sister of." Sing. const. of irregular fem. noun, אָחוֹת. Why does conjunctive וְ use ֲ ?

II. Grammar

1. The subject of a passive verb.

The subject of a passive verb, which would be the object if
that verb were active, should be preceded by אֵת which is the
sign of the direct and definite object.

E. g. וַיִּוָּלֵד לַחֲנוֹךְ אֶת־עִירָד "And Irad was born to Enoch"
(vs. 18).

2. The Lamed-Alef (ל"א) verb. (See paradigm pp. 136, 137.)

a. This verb is cognate to the ל"ה verb and hence there are
many similarities. In the Aramaic it is identified with and
treated the same as the ל"ה.

b. The final א always quiesces losing its consonantal force,
the stem vowel becoming ָ. קָטַא (kātă) with א quiescing
becomes קָטָא (kātā), where the stem vowel in the strong
verb was ַ.

c. The א when medial is treated as a consonant when it introduces a syllable. E. g. קָטְאָה.

d. When א closes a syllable, it quiesces. E. g. קָטְאָתָ.

e. ֵ is used instead of ַ as the stem vowel in all of the Perfects
except the Kal. E. g. נִקְטֵאתָ. The 3rd mas. sing. forms of
course, are exceptions.

f. ֶ, following the analogy of the ל"ה verb, is used as the
stem vowel in all 2d and 3d feminine plural imperfects and
imperatives. E. g. תִּקְטֶאנָה.

III. Vocabulary

416. אֹהֶל tent, tabernacle (m)

417. קָנָה he obtained, gained, purchased

418. מִקְנֶה possessions, wealth

419. כִּנּוֹר harp (m)

420. עוּגָב flute (m)

421. תָּפַשׂ he laid hold of, performed

422. לָטַשׁ he sharpened

423. חָרַשׁ he scratched, engraved, plowed

424. חֹרֶשׁ cutting instrument (m)

425. חָרָשׁ engraver, worker (m)

426. נְחֹשֶׁת copper, brass (m)

427. בַּרְזֶל iron (m)

428. שְׁתַּיִם two (f)

PART THREE — LESSON ELEVEN

I. Reading Lesson — Gen. 4:23–26.

403. לְ נָ שָׁ יו   "to wives his." Construct plural of נָשִׁים used with 3rd per. sing. pronominal suffix וֹ and with preposition לְ. Cf. No. 393.

404. שְׁ מַ עַ ן   "hear ye." Irregular Kal imperative 2nd per. fem. plural for שְׁמַעְנָה from verb root שׁמע (hear). This is a לְ guttural verb. Cf. קְטֹלְנָה.

405. הַ אֲ זֵ נָּ ה   "cause to give ear." This is a shortened form for הַאֲזֵנְנָה the nun being assimilated in closing a syllable. This is the Hifil imperative 2nd per. fem. plural from verb root אזן (give ear), a פ guttural verb.

406. לְפִצְעִי   "for my wound." Mas. sing. const. of פֶּצַע
and used with 1st per. sing. pronominal
suffix.

407. לְחַבֻּרָתִי   "for my hurt or bruise." Fem. sing. construct of חַבּוּרָה used with 1st per. sing.
pronominal suffix. Note ֻ a defective
writing of וּ.

408. יֻקַּם   "(he) shall cause to be avenged." Hofal
imperfect, 3rd mas. sing. from verb root
נקם (avenge). This is a פ"ן verb.

409. שָׁת   "(he) put." Kal pft. 3rd mas. sing.
from verb root שִׁית (put). This is an ע"י
verb.

410. הֲרָגוֹ   "(he) killed him." Kal pft. 3rd masc. sing.
used with 3rd per. sing. pronominal suffix וֹ.
Cf. No. 385.

411. הוּחַל   "(he) caused to cease." Hofal pft. 3rd mas.
sing. from verb root חוּל (cease). This is
a פ guttural and ע"ו verb. Could be from
חָלַל (begin).

II. The chief characteristics of Hebrew poetry.

Instead of *rhyme* is *sound*. Hebrew poetry "rhymes" in
thought, which is called "parallelism." There are three chief
kinds, namely:

1. When the second line repeats the thought of the first
line, it is called "synonymous." Cf. vs. 23.

2. When the second line completes the thought of the first line, it is called "synthetic." Cf. vs. 24.

3. When the second line is in direct contrast in thought from the first line, it is called "antithetic." Cf. Prov. 10:1.

III. Grammar — the Lamed-Aleph (לֹ"א) verb (continued).

    1. Review and practice application of rules.

    2. Select one of the following verbs and work out in full.

1. בָּרָא — create	9. נָבָא — prophesy
2. חָבָא — hide	10. פָּלָא — be wonderful
3. חָטָא — sin	11. צָמָא — be thirsty
4. טָמָא — be unclean	12. קָנָא — be jealous
5. מָלֵא — fill	13. קָרָא — call
6. כָּלָא — restrain	14. רָפָא — heal
7. מָצָא — find	15. שָׂנֵא — hate
8. נָשָׂא — lift up	

IV. Vocabulary

429.	אָז then	434.	פֶּצַע wound (m)
430.	אָזַן he gave ear	435.	חַבּוּרָה hurt, bruise
	(used only in		(f)
	Hifil)	436.	חוּל he ceased
431.	אֹזֶן ear (f)	437.	חָלַל he began
432.	אַחֵר other, another	438.	שִׁבְעָתַיִם sevenfold (c)
433.	פָּצַע he wounded		

PART THREE — Lesson Twelve

I. Weekly oral or written review of words, Nos. 416–438.

II. Written review of rules and paradigms of ל״ה and ל״א verbs.

III. Sentences to be translated into Hebrew and written in exercise book:

1. When the woman sinned, God said, Thou art unclean.

2. Tubal who was the son of Ada became a dweller of tents and had large possessions.

3. Jubal, his brother, played the harp and the flute.

4. Tubal Cain was born to Zillah and he became a blacksmith who made every engraving tool of bronze and iron.

5. Listen to me, wives of Lamech, I have killed a youth for wounding me.

6. Why will Lamech be avenged seventy and seven and Cain only (רַק) sevenfold?

7. Seth became the father of the good men in the place of Abel.

8. Men began to call in the name of Jehovah and brought an offering to Him.

9. Eve named her son Seth because God had put to her another seed instead of Abel.

10. Why didst thou kill the good man who brought an offering to me from firstlings of his flock?

11. Cain heard the voice of the blood of his brother crying unto him from the dry land.

12. God cursed the ground and it did not give her strength to Cain.

PART THREE — Lesson Thirteen

I. Reading Lesson — Gen. 5:1–16.

412.   בָּרֹא   "(to) create." Kal. inf. const. from verb root בָּרָא (create). This is an ע guttural and ל"א verb. Cf. קְטֹל.

413.   הִבָּרְאָם   "(to) be created them." Nifal inf. const. from above verb root (cf. No. 412). It is used with the 3rd person mas. plural pronominal suffix ם.

414.   אַחֲרֵי   "after." A plural noun construct form used as a preposition.

415.   הוֹלִידוֹ   "his causing to beget." Hifil inf. const. from verb root יָלד (bear). This is a פ"ו verb and used with 3rd mas. sing. pronominal suffix וֹ. Cf. הַקְטִיל.

416.   וַיָּמָת   "and he died." Kal jussive impft. 3rd mas. from verb root מוּת (die). The regular impft. form is יָמוּת. It is a ע"ו verb and used with the waw conversive.

II.　Grammar

1. The Numerals and Ordinals.

a. The numeral אֶחָד (one) is treated as an adjective standing after and agreeing with its noun. It may be used as a noun and stand in the construct state.

b. The remaining numerals are nouns.

   (1) They regularly stand before the nouns they limit though sometimes they are found to stand after. With "two" to "ten" their nouns are in the plural, and from "eleven" upwards their nouns are in the singular when they stand before but in the plural when following.

   (2) One and two always agree in gender with the noun they limit, but three and upwards always are in the opposite gender. See table of numerals.

   (3) The numerals one to ten, hundred or hundreds, thousand or thousands, are used in the construct as well as the absolute. ALL others are used only in the absolute.

c. The tens, except twenty which is the plural of ten (עֶשְׂרִים plural of עֶשֶׂר), are formed by adding ־ִים to the units.

d. The ordinals two to ten, except "first" (רִאשׁוֹן from רֹאשׁ head), are formed by adding ־ִי to the units. Above ten, the regular numerals are used.

2. Table of numerals.

	FEMININE		MASCULINE	
	(Use with masculine nouns)		(Use with feminine nouns)	
	Absolute	Construct	Absolute	Construct
1.	*אֶחָד	*אַחַד	**אַחַת**	**אַחַת**
2.	*שְׁנַיִם	*שְׁנֵי	**שְׁתַּיִם**	**שְׁתֵּי**
3.	שְׁלֹשָׁה	שְׁלֹשֶׁת	שָׁלֹשׁ	שְׁלֹשׁ
4.	אַרְבָּעָה	אַרְבַּעַת	אַרְבַּע	אַרְבַּע
5.	חֲמִשָּׁה	חֲמֵשֶׁת	חָמֵשׁ	חֲמֵשׁ
6.	שִׁשָּׁה	שֵׁשֶׁת	שֵׁשׁ	שֵׁשׁ
7.	שִׁבְעָה	שִׁבְעַת	שֶׁבַע	שְׁבַע
8.	שְׁמֹנָה	שְׁמֹנַת	שְׁמֹנֶה	
9.	תִּשְׁעָה	תִּשְׁעַת	תֵּשַׁע	תְּשַׁע
10.	עֲשָׂרָה	עֲשֶׂרֶת	עֶשֶׂר	עֶשֶׂר
11.	{ אַחַד עָשָׂר / עַשְׁתֵּי עָשָׂר		{ אַחַת עֶשְׂרֵה / עַשְׁתֵּי עֶשְׂרֵה	
12.	{ שְׁנֵים עָשָׂר / שְׁנֵי עָשָׂר		{ שְׁתֵּים עֶשְׂרֵה / שְׁתֵּי עֶשְׂרֵה	
13.	שְׁלֹשָׁה עָשָׂר		שְׁלֹשׁ עֶשְׂרֵה	

100	מֵאָה fem; Const. מֵאַת; pl. מֵאוֹת	400	אַרְבַּע מֵאוֹת	
		1,000	אֶלֶף; pl. אֲלָפִים	
200	מָאתַיִם dual (for מְאָתַיִם)	2,000	אַלְפַּיִם (dual)	
300	שְׁלֹשׁ מֵאוֹת	3,000	שְׁלֹשֶׁת אֲלָפִים	

*Masculine forms used with masculine nouns. See II; 1, b, (2) above.
**Feminine forms used with feminine nouns. See II, 1, b, (2) above.

4,000 אַרְבַּעַת אֲלָפִים   20.000 רִבֹּתַיִם (dual) also

רְבָבָה, but in later books,   שְׁתֵּי רִבּוֹת

10,000 רְבוֹ, רְבּוֹא;   30,000 שְׁלֹשׁ רִבֹּאוֹת

pl. רִבֹּאוֹת (contracted)   40,000 אַרְבַּע רִבֹּאוֹת

רִבּוֹת   60,000 שֵׁשׁ־רִבֹּאוֹת

3. The Ayin-Doubled (ע״ע) verb (See paradigm pp. 138, 139).
This verb is strictly a triliteral verb as seen in the compensation given for the contraction. The term "bi-literal" is confusing.

a. The second and third radicals are contracted. This takes place in ·

(1) Kal — Kal Perfect regular form,   קָטַט (kătăt).

         contracted form,   קַטַּ (kāttă). stem

         vowel displaces pretonic vowel,   קַטּ (kătt); since no

         final consonant should be

         doubled hence,   קַט (kăt).

(a) Except in Kal Perfect of verbs of action and movement. Some grammarians state that this is optional. E. g. גֲּלְלוּ (Gen. 29:3).

(b) Except in Kal Participle, Gerundive and Infinitive Absolute.
Forms which contain naturally long vowels are not contracted.

(c) Except in Kal Perfect occurring in pause or for emphasis. E. g. בָּזָזוּ (Num. 31:9).

(2) Nifal, Hifil, and Hofal.

 (a) נִקְטַט becomes נְקַט.

 (b) הִקְטֶט becomes הִקַט (Note ‑ָ‑ instead of יִ‑ as in strong verb. This is regular).

 (c) הָקְטַט becomes הוּקַט. See d. (4).

b. *The second radical is doubled* whenever possible in the Kal, Nifal, Hifil, and Hofal stems.

(1) Except when final, as קַט for קָט.

(2) Except in Kal Imperfect of some verbs where the first radical is doubled. This occurs as an adaptation from the Aramaic which regularly does this. Hence it is called the Aramaic Imperfect, but it is not the regular Imperfect. E. g. יִקֹּט for יִקְטֹט.

The daghe̬s-forte used is called the daghe̬s-conservative, in that it is so used that the short vowel, ‑ִ‑, in the preformative syllable may be retained.

c. *The stem vowel*, after contraction, displaces the pretonic long vowel or attenuated ‑ִ‑.

(1) In Nifal Imperfect and Imperative where ‑ָ‑ appears in the strong verb, the original ‑ִ‑ is unchanged. E. g. יִקַט for יִקָּט.

(2) In the Hifil throughout, the attenuated ‑ִ‑ is not lengthened to יִ‑ as in the strong verb, but

 (a) is lengthened to ‑ֵ‑ when it has the accent or tone;

(b) is retained as ⫶ when losing the accent in adding affixes or suffixes; e. g. יִקְטֹו.

(c) is deflected to ⫶ when the accent has receded on account of adding Waw Conversive. E. g. וַיָּ֫קָם ט.

d. *The preformative vowel*, after contraction, standing in an open syllable is heightened.

(1) In regular Kal Imperfect; Nifal Perfect and Participle; and Hifil Imperfect, Imperative, and Infinitive, the original ⫶ is lengthened to ⫶ when pretonic; but is reduced to Sheʷwa when the accent or tone shifts away. (See paradigm.)

(2) In the Nifal Imperfect, Imperative, and Infinitive, and in the Aramaic Kal Imperfect, the original ⫶ is attenuated to ⫶, in all instances the first radical being doubled. (See paradigm.)

(3) In the Hifil Perfect and Participle, the original ⫶ is attenuated to ⫶ and lengthened to ⫶ when pretonic, but when the tone is shifted away, the original ⫶ is reduced to compound Sheʷwa (⫶). (See paradigm.)

(4) In the Hofal the ⫶ regularly lengthens to וֹ. This is due to the close relation of עַ״ע and עַ״ו verbs. (See paradigm.)

e. *Before consonant terminations* a separating vowel is inserted to retain doubling of the radical.

(1) In the Perfect וֹ is used.

(2) In the Imperfect before נָה, יֶ״ is used.

(3) The separating vowels regularly have the tone except before the heavy affixes כֶּם and כֶּן.

(4) In adding afformatives the tone shifts from the tone syllable, hence,

(a) tone-long ־ָ and ־ֵ shorten to ־ַ and ־ֶ as in the Kal and Hifil second and third person feminine plural Imperfect and Imperative, and in Hifil Perfect.

(b) tone-long preformative vowels are reduced to Sheʷwa. (For examples see paradigm.)

f. *Intensive stems assume special forms*, although the regular Piel, Pual, and Hithpael are very frequently found.

(1) The Poel stem, as active, with its middle or reflexive Hithpoel. E. g. קוֹטֵט and הִתְקוֹטֵט.

(2) The Poal stem, as passive, with its reflexive Hithpoal. E. g. קוֹטַט and הִתְקוֹטַט.

(3) The Palpel stem in which the contracted stem is reduplicated. E. g. גִּלְגַּלְתִּי (Jer. 51:25).

III. Vocabulary

439. סָפַר he wrote, numbered
440. סֵפֶר book, writing (m)
441. מִסְפָּר number (m)
442. לֵב heart (m)
443. אַחֲרֵי after

444. מֵאָה   hundred (f)

445. נָחַם   he comforted, sighed. (Kal not used).

(Nifal — he repented)

446. מַעֲשֶׂה   labor, work (m)

PART THREE — LESSON FOURTEEN

I. Reading Lesson — Gen. 5:17–32.

417.   וַיִּתְהַלֵּךְ   "and he walked." Hithpael jussive impft. 3rd mas. sing. from verb root הלך (walk). This is a פ guttural verb and used with the waw conversive. See p. 181, II, 1.

418.   וְאֵינֶנּוּ   "and nothing he." See p. 181, II, 2.

419.   יְנַחֲמֵנוּ   "(he) will cause to comfort us." Piel impft. 3rd mas. sing. from verb root נחם (sigh). This is an ע guttural verb and used with the 1st per. plu. pronominal suffix נו.

420.   מִמַּעֲשֵׂנוּ   "from work our." Mas. sing. noun מַעֲשֶׂה (work), used with preposition מִן and 1st per. plu. pronominal suffix נו.

421.   וּמֵעִצְּבוֹן   "from toil of." Mas. sing. noun עִצָּבוֹן (travail, toil) used with the preposition מִן and conjunction וְ. Explain usage.

422.   יָדֵינוּ   "hands our." Plural const. of mas. noun יָד (hand) and used with 1st per. plural pronominal suffix נו.

423.   אָרְרָה   "cursed it." Piel pft. 3rd mas. sing. from
verb root אָרַר (curse). This is a פ guttural
and ע"ע verb and used with 3rd fem. sing.
pronominal suffix הָ.

II. Grammar.

1. The use of the Hithpael stem in vss. 22 and 24.

This stem is reciprocal and here denotes companionship or
fellowship with God. Walking with God implies unanimity
with Him in thought, word and deed. In 1 Samuel 25:15, it is
translated "were conversant," hence walking implies as its
natural condition that his manner of life was such as God
approved. It perhaps denotes character of life.

2. The use of the Nun Epenthetic in vs. 24.

This is used to give emphasis. אֵין is the construct form of אַיִן
meaning "nothing," from אוּן, "to be nothing." To this ֶנ־
was added for emphasis before the pronominal suffix הוּ (him).
הוּ plus ֶנ־ plus אֵין equals אֵינֶנּוּ with the ה assimilated as shown
by the daghes-forte.

3. The Ayin-Doubled (ע"ע) verb (continued).

   a. Review and practice application of rules.

   b. Select one of the following verbs and work out in full.

1. בָּלַל — confound   6. סָבַב — surround
2. גָּלַל — roll   7. סָכַךְ — cover
3. דָּמַם — be dumb   8. פָּלַל — pray
4. מָדַד — measure   9. פָּרַר — break
5. נָדַד — wander   10. צָרַר — distress

11. קָדַד — bow the head
12. קָלַל — be light
13. רָנַן — sing
14. שָׁדַד — destroy
15. שָׁמֵם — astonish
16. אָרַר — curse
17. הָלַל — praise

18. חָגַג — dance
19. חָלַל — begin
20. חָנַן — be gracious
21. חָתַת — be dismayed
22. רָבַב — be many
23. רָעַע — be evil

III. No vocabulary lesson.

PART THREE — LESSON FIFTEEN

I. Oral or written review of words Nos. 439–446.

II. Review thoroughly the rules and paradigm of the ע"ע verb.

III. Sentences to be translated into Hebrew and written in exercise book:

1. According to this book God created the generations of man in his likeness.

2. In the day of their creation He blessed them and named them Adam and Eve.

3. He lived in Eden 117 years after he had begotten sons and daughters.

4. After God drove them from that garden they dwelt in that place 875 years.

5. He walked with the God, and his wife did not find him because he was not.

6. Jehovah took Enoch into heaven because he knew him to be a good man.

7. This is the son who will comfort us from our work in the field.

8. Noah begat three sons who became dwellers of the great land eastward of Eden.

9. He walked with his wife in the garden 145 years.

10. The man begat seven sons and nine daughters after he was driven from the presence of God.

11. All the days which the woman lived after sons and daughters were born to her were 114 years.

12. Will Noah and Lamech be a comfort in my labor in the field?

PART THREE — LESSON SIXTEEN

I. Reading Lesson — Gen. 6:1–8.

424.   הֵחֵל   "(he) caused to begin." Hifil pft. 3rd mas. sing. from verb root חלל (begin). This is a פ guttural and ע"ע verb.

425.   לָרֹב   "to multiply." Kal inf. construct from verb root רבב (multiply). This is an ע"ע verb and used with the preposition לְ. Why is the vowel of the preposition long?

426.   וַיִּקְחוּ   "And they took." Kal jussive impft. 3rd mas. plu. from verb root לקח (take). The ◌ֽ is a "rafe" indicating the omission of daghes-forte. This verb follows the analogy of the פ"נ verbs, except in the Nifal.

427.　בֶּחָרוּ　Kal perf. pausal form, third com. plu. from verb root בחר (choose, select, examine). This is a ע and ל guttural verb.

428.　יָדוֹן　Kal impft. third mas. sing. from דוֹן (judge contend, strive, keep down by moral force). Some scholars offer "remain" as a mean ing and reject "strive". This is an ע״ו verb.

429.　בְּשַׁגָּם　"In which also." A contraction בַּאֲשֶׁר and גַּם. However many scholars hold that שַׁגָּם is the Kal inf. const. from verb root שגג (err) used with 3rd per. mas. plu. pro nominal suffix ם. Hence it is translated "on account of them to err."

430.　הַנְּפִלִים　Who were the Nephilim? This noun is from נָפַל meaning "to fall," hence noun literally means "fallers upon," i. e. robbers. Note the use of the remote demonstrative pronoun as an adjective with בַּיָּמִים.

431.　רַע　"evil" from רעע meaning "to do harm, injure." Every use of this noun indicates injury.

432.　וַיִּנָּחֶם　"and it grieved." Nifal Impft. 3rd mas. sing. with waw conversive, from verb root נחם (to pant or sigh), hence "to grieve, pity, comfort and sometimes 'repent'." This is an ע guttural verb.

433. נֶחָמְתִּי "it grieves me." Nifal pft. 1st per. com.
from verb root נחם. See No. 432.

II. Grammar — The Ayin-Waw (ע"ו) and Ayin-Yodh (ע"י) verbs.
(See paradigm pp. 140, 141.)
This is a triliteral verb. The ו or י becomes a part of the stem
vowel after contraction. This is due to these weak consonants
contracting with whatever vowel they may follow, forming
in reality a diphthong. They keep their consonantal force
when doubled, or begin a syllable.

Further, these verbs, being "contracted" verbs, are similar to
the ע"ע verbs having many striking resemblances and even
to interchange of forms.

1. *The second radical and stem vowel contract* whenever possible
   forming an unchangeable long vowel, as
   Kal 3rd per. mas. sing. Imperfect (strong verb form)

   יַקְוֻל (yăkwŭl) Stem vowel and 2nd radical contracting
   יַקוּל (yăkŭl)

   Preformative vowel in pretonic syllable must be lengthened
   hence

   יָקוּל (yākŭl).

   This stem vowel, however, is deflected for euphony in the
   Kal and Nifal perfects when consonant terminations are
   added. E. g. קָלְתָ becomes קַלְתָ .

2. *When consonant terminations are added*, separating vowels
   are used, which in the Nifal and Hifil perfect is ו and in the
   Kal and Hifil Imperfect is י ִ . (See paradigm.)

3. *The preformative vowel* thus standing in an open syllable is lengthened but reduced to Shᵉwa when ante-pretonic.

E. g.　　תָּקוּל becomes　תְּקוּל but תְּקוּלֶינָה becomes תְּקוּלֶינָה.

4. *In the Hofal* it seems that the ו or י has been transposed and contracted with the preformative vowel becoming וֹ.

5. *The intensive stems* are similar in form to the ע״ע verb and differ only in name. They are called Polel, Polal, and Hithpolel.

6. The only forms in which the ע״י differs from the ע״ו are in the Kal Imperfect, Jussive, Imperative, and Infinitive Construct, יָקִיל becoming יָקִיל. Otherwise it follows as analogy of the ע״ו verb.

III.　Vocabulary

447. בָּחַר he chose, examined

448. בָּחוּר youth (m)

449. דּוּן to judge, strive, contend

450. דִּין judgment (m)

451. אָדוֹן lord, master (m)

452. מָדוֹן contention, strife

453. מְדִינָה province, country

454. חָנַן he was gracious

455. חֵן grace, favor (m)

456. חַנָּה grace, favor (m)

457. חָשַׁב he thought

458. מַחֲשָׁבָה thought (f)

459. מָחָה he destroyed, wiped out

460. רָבַב he multiplied

461. רָעָה wickedness (f)

462. רַק only

463. שֶׁ who, which, what

PART THREE — Lesson Seventeen

I. Reading Lesson — Gen. 6:9–15.

434. בְּדֹרֹתָיו   "in generations his." Plural const. of דּוֹר
used with preposition בְּ and 3rd per. sing.
pronominal suffix וֹ.

435. וַתִּשָּׁחֵת   "and was corrupted." Nifal jussive impf.
3rd fem. sing. from verb root שׁחת (corrupt,
spoil by rotting). The Hifil means "to
destroy." Used with waw conversive. This
is an ע guttural verb. Cf. following verbs
in verse 12. וַתִּמָּלֵא also נִשְׁחָתָה and
הִשְׁחִית and in vs. 13. מַשְׁחִיתָם.

436. תֵּבָה   "and ark or chest" from תבה (to be hollow).
If the ancient cubit was 1.8 feet, then the
ark was 540 feet long, 90 feet wide, and
54 feet high.

437. מִבַּיִת   "within" — adverbial idiom literally meaning "from house."

438. מָחוּץ   "without" — adverbial idiom literally
meaning "from street."

II. Grammar — the Ayin-Waw (ע"ו) and Ayin-Yodh (ע"י) verbs
(continued).

1. Review and practice application of rules.

2. Select one of the following verbs and work out in full.

1. אוֹר — shine
2. בּוֹא — go in
3. בּוֹז — despise
4. בּוֹשׁ — ashamed
5. גּוּר — sojourn
6. דִּין — judge
7. דּוּשׁ — thresh
8. זוּב — flow
9. זוּד — boil
10. חוּל — bring forth
11. טוֹב — be good
12. פּוּל — contain
13. כּוּן — prepare
14. מוּג — melt
15. לוּץ — scorn
16. מוֹט — be moved
17. מוּל — circumcise
18. מוּשׁ — depart

19. מוּת — die
20. נוּחַ — rest
21. נוּס — flee
22. נוּעַ — nod
23. נוּף — sift
24. סוּג — turn back
25. סוּר — turn aside
26. עוּד — testify
27. עוּף — fly
28. עוּר — awake
29. פּוּץ — scatter
30. צוּם — fast
31. צוּר — besiege
32. קוּם — arise
33. רוּם — be high
34. רוּעַ — shout
35. רוּץ — run
36. שׁוּב — turn

III. Vocabulary

464. אָרַךְ it became long
465. אֶרֶךְ length (m)
466. אֹרֶךְ length (m)
467. אַמָּה cubit (f)
468. גֹּפֶר gopher, pine (m)
469. חוּץ street, field (m)
470. מְחוּץ outside (adv.)

471. מִבַּיִת inside (adv.)
472. חָמַס he injured, did violence
473. חָמָס violence, injury (m)
474. כָּפַר he covered, pardoned

475. כְּפָר pitch, village (m)

476. כִּפּוֹר bowl, cup (m)

477. כַּפֹּרֶת the mercy seat (m)

478. קָנַן it nested (used in Piel and Pual only)

479. רָחַב it was wide, spacious

480. קֵן nesting place, room (m)

481. רֹחַב width, breadth (m)

482. רָחָב width, breadth (m)

483. תֵּבָה ark, chest (f)

484. שָׁחַת he corrupted, spoiled by rotting (Hif. destroyed)

485. תָּמַם he completed

486. תָּמִים complete, perfect (m)

PART THREE — LESSON EIGHTEEN

I. Oral or written review of words, Nos. 447–486.

II. Review thoroughly the rules and paradigm of the ע״ו and ע״י verbs.

III. *Now* is the time to prepare for the final examination.

PART THREE — LESSON NINETEEN

I. Reading Lesson — Gen. 6:16–22.

439.   צֹהַר   "a window" from צָהַר "to shine." Note that only height of window is given, and not length.

440.   תְּכַלֶּנָּה   "thou shalt finish it." Piel impft. 2nd per. mas. sing. from verb root כלה (finish). It is used with the 3rd fem. sing. suffix הָ and the

nun epenthetic. Note contraction takes place.

441. מִלְמַעְלָה   "from to upwards." A composite adverb. Literally מִן (from) and לְ (to) and מֵעַל (upwards) and הָ‍ (towards — he-directive).

442. בְּצִדָּה   "in side her." Mas. sing. noun צַד used with preposition בְּ (in) and 3rd fem. sing. pronominal suffix הָ.

443. הִנְנִי   "behold I." Interjection הִנֵּה with 1st per. sing. pronominal suffix נִי. With the 1st per. sing. and plu. there are two forms used with and without daghes̆-forte.

444. מֵבִיא   "about to bring." Hifil participle from verb root בּוֹא (go in). The participle is often used to designate action which is soon to take place.

445. לְשַׁחֵת   "to destroy." Piel inf. const. from verb root שׁחת (break in pieces, destroy). Used with preposition לְ.

446. יִגְוַע   "shall expire." Kal impft. 3rd mas. sing. from verb root גּוע (expire). Though an ע"ו verb it follows in all extant forms that of the ל guttural verb.

447. וַהֲקִמֹתִי   "And I will establish." Hifil pft. 1st per. sing. from verb root קוּם (stand) and used

with waw conversive וָ. Why is ־ְ in וָ changed to ־ֶ? Note defective writing of ־ָ and ־ִי.

448.   וּבָאתָ   "And thou shalt go in." Kal pft. 2nd per. mas. sing. from verb root בּוֹא (go in). Note use of waw conversive וָ and why is it changed to וּ?

449.   לְהַחֲיִת   "to cause to keep alive." Hifil inf. const. from verb root חיה (live) and used with preposition לְ.

II.   Grammar — review of the פ"ן and פ"וּ verbs.

1. Remember to study rules and application of same in relation to the strong verb. The basis is the strong verb.

2. Be able to apply rules to any given verb from lists assigned for study.

III.   Vocabulary

486. אָסַף   he gathered, collected
487. אָסֵף   ingathering, harvest (m)
488. אֲסֵפָה assembly, council (f)
489. בָּרָה   he cut
490. בְּרִית covenant, league (f)
491. גָּוַע   he expired, died
492. יָבַל   it flowed (Kal not used. In causative stem—to lead, bring)

493. יְבוּל   produce, increase (m)
494. מַבּוּל flood (m)
495. מַפְתֵּחַ key (m)
496. צַד   side (m)
497. צֹהַר   window (m)
498. תַּחְתִּי lower of two, lowest of three (m)

PART THREE — LESSON TWENTY

I. Reading Lesson — Gen. 7:1–8.

450. שִׁבְעָה שִׁבְעָה   "by sevens" lit. seven seven Cf. vs. 9.
שְׁנַיִם שְׁנַיִם   "by twos."

451. מַמְטִיר   "about to cause to rain." Hifil participle
from verb root מטר (rain). Cf. with No.
444 as to usage.

452. הַיְקוּם   "the living (standing) thing." Mas. sing.
noun יְקוּם used with the article. Why is
daghes̆-forte omitted from יְ? See p. 15,
II, 2, b, (2).

453. צִוָּהוּ   "(he) commanded him." Piel pft. 3rd mas.
sing. from verb root צוה (command) used
with 3rd mas. sing. pronominal suffix הוּ
(him).

454. אֵינֶנָּה   "nothing it." Compare with No. 418, noting
that 3rd fem. sing. pronominal suffix הָ
is used.

II.   Grammar — review of ל"ה and ל"א verbs.

1. Thoroughly review these verbs and apply rules in relation to the strong verb.

2. Practice with verbs from verb lists.

III. Vocabulary

499. צָדַק he was just

500. צַדִּיק righteous (m) adj. (adj. of this voweling express
personal quality)

501. צֶדֶק righteousness (m)

502. טָהֵר it was clean, pure

503. טֹהַר brightness, purification (m)

504. טָהוֹר clean (m) adj.

PART THREE — Lesson Twenty One

I. Oral or written review of words, Nos. 486–504.

II. Grammar — review of ע״ע verb.

1. Thoroughly review and practice application of the rules in
relation to strong verb.

2. Practice with verbs from verb list.

III. For examination prepare Gen. 6 as to literal translation and
parsing of all verbs therein.

PART THREE — Lesson Twenty-Two

I. Reading Lesson — Gen. 7:9–16.

455.   לְ שִׁ בְ עַ ת   "to seven of" i. e. "a week of." This is
the sing. const. of שִׁבְעָה.

456.   מֵ י   "waters of." Construct of מַיִם irregular
plu. noun.

457.   בִּשְׁנַת   "in year of." Noun sing. const. of feminine noun שָׁנָה. It is used with preposition
בְּ (in). Why does the preposition use ﹖

458.   לְחַיֵּי   "to (the) lives of." Plural const. of mas.
noun חַי (life) used with preposition לְ.

459.   נִבְקְעוּ   "were broken up." Nifal perfect 3rd
common plu. from verb root בקע (hatch,
break up).

460.   מַעְיְנוֹת   "fountains." עַיִן (fountain) with מ prefixed indicates source of fountains.

461.   בְּעֶצֶם   "in (the) bone of." Sing. construct of
עֶצֶם. It is used as an idiom meaning "in
very," i. e. "in this very day."

462.   בָּא   "went in." Kal pft. mas. 3rd per. sing. from
verb root בוא (go in). Note that this form
is used with several subjects connected by וְ
(and). Either sing. or plu. form of verb
may be used.

463.   הַבָּאִים   "The going in ones" i. e. those that went
in. Kal participle of verb above (No.
462) used as a masculine plural noun.

II. Grammar — review of עו"ו and עי"ע verbs.

1. Thoroughly review and practice application of rules using the
strong verb as a basis.

2. Practice with verbs from verb list.

III. Vocabulary

505. אֲרֻבָּה window (f)

506. בְּעַד around, behind

507. בָּקַע it broke up, hatched

508. גֻּשַׁם it rained (used only in Hifil)

509. גֶּשֶׁם rain (m)

510. חָדָשׁ new, fresh (m) adj.

511. חֹדֶשׁ month, new moon (m)

512. מַעְיָן fountain (m) (c. in plu.)

513. צָפַר it chirped

514. צִפּוֹר sparrow, little bird (c)

PART THREE — LESSON TWENTY-THREE

I. Reading Lesson — Gen. 7:17–24.

464.   וַיִּשְׂאוּ   "and they lifted up." Kal jussive impft. 3rd mas. plural from verb root נשׂא (lift up) and used with waw conversive.

465.   וַתָּרָם   "and it was high." Kal jussive impft. 3rd fem. sing. from verb root רוּם (be high) and used with waw conversive. Regular impft. form is תָּרוּם.

466.   וַיִּגְבְּרוּ   "and (they) became strong." Kal jussive impft. 3rd mas. plu. from verb root גבר (be strong) and used with waw conversive.

467. מְאֹד מְאֹד   "exceedingly, exceedingly." Words are often repeated to express emphasis or intensification.

468.　　וַיְכֻסּוּ　　"and were covered." Pual jussive impft. 3rd mas. plu. from verb root כסה (cover) and used with the waw conversive.

469.　　הֶהָרִים　　"the mountains." Plural absolute of masculine noun הַר (mountain). Note use of ‎ֶ with the article. Why?

470.　　הַגְּבֹהִים　　"the high." An adjective agreeing with the noun it modifies. Note position and change of vowels. Why? וֹ (ô) is written defectively as ‎ֹ.

471.　　בֶּחָרָבָה　　"on the dry land." Note use of article with preposition. Why?

472.　　וַיִּמַח　　"and he destroyed." Kal jussive impft. 3rd mas. sing. from verb root מחה (destroy, wipe out), and used with the waw conversive. Raphe ‎ַ is used over מ to prevent it from being considered a Nifal form.

473.　　וַיִּמָּחוּ　　"and they were destroyed." Nifal jussive impft. 3rd mas. plural from above verb root (Cf. No. 472.) and used with waw conversive.

474.　　וַיִּשָּׁאֵר　　"and there was left." Nifal jussive impft. 3rd mas. sing. from verb root (he left) and used with the waw conversive.

II.   Grammar — general review of weak verbs

1. Learn to state concisely principles of each verb and to apply
   same using strong verb as basis.

2. Work out a synopsis of paradigm of each verb and compare same
   with that of the strong verb.

III.   Vocabulary

515.   גָּבַהּ it was high, lofty

516.   גֹּבַהּ height, majesty
               pride (m)

517.   גָּבֹהַּ high, proud,
               majestic (adj.)

518.   הַר mountain (m)

519.   חָרָבָה dry land (f)

520.   כָּסָה he covered,
               concealed

521.   כְּסוּת covering, gar-
               ment (f)

522.   רוּם to be high, lofty

523.   רָמָה high place (f)

524.   מָרוֹם height, altitude
               (m)

525.   שָׁאַר he remained

526.   שְׁאֵרִית remnant (f)

PART FOUR — Lesson One

I. Reading Lesson — Gen. 8:1–7.

476.   וַיַּעֲבֵר   "and (he) caused to pass over." Hifil jussive impft. from verb root עבר (pass over) and used with waw conversive.

477.   וַיָּשֹׁכּוּ   "and (they) assuaged." Kal jussive impft. from verb root שכך (assuage, subside) and used with the waw conversive.

478.   וַיִּסָּכְרוּ   "and were shut up." Nifal juss. impft. from verb root סכר (shut or stop up) and used with waw conversive.

479.   וַיָּשֻׁבוּ   "and (they) returned." Kal jussive impft. from verb root שוב (turn, return) and used with waw conversive. Note that $-$ is a defective writing for וּ.

480.   הָלוֹךְ   "going." Kal inf. absolute from verb root הלך (go). When the inf. abs. follows the finite verb it has the same action as a participle.

481.   מִקְצֵה   "from end of." Sing. const. from mas. noun קָצֶה and used with the preposition מִן. Why is the daghes-forte omitted from ק?

482.　　　וַתָּנַח　　"and (she) rested." Kal. juss. impft. from verb root נוח (rest) and used with waw conversive. Regular Kal impft. form is תָּנוּחַ.

483.　　　הָרֵי　　"(the) mountains of." Plu. const. of mas. noun הַר. Why does the — remain long?

484.　　　רָאשֵׁי　　"(the) heads of." Irregular plu. const. of mas. noun רֹאשׁ.

485.　　　יְבֶשֶׁת　　"dry." Fem. Kal inf. const. from verb root יבשׁ (be dry).

II. Grammar — the origin and inflection of nouns

1. Nouns are inflected instead of being declined, as in Arabic. This is because the case endings have been discarded except for a few instances listed below.

  a. The nominative ending is וֹ, but there are no definite traces found.

  b. The genitive ending is ִי—, and is found in a few compound nouns, as מַלְכִּי־צֶדֶק(king of righteousness).

  c. The accusative ending is הָ— and is found in the so-called He-directive. This syllable, הָ—, is added to nouns to denote place where or motion toward. E. g. יָמָּה(seaward);הַנֶּגְבָּה the(southward).

2. The origin and inflection of nouns includes four things.

  a. The formation of noun stems from verb roots or from other nouns.

b. The addition of affixes indicating gender and number.

c. The formation of the construct state.

d. The addition of pronominal suffixes.

3. The origin and formation of nouns.

a. From verb roots (deverbals).

(1) The insertion of one or more vowels.

Long or short vowels are inserted. It is to be noted that the long vowels become naturally long and the short vowels, when lengthened, become tone-long.

(a) Nouns given one originally short vowel.

These vowels become tone-long, ◌ַ becoming ◌ֶ◌ֶ, ◌ִ becoming ◌ֵ, and ◌ֻ becoming ◌ֹ.

When inserted after first radical there is added ◌ֶ to facilitate pronunciation (◌ַ with gutturals). E. g. מַלְךְ became מֶלֶךְ (king); סִפְר became סֵפֶר (book); קֻדְשׁ became קֹדֶשׁ (holiness); and זַרְע became זֶרַע (seed). These nouns are called Segholates, taking their name from the helping vowel ◌ֶ. (See p. 49.) When inserted after the second radical, the vowel remains short or becomes tone-long. Sh^ewa is inserted after first radical to assist pronunciation. E. g. דְּבַשׁ (honey); בְּאֵר (well).

The above nouns are all masculine. The feminine form retains the original vowel and the feminine ending, ◌ָה is added. E. g. מַלְכָּה (queen); אָכְלָה (food).

(b) Nouns given one originally long vowel.

This occurs where the second radical is a vowel letter and contracts with the vowel, or when the noun is based on the Infinitive Absolute and the participial form of the verb. E. g. שׁוֹר (ox); מֵת (dead); רִיב (strife).

(c) Nouns given two originally short vowels.

These vowels became tone-long. E. g. דְּבַר became דָּבָר (word); זָקֵן became זָקֵן (old man); עֶרֶם became עָרֹם (naked); לְבַב became לֵבָב (heart).

The feminine forms add the regular ending הָ– with resultant changes due to the tone, as דָּבָר changes to דְּבָרָה.

(d) Nouns given one originally short and one originally long vowel. E. g. גָּדַל became גָּדוֹל (great); יַמִין became יָמִין (right hand).

(e) Nouns given one originally long and one originally short vowel. E. g. עָלָם became עוֹלָם (eternity); כָּהֵן became כּוֹהֵן (priest).

The nouns based on the Kal Active Participle usually have the וֹ defectively written.

(2) The reduplication of one or more radicals of the root.

(a) The reduplication of the second radical.

These are nouns built on the Piel and Pual stems, and have the same intensive meaning. E. g. אִלֵּם (dumb); גִּבּוֹר (hero); נִחֻמִים (consolation).

(b) The reduplication of the third radical.

These have also the same significance in meaning as above. E. g. שַׁאֲנָן (tranquil); שַׁפְרוּר (splendor).

(c) The reduplication of the second and third radicals. These nouns are built on the Pilpel stem of the verbs. E. g. עֲקַלְקַל (crooked).

III. Vocabulary

527. חָלַל he wounded, opened, loosed

528. חָלָל pierced, wounded, adj. (m)

529. חַלּוֹן window, opening (m)

530. חָסַר he decreased, diminished

531. חָסֵר wanting, lacking, adj. (m) want, lack (m)

532. כָּלָא he restrained, withheld

533. כֶּלֶא prison (m)

534. מִכְלָה sheep fold (m)

535. קָצַץ he cut off

536. קֵץ end (m)

537. קָצֶה end (m)

538. עָבַר he passed over

539. עֵבֶר region beyond (m)

540. סָכַר he shut, stopped

541. שָׁכַךְ he assuaged, abated, decreased

542. שׁוּב to turn, return

PART FOUR — Lesson Two

I. Reading Lesson — Gen. 8:8–14.

486.   מֵאִתּוֹ   "from with him." The prepositions מִן and אֵת used with the 3rd sing. mas. pronominal suffix.

487. הֲקַלּוּ "(if) were diminished." Kal pft. from verb root קלל (diminish) and used with the He-interrogative.

488. וַתָּשָׁב "and (she) returned." Kal juss. impft. from verb root שׁוב and used with waw conversive. Cf. Nos. 465 and 479.

489. וַיִּקָּחֶהָ "and he took her." Kal juss. impft. from verb root לקח (take). It is used with waw conversive and 3rd fem. sing. pronominal suffix הָ.

490. וַיָּחֶל "and he waited." Hifil juss. impft. from verb root חול (wait) and used with waw conversive.

491. וַיֹּסֶף "and he caused to add." Hifil juss. impft. from verb root יסף (add) and used with waw conversive. Note that ו is written defectively and that following infin. const. has the preposition לְ understood.

492. וַיִּיָּחֶל "and it was waited." Nifal juss. impft. from verb root יחל (wait) and used with waw conversive.

493. וַיָּסַר "and (he) removed." Kal juss. impft. from verb root סור (wait) and used with waw conversive.

494. חָרְבוּ "were drained." Kal pft. from verb root חרב (drain, be dry), a stative verb. Cf. יָבֵשׁ (be fully dry).

II. Grammar — The origin and inflection of nouns (continued
from previous lesson).

3. The origin and formation of nouns (continued).

  a. From verb roots — deverbals (continued).

    (3) The prefixing of consonants with vowels to the root.

      (a) The prefixing of א, ה, and י with vowels. E. g.
אֶצְבַּע (finger); הַכָּרָה (aspect); יַלְקוּט (pouch).
The additions are purely euphonic, except the ה
which is the sign of the causative stems.

      (b) The prefixing of מ with vowels to the root.
These nouns are based on the intensive and causative Participles.

The מ, in addition to the above, signifies further:

        aa. The subject of an action — based on the active
or middle stem of the verb. E. g. מַשְׂכִּיל (a
teaching poem).

        bb. The object of an action — based on the passive
stem of the verb. E. g. מַאֲכָל (food).

        cc. The means of an action. E. g. מַלְמֵד (goad).

        dd. The place of an action. E. g. מָקוֹם (place).

        ee. The quality contained in an action. E. g. מִישָׁר
(straightness).

      (c) The prefixing of ת with vowels.
The addition of this prefix indicates in the main the
abstract idea. Most of these nouns are feminine,

as there is no neuter gender in the Semitic languages.
E. g. תּוֹרָה (law); תִּקְוָה (hope); תַּרְדֵּמָה (deep
sleep).

(4) The affixing of consonants with vowels to the root.

(a) The addition of ל, מ, and נ.

The addition of ל and מ has no special significance.
E. g. בַּרְזֶל (iron); חַרְטֹם (scribe).

The addition of נ indicates either an adjective or an
abstract noun. E. g. רִאשׁוֹן (first); כִּשָׁרוֹן (suc-
cess).

(b) Nouns with four or five radicals.

These have no special significance, and many are
of foreign origin. E. g. גִּזְבָּר (treasurer); אַרְגָּמָן
(purple).

(c) Compound nouns.

The majority of these are proper names; only a few
are common nouns. E. g. מַלְכִּי צֶדֶק (Melchizedek),
בְּלִיַּעַל (worthlessness).

b. From other nouns (denominals).

These are nouns that are formed from other nouns, which
original nouns may be either primitive (as onomatopoeic) or
deverbal.

(1) Nouns denoting agency are formed by adding vowels of
Kal Active Participle. E. g. בֹּקֵר (herdsman) from בָּקָר
(cattle); שֹׁעֵר (gate keeper) from שַׁעַר.

(2) Nouns indicating place where or source are prefixed with מ. E. g. מַעְיָן (fountain) from עַיִן (fountain); hence this word really means source of fountain.

(3) Nouns and adjectives are formed by adding וֹן, ָ־ן, or וּן. The latter affix is seldom used. E. g. קַדְמוֹן (eastern) from קֶדֶם (east); לִוְיָתָן (serpent) from לִוְיָה (a winding).

(4) Adjectives as ordinals, patronymics and gentilics are formed by adding ־ִי. E. g. שִׁשִּׁי (sixth) from שֵׁשׁ (six); מוֹאָבִי (Moabite) from מוֹאָב (Moab); פְּרָזִי (country man) from פְּרָזָה (open country).

(5) Abstract nouns are formed by adding ־ִית or וּת. E. g. רֵאשִׁית (beginning) from רֹאשׁ (head); מַלְכוּת (kingdom) from מֶלֶךְ (king). This is similar to the English language which also forms abstract nouns by the addition of "th."

III. Vocabulary

543. יוֹנָה dove (f)

544. מָנוֹחַ resting place (m)

545. כַּף the hollow — hence sole, palm (f)

546. רֶגֶל foot (f)

547. זַיִת olive (m)

548. טָרָף fresh, new (adj.)

549. יָחַל he waited, stayed חוּל (These verbs are cognate)

550. עָדָה it went or passed by

551. עֵת time (c) — from עָדָה

552. קָלַל it was light, lessened dimi- nished

553. סוּר to remove, turn away

554. מִכְסֶה covering (m)

PART FOUR — Lesson Three

I. Weekly oral or written review of words, Nos. 527–554.

II. Written review of the origin and formation of nouns. Study following outline.

    1. *Inflection:* **(1.)** Formation of noun stems, deverbals and denominals

        (2.) Affixes for gender and number

        (3.) Formation of construct state

        (4.) Addition of pronominal suffixes

    2. *Formation of Noun Stems:*

      A. *Deverbals:*

        (1) Insertion of vowels:

          (a) 1 short vowel becoming tone long (Segholates)

          (b) 1 long vowel becoming unchangeably long

          (c) 2 short vowels becoming tone long

          (d) 1 short vowel and 1 long vowel becoming tone and naturally long, respectively

          (e) 1 long vowel and 1 short vowel becoming naturally and tone long, respectively

        (2) Reduplication of consonants (Intensive stems)

        (3) Prefixing consonants:

          (a) א, ה, and י no signification.

          (b) מ(1.) subject

             (2.) object

           (3.) means of an action

           (4.) place

           (5.) quality

        (c) ת abstract

    (4) Affixing of consonants:

        (a) ל, ם or ן (ן = adjective or abstract noun)

        (b) 4 or 5 radicals (mostly foreign)

        (c) compound (mostly proper names)

  B. *Denominals:*

    (1) Agency by use of vowels of קְטֵל

    (2) Source by prefixing מ

    (3) Nouns and adjectives by adding, וֹן, ָן, and וֹן

    (4) Adjectives, or ordinals, or patronymics by adding
        ִי

    (5) Abstract by adding ִית or וּת

III. Sentences to be translated into Hebrew and written in exercise
book:

  1. Jehovah sent the great wind to diminish the waters on the
earth.

  2. He thoroughly shut the windows of the heavens and it did
not rain.

  3. The waters diminished returning and going to the sources
of the great fountains.

  4. Noah had a hard time sending forth a raven which did
not return to the ark.

5. The dove found the small olive leaf and brought it in her mouth to him.

6. The covering of the large ark was removed after another week.

7. The ark landed in the mountains of Ararat after 365 days.

8. Noah and those with him did not expire because he had walked with the God.

9. He securely stopped up the fountains in the deep and from the skies held back the rain.

10. The dove returned with an olive leaf in her mouth by which he knew that the earth was drained.

11. Because Noah did what God commanded him, he and his family went into the ark.

12. The rain ceased after forty-two days, but the water kept on increasing for 125 days.

PART FOUR — Lesson Four

I. Reading Lesson — Gen. 8:15–22.

495.   יְדַבֵּר   "and spoke." Piel impft. from verb root דבר (speak). What is the force of the Piel stem?

496.   צֵא   "go out." Kal imperative from verb root יצא (go out). Why is the first radical of this verb form missing?

497.   הַוְצֵא   "cause to go out." Hifil imperative from same verb root as above (No. 496). This is an irregular form for הוֹצֵא.

498.   וַיֵּצֵא   "and (he) went out." Kal jussive impft. from same verb root as in No. 496. Why is the first radical of this verb form missing?

499. לְמִשְׁפְּחֹתֵיהֶם   "according to their families." Plural const. form of fem. noun מִשְׁפָּחָה and used with preposition and 3rd mas. plu. suffix הֶם. It is a deverbal from verb root שׁפח (to join, associate). Note defective writing of וֹ as ־ֹ.

500.   וַיַּעַל   "and (he) caused to offer." Hifil, not Kal, jussive impft. from verb root עלה (go up, offer) and used with waw conversive. Both Kal and Hifil have the same form.

501.   וַיָּרַח   "and (he) smelled." Hifil jussive impft. from verb root רוח (to breathe, inhale, smell). The Hifil is the only stem used in the Old Testament.

502.   רֵיחַ   "odor, smell, scent." A deverbal noun from above verb root. (No. 497)

503.   אֹסֵף   "I will cause to add." Hifil impft. from verb root יסף (add). Note defective writing

of both vowels, —ִ for יְ— and —ִ for וֹ. Cf. No. 491.

504.   לְקַלֵּל   "to curse." Piel inf. const. from verb root קלל (curse). Note that Piel form is used. There is no extant usage of the poel form.

505.   לְהַכּוֹת   "to smite." See No. 348.

506.   קָצִיר   "harvest." Deverbal mas. noun from verb root קצר (to cut down, harvest).

507.   קַיִץ   "summer." Deverbal mas. noun from verb root קוץ (to cut down). The verb form is not used in the O. T.

508.   חֹרֶף   "winter." Deverbal mas. noun from verb root חרף (to gather, reap, pass the autumn).

II. The inflection of nouns

1. The affixes for gender and number.

There are two genders only in the Hebrew, as in all the Semitic languages, namely the masculine and the feminine. The feminine is most commonly the gender used to indicate what would be neuter.

There are three numbers in the Hebrew, namely singular, plural and dual.

a. The masculine singular.

There is no special form or mark of distinction to indicate this gender in the singular.

b. The feminine singular.

The original ending was תֹ_, following the analogy of the third feminine singular Perfect of the verb. Like the verb form, it came to be substituted by the ending הָ_, but is retained when adding pronominal suffixes.

There are modified forms of תֹ_, namely: תֶ_ (with gutturals תַ_) used in final unaccented syllables, either in Infinitive Construct or construct of some nouns; and תָ_ used almost exclusively in poetry.

E. g. with תֶ_ = קָאַת, pelican; שִׁפְעַת, crowd.

with תֶ_ = שֶׁבֶת, Kal Infinitive Construct of יָשַׁב, to dwell.

with תָ_ = עֶזְרָת help (Ps. 60:13).

with הָ_ = פָּרָה, heifer.

c. The masculine plural ending is יִ_ם in the absolute and יֵ_ in the construct state. E. g. דְּבָרִים, words; דִּבְרֵי, words of. The original ending of the construct was יֵ_.

d. The feminine plural both absolute and construct is וֹת. E. g. דְּבָרוֹת, causes, דִּבְרוֹת, causes of.

e. The dual endings are יִ_ם in the absolute, and יֵ_ in the construct state. E. g. סוּסַיִם, pair of horses.

III. Vocabulary

555.   דָּבַר he spoke
556.   דָּבָר word, command (m)
557.   דְּבִיר oracle (m)

558.   זָבַח he slaughtered (Piel—sacrificed)
559.   זֶבַח slaughtering, sacrifice (m)

560. מִזְבֵּחַ altar (m)

561. נִיחֹחַ pleasant, delight (m)

562. נְעוּרִים youth, early life (m) used only in plural

563. שָׂפַח he joined, associated

564. מִשְׁפָּחָה family, clan (f)

565. חָמַם it was or grew warm

566. חָם hot, warm, adj. (m)

567. חֹם heat, warmth (m)

568. חָרַף he gathered, reaped, it passed the autumn

569. חֹרֶף autumn, frequently including winter (m)

570. קָצַר he cut down, reaped

571. קָצִיר harvest (m)

572. קַיִץ summer, fruit harvest

573. קֹר cold (m)

574. רוּחַ to smell

575. רֵיחַ odor, scent, smell (m)

PART FOUR — LESSON FIVE

I. Reading Lesson — Gen. 9:1–10.

509. מוֹרַאֲכֶם "fear of you." Sing. const. of mas. deverbal noun מוֹרָא (fear, terror, awe, respect, reverence) from verb root ירא (to eye with suspicion; hence "to fear") and used with 2nd mas. plu. suffix כֶם.

510. חִתְּכֶם "dread of you." Sing. const. of mas. deverbal noun חַת (dread, terror) from verb root חתת (to terrify, be dismayed, broken) and used with 2nd per. mas. plural suffix כֶם.

511. בְּיֶדְכֶם "into your hand." Irregular form for בְּיֶדְכֶם. It is the sing. const. form of יָד (hand) and used with preposition בְּ and suffix כֶם.

512. אַךְ "only, nothing but, but, or surely." An adverbial particle.

513. אֶדְרֹשׁ "I will require." Kal impft. from verb root דרשׁ (require, demand back). Note usage of same form in the verse with nun epenthetic.

514. שֹׁפֵךְ "one or whoever shedding." Kal participle from verb root שׁפֵךְ (shed, put out) and used as a noun.

515. מֵקִים "about to establish." Hifil participle from verb root קוּם (stand). In Hifil it means "to cause to stand," hence "to establish."

516. יֹצְאֵי "the ones going out of." Kal participle from verb root יצֵא (go out). Here it is used as a noun in the plural mas. construct state.

II. Grammar

1. The absolute and construct states. (See statements on p. 10.)

Instead of changing the second of two nouns when one depends on the other for its meaning as does the genitive case in Indo-European languages, the Hebrew language changes the first of these two nouns. This first noun which suffers change, if possible, in form of vowels is said to be in a state of construction with the following noun which does not suffer change. Hence this latter noun is said to be in the absolute state, and the first in the construct state. E. g. דִּבְרֵי מֶלֶךְ, words of a king.

The noun in the construct never takes the article, and is always dependent upon the noun in the absolute for its definiteness. A noun in the absolute is definite when it has the article, a pronominal suffix, or when it is a proper name.

E. g.   דִּבְרֵי מֶלֶךְ, words of a king.

דִּבְרֵי הַמֶּלֶךְ, the words of the king.

דִּבְרֵי מַלְכּוֹ, the words of his king.

If adjectives are used with the construct, they must follow the noun in the absolute.

E. g. יַד אֱלֹהִים הַטּוֹבָה, the good hand of God.

גַּל אֲבָנִים גָּדוֹל, a great heap of stones.

2. Classification of nouns.

a. Nouns having one original, changeable vowel are called FIRST class. E. g. יָם, מֶלֶךְ, מָוֶת, זַיִת, פְּרִי, תֹּהוּ.

b. Nouns having two original, changeable vowels are called SECOND class. E. g. זָקֵן, שָׂדֶה, דָּבָר.

c. Nouns having one original, unchangeable vowel in the penult and one original, changeable vowel in the ultima are called THIRD class. E. g. אֵלֶם, מִשְׁפָּט, שַׁבָּת, עוֹלָם.

d. Nouns having one original, changeable vowel in the penult and one original, unchangeable vowel in the ultima are called FOURTH class. E. g. עָנִי, מָאוֹר, אָרוּר, גָּדוֹל.

e. Nouns having all vowels unchangeable are called FIFTH class. E. g. גִּבּוֹר, תַּלְמִיד , כְּתָב, סוּס.

3. The inflection of nouns with one unchangeable vowel. These are fifth class nouns.

Paradigm of סוּס

	Masculine		Feminine	
	Singular	Plural	Singular	Plural
Abs.	סוּס	סוּסִים	סוּסָה	סוּסוֹת
Const.	סוּס	סוּסֵי	סוּסַת	סוּסוֹת
Sing. 1 c.	סוּסִי	סוּסַי	סוּסָתִי	סוּסוֹתַי
2 m.	סוּסְךָ	סוּסֶיךָ	סוּסָתְךָ	סוּסוֹתֶיךָ
2 f.	סוּסֵךְ	סוּסַיִךְ	סוּסָתֵךְ	סוּסוֹתַיִךְ
3 m.	סוּסוֹ	סוּסָיו	סוּסָתוֹ	סוּסוֹתָיו
3 f.	סוּסָהּ	סוּסֶיהָ	סוּסָתָהּ	סוּסוֹתֶיהָ
Plu. 1 c.	סוּסֵנוּ	סוּסֵינוּ	סוּסָתֵנוּ	סוּסוֹתֵינוּ
2 m.	סוּסְכֶם	סוּסֵיכֶם	סוּסַתְכֶם	סוּסוֹתֵיכֶם
2 f.	סוּסְכֶן	סוּסֵיכֶן	סוּסַתְכֶן	סוּסוֹתֵיכֶן
3 m.	סוּסָם	סוּסֵיהֶם	סוּסָתָם	סוּסוֹתֵיהֶם
3 f.	סוּסָן	סוּסֵיהֶן	סוּסָתָן	סוּסוֹתֵיהֶן

a. The relation between the noun and its pronominal suffix is the construct relation. Pronominal suffixes are thus added to the construct form, all tone-long vowels subject to change when the tone changes.

b. The vowel of this noun itself does not change, since it is a naturally long vowel, סוּס.

c. The masculine singular construct adds pronominal suffixes as follows:

   (1) וֹ and ִי‑ do not need a connecting vowel, and are added directly.

   (2) ךָ, כֶם, and כֶן use ְ‑ as connecting vowel.

   (3) הָ, ם, and ן, use ָ‑ as connecting vowel, but הָ and ָ‑ contract to הָ‑.

   (4) ךְ and נוּ use ֵ‑ as connecting vowel.

d. The feminine singular construct follows the same method as the masculine singular. The ַ‑ becomes tone-long ָ‑ when pretonic, and remains ַ‑ when ante-pretonic.

e. The masculine plural and the dual add pronominal suffixes to their construct forms as follows:

   (1) ִי‑ contracts with the original construct ending ֵי‑ making ַי‑.

   (2) ךָ and הָ use ֶ‑ as a connecting vowel, which contracts with ֵי‑ making ֶיָ‑. This ֶיָ‑ is of the tone-long "A" class, but it becomes part of an unchangeable diphthong.

   (3) ךְ uses ֵ‑ as its connecting vowel and is added to original ending ֵי‑.

(4) וֹ contracts with ־ֶי making the unchangeable diphthong וָֹי.

(5) All the plural pronominal suffixes are added directly to the construct form.

f. The feminine plural adds pronominal suffixes to its construct וֹת, which is unchangeable, using both the construct ending and connecting vowels of the masculine plural.

IV. Vocabulary

576. חָתַת he was terrified, dismayed

577. חִתָּה dread, fear (f)

578. אַךְ only, nothing but, but, surely (adv.)

579. דָּרַשׁ he required, demanded, sought

580. שָׁפַךְ he shed, poured out

PART FOUR — LESSON SIX

I. Oral or written review of words, Nos. 555–580.

II. Written review of the paradigm סוּס. This paradigm must be mastered.

PART FOUR — LESSON SEVEN

I. Reading Lesson — Gen. 9:11–19.

517.   יִכָּרֵת   "will be cut off." Nifal impft. from verb root כרת (cut off, destroy)

518.   לְדֹרֹת   "to generations or ages." Plural construct of דּוֹר used with prep. לְ (to). Note defective writing of וֹ. See No. 434.

519.   קַשְׁתִּי   "my bow or rainbow." Singular const. form of קֶשֶׁת and used with 1st per. pronominal suff. יְ—. It is a deverbal noun from verb root קוֹשׁ (to be curved, bent).

520.   בֶּעָנָן   "in the cloud." A deverbal noun from verb root עֲנַן (to cover, cast over). Piel form is עִנֵּן "to cloud or bring a cloud."

521.   בְּעַנְנִי   "in my clouding." Piel inf. const. of above verb root (No. 520), used with preposition and pronominal suffix.

522.   לְמַבּוּל   "for a flood, deluge or innundation." A deverbal noun from verb root נבל (to gush or flow out).

523.   הַיֹּצְאִים   "the ones going out." Kal participle from verb root יצא (go out). It is the mas. plu. form and used with the article.

524.   כְּנַעַן   "Canaan." A deverbal noun from verb root כנע (be low.) Hence it means literally "a low lander."

525.   נָפְצָה   "(she) scattered." Kal pft. from verb root נפץ (to scatter, spread). Cf. פוץ "to scatter, spread."

III. Grammar

1. The inflection of nouns with two changeable vowels. These are second class nouns.

Paradigm of דָּבָר (word) and דְּבָרָה (cause)

	Masculine		Feminine	
	Singular	Plural	Singular	Plural
Abs.	דָּבָר	דְּבָרִים	דְּבָרָה	דְּבָרוֹת
Const.	דְּבַר	דִּבְרֵי	דִּבְרַת	דִּבְרוֹת
Sg. 1 c.	דְּבָרִי	דְּבָרַי	דִּבְרָתִי	דִּבְרוֹתַי
2 m.	דְּבָרְךָ	דְּבָרֶיךָ	דִּבְרָתְךָ	דִּבְרוֹתֶיךָ
2 f.	דְּבָרֵךְ	דְּבָרַיִךְ	דִּבְרָתֵךְ	דִּבְרוֹתַיִךְ
3 m.	דְּבָרוֹ	דְּבָרָיו	דִּבְרָתוֹ	דִּבְרוֹתָיו
3 f.	דְּבָרָהּ	דְּבָרֶיהָ	דִּבְרָתָהּ	דִּבְרוֹתֶיהָ
Pl. 1 c.	דְּבָרֵנוּ	דְּבָרֵינוּ	דִּבְרָתֵנוּ	דִּבְרוֹתֵינוּ
2 m.	דְּבַרְכֶם	דִּבְרֵיכֶם	דִּבְרַתְכֶם	דִּבְרוֹתֵיכֶם
2 f.	דְּבַרְכֶן	דִּבְרֵיכֶן	דִּבְרַתְכֶן	דִּבְרוֹתֵיכֶן
3 m.	דְּבָרָם	דִּבְרֵיהֶם	דִּבְרָתָם	דִּבְרוֹתֵיהֶם
3 f.	דְּבָרָן	דִּבְרֵיהֶן	דִּבְרָתָן	דִּבְרוֹתֵיהֶן

a. With affixes for gender and number absolute, other than masculine singular, and with light suffixes added to the masculine, tone shifts *one place*. Then penultimate vowel reduces to Shᵉwa, and ultimate tone-long vowel becomes pretonic.

E. g. דְּבָרִים — devārîm; דְּבָרִי — devārî.

b. With affixes for gender and number construct, other than masculine singular, and with grave suffixes attached to plural masculine nouns, tone shifts *two places*. Ultimate vowel reduces to Shᵉwa, and penultimate vowel in unaccented closed syllable shortens, usually being attenuated.

E. g. דִּבְרֵי — dĭverê; דִּבְרֵיכֶם — dĭverêkĕm.

c. In masculine construct singular, and with grave suffixes attached to singular nouns, tone shifts *one place*. Penultimate vowel reduces to Shᵉwa; ultimate vowel gives way to —.

E. g. דְּבַר — devăr; דְּבַרְכֶם — devărekĕm.

d. The feminine adds its pronominal suffixes to the construct forms. The vowel — of the singular construct is long when pretonic and short when ante-pretonic. (See paradigm of דָּבָר.)

III. Table showing vowel inflections in *second class nouns*.

	Word	Old Man	Wise	Righteousness
The Noun	דָּבָר	זָקֵן	חָכָם	צְדָקָה
Original Voweling	דַּבַר	זַקֵן	חַכַם	
1. Mas. Sing. Absolute	*** ָ ָ	*** ֵ ָ	*** ָ ָ	None
2. a — Mas. Sing. Construct. TONE MOVES b — Mas. Sing. ONE with grave PLACE suffixes.	*** ְ ִ	a — *** ֵ ְ b — *** ֲ ְ	*** ֲ ַ	None
3. a — All absolutes except Mas. Sing. TONE MOVES b — With all light ONE suffixes in Mas. PLACE Sing. and Plural.	*** ָ ְ	*** ֵ ְ	*** ָ ֲ	a — צְדָקָה b — None.
4. a — All Consts. except Mas. Sing. TONE b — With grave MOVES suffixes in Mas. TWO Plu. PLACES c — All fem. forms adding suffixes to const.	*** ְ ִ	*** ְ ִ	*** ְ ַ	a — *** ִ ְ b — None c — *** ִ ְ

IV. Vocabulary

581. כָּרַת he cut off, destroyed

582. דּוּר to dwell

583. דּוֹר generation, age (m)

584. קֶשֶׁת bow, rainbow (c)

585. עָנַן to cloud, cast over (only used in Piel)

586. עָנָן cloud (m)

587. נָפַץ he scattered, spread

PART FOUR — Lesson Eight

I. Reading Lesson — Gen. 9:20–29.

526. וַיָּחֶל   "and (he) began." Hifil jussive impft. from verb root חלל (begin).

527. וַיֵּשְׁתְּ   "and he drank." Kal jussive impft. from verb root שתה (drink). Regular Kal impft. form is יִשְׁתֶּה.

528. וַיִּשְׁכָּר   "and he was drunken." Kal jussive impft. pausal form, from verb root שכר (drink to the full or to hilarity).

529. וַיִּתְגַּל   "and he uncovered himself." Hithpael jussive impft. from verb root גלה (uncover, make bare). Regular Hithpael impft. is יִתְגַּלֶּה.

530.   וַיַּגֵּד   "and he caused to tell." Hifil jussive impft. from verb root נגד (tell). Cf. No. 288.

531.   בַּחוּץ   "outside." Literally "in the street, open place, or out of doors." Cf. No. 438.

532.   וַיִּיקֶץ   "and he awoke." Kal jussive impft. from verb root יקץ (awake).

533.   יַפְתְּ   "will enlarge." Hifil jussive impft. from verb root פתה (open wide). The Hifil means "to make wide or enlarge." Regular Hifil impft. form is יַפְתֶּה.

534.   לָמוֹ   "to him." This is a poetical form for לוֹ and is used 55 times in the Old Testament.

II. Grammar

Nouns for practice. Work out in full.

Sing. Abs.	Sing. Const.	Plu. Abs.	Plu. Const.
1. בָּקָר — cattle	— בְּקַר —	בְּקָרִים —	בִּקְרֵי
2. חָכָם — wise	— חֲכַם —	חֲכָמִים —	חַכְמֵי
3. זָקֵן — old man	— זְקַן —	זְקֵנִים —	זִקְנֵי
4. צְדָקָה — righteousness	— צִדְקַת —	צְדָקוֹת —	צִדְקוֹת
5. רָעָב — hunger	— רְעַב —	רְעָבִים —	רַעֲבֵי
6. רָשָׁע — wicked	— רְשַׁע —	רְשָׁעִים —	רִשְׁעֵי

III. Vocabulary

588. אֲחֹרַנִּית backward (adv.)   595. גָּלָה he uncovered,

589. כֶּרֶם vineyard (m)   made bare

590. יַיִן wine (m)   596. עָרָה he uncovered,

591. שָׁכַר he was drunken   made bare

592. שֵׁכָר strong drink   597. עֶרְוָה nakedness (f)

           (m)   598. שִׂמְלָה garment (f)

593. שִׁכֹּר drunken (m)   599. שְׁכֶם shoulder, part

594. שָׁתָה he drank,   (m)

           banqueted   600. יָקַץ he awoke

PART FOUR — Lesson Nine

I. Weekly oral or written review of nouns, Nos. 581–600.

II. Drill and review of rules and paradigm of דָּבָר and kindred nouns.

III. Sentences to be translated into literal Hebrew and written in exercise book:

1. The porter has not often opened the gates to the garden.

2. The fear of Noah and his sons was upon every living creature upon the earth and in the heavens.

3. God will require the lives of the men who shed the blood of their brothers.

4. When God has cast over a cloud in the sky, the rainbow will be seen.

5. The rainbow is the sign of God's covenant with all flesh.

6. Noah cursed (Piel) Ham, his youngest son, but blessed (Piel) the God of Shem.

7. When Noah awakened from his wine, he was not seen by Shem and Japheth.

8. The herdsmen drove her cattle from their small garden to his large field.

9. God established His covenant with all mankind after the water of the flood had been drained from the ground.

10. Jehovah will cut off again all flesh from the earth.

PART FOUR — Lesson Ten

I. Reading Lesson — Gen. 10:1–11.

Finish the reading of verses 12–32 and report on same at next lesson.

535.　נִפְרְדוּ　　"were divided." Nifal pft. from verb root פרד (divide, separate).

536.　אִיֵּי　　"coast lands of, shore lands, or land reached or bounded by water." It is the plural construct of deverbal noun אִי from verb root איה (to mark off or bound by water).

537.　הֵחֵל　　"(he) began." Hifil perfect from verb root חלל (begin).

538.　גִּבּוֹר　　"mighty one, hero, warrior." A deverbal from Piel stem of verb root גבר (bind, twist together, hence to be strong, mighty).

539.   צָיִד   "a hunter." A deverbal from verb root צוּד (set snares or nets, hunt).

540. מַמְלַכְתּוֹ   "his kingdom." Sing. const. of deverbal noun מַמְלָכָה from verb root מלך (rule) and used with pronominal suffix וֹ.

II. Grammar — The inflection of nouns with one original short vowel. These are first class nouns, called Segholates.

1. Masculine singular absolute form remains unchanged in masculine singular construct, when consonants are strong or gutturals. E. g. מֶלֶךְ (king) — mêlĕk.

2. In singular before all suffixes, and in the plural construct and before its grave suffixes, the noun takes the primary form. (Note that in spirant consonants in the plural construct and before grave suffixes, the dagheš-lene is missing.)

E. g.   מַלְכִּי — mălkî

           מַלְכֵי — mălkê

       מַלְכֵיהֶם — mălkêkĕm

3. Before plural affixes absolute and light suffixes added to the plural masculine, pretonic $\bar{\ }$ is inserted and the primary vowel reduces to Shewa. E. g. מְלָכִים — mᵉlākîm

          מְלָכֵינוּ — mᵉlākênû

4. The feminine adds its suffixes directly to the construct forms. Note that $\bar{\ }$ of singular construct affix is long when pretonic and short when ante-pretonic.

E. g. Sing. abs. מַלְכָּה; sing. const. מַלְכַּת; with suffix מַלְכָּתִי

    Plu. abs. מְלָכוֹת; plu. const. מַלְכוֹת; with suffix מַלְכוֹתַי

III. Table showing vowel inflections in *Segholate nouns*

	King	Book	Holiness	Youth
The Noun	מֶלֶךְ	סֵפֶר	קֹדֶשׁ	נַעַר
Original vowels	מַלְךְּ	סִפְר	קֻדְשׁ	נַעַר
1. Mas. sing. ab. and const. unchanged	***	***	***	***
2. (1) All suffixes to mas. sing. (2) Mas. plu. const. and with its grave suffixes (3) All fem. forms, except plu. ab. Note all suffixes above added to original form	***	***	***	***
3. (1) Mas. plu. ab. and with its light suffixes (2) Fem. plu. ab. (Note that the pretonic ָ forces stem vowel to become ְ)	***	***	*** or ***	***

IV. Vocabulary

601. אִי coastland, island (m)

602. גּוֹי nation, people (m)

603. לָשׁוֹן tongue, language (c)

604. מָלַךְ he was king, reigned

605. מֶלֶךְ king (m)

606. מַלְכָּה queen (f)

607. מַמְלָכָה kingdom (f)

608. צוּד to hunt, snare

609. צַיִד hunting, game (m)

PART FOUR — Lesson Eleven

I. Reading Lesson — Gen. 11:1–10.

Finish reading of verses 11–32 and report on same at next lesson.

541.   בְּנָסְעָם   "in their traveling." Kal infinitive construct from verb root נסע ("pull up tent pegs," hence "to journey, travel").

542.   בִּקְעָה   "sunken ground, valley" (a split or rent in the hills), "a depression"; also "a wide open country, a plain."

543.   הָבָה   "come on." Kal imperative with הָ‑ cohortative from verb root יהב (give, set, place). Here it means, as an idiom, "go to" or "come on."

544.   נִלְבְּנָה   "let us make brick." Kal imperfect with הָ‑ cohortative from verb root לבן (make brick).

545.   חֵמָר   "pitch, asphalt, bitumin." A deverbal from verb root חמר (to burn, be hot, boil, bubble, foam, swell).

546.   חֹמֶר   "clay, mortar, cement," from same verb as above.

547.   וַיֵּרֶד   "and (he) went down." Kal imperfect of verb root ירד (go down, descend).

548.   לְכֻלָּם   "to all of them." לְ (to) plus כֹּל (all) plus ‑ם them.

549.   הַחִלָּם   "to cause to begin them." Hifil infinitive construct from verb root חלל (begin).

550.   יִבָּצֵר   "will it be restrained." Nifal imperfect from verb root בצר (restrain, cut off).

551.   יָזְמּו   "they purpose" for יָזֹמּו. Kal imperfect from verb (hum, mutter), hence, "to meditate, consider, purpose, especially of evil." (זמם)

552.   נָבְלָה   "let us confuse." For נָבְלָה Kal imperfect from verb root בלל (pour together), hence "confound, confuse."

553.   וַיַּחְדְּלּו   "and they stopped." Kal imperfect from verb root חדל (leave off, cease, stop, desist).

554.   הֲפִיצָם   "he caused to scatter them." Hifil perfect הֵפִיץ from verb root פוץ (scatter) and used with pronominal suffix ם‑.

II. Grammar

Nouns for practice; work out in full.

Sing. Abs.		Sing. Const.	Plu. Abs.	Plu. Const.
1. מֶלֶךְ — king	—	מֶלֶךְ —	מְלָכִים —	מַלְכֵי
2. סֵפֶר — book	—	סֵפֶר —	סְפָרִים —	סִפְרֵי
3. קֹדֶשׁ — holiness	—	קֹדֶשׁ —	קָדָשִׁים —	קָדְשֵׁי (Note ָ for ֳ)
4. נַעַר — youth	—	נַעַר —	נְעָרִים —	נַעֲרֵי
5. מַלְכָּה — queen	—	מַלְכַּת —	מְלָכוֹת —	מַלְכוֹת
6. חֶרְפָּה — reproach	—	חֶרְפַּת —	חֲרָפוֹת —	חֶרְפוֹת

III. Vocabulary

610. לָבַן he made brick

611. לְבֵנָה brick, tile (f)
(plu. ‍ים_.)

612. שָׂרַף he burned

613. שְׂרֵפָה a burning (f)

614. מִגְדָּל tower, fortress (m)

615. נָסַע he pulled up tent
pegs, jour-
neyed, travelled

616. מִסַּע a removing,
journey (m)

617. בָּקַע he divided, split

618. בִּקְעָה sunken ground,
valley, plain (f)

619. בָּצַר he cut off, restrained

620. זָמַם he hummed,
muttered,
he mediated,
purposed, con-
sidered

621. זִמָּה device, plan, sin (f)

622. שָׂפָה shore (f)

623. בָּלַל he confused, con-
founded, mixed

624. פוּץ to scatter

625. חָדַל he left off,
stopped

PART FOUR — LESSON TWELVE

I. Oral or written review of words, Nos. 601–625.

II. Drill and thoroughly review inflection and paradigm of Segholate nouns.

PART FOUR — LESSON THIRTEEN

I. Reading Lesson — Gen. 12:1–10.

554.   אָאֹר   Kal imperfect, from verb root אָרַר (curse).
Cf. קָלַל (lightly esteem, despise, bemean).

555.   רְכוּשָׁם   "their substance, property, wealth." A deverbal noun from verb root רכש (get,
gain, acquire) and used with 3rd per. plu.
pronominal suffix.

556.   לָלֶכֶת   Kal infinitive construct from verb root ילך
(to go).

557.   אַרְצָה   "landward." Note the use of the He-
directives in verse 5.

558.   עַד   "into" or "unto."

559.   אָז   "then."

560.   אֵלוֹן   "oak tree" from verb root אול meaning
"to be lasting, strong."

561.   וַיֵּרָא   "and appeared." Nifal jussive imperfect
with waw conversive (full form יֵרָאֶה)
from verb root ראה (see).

562.   הַנִּרְאֶה   Nifal participle of the above verb.

563.   וַיַּעְתֵּק   "and he removed." Hifil jussive imperfect from verb root עתק (remove, break
camp).

564.   וַיֵּט   "and he pitched." Kal jussive imperfect,
from verb root נטה (spread or stretch
out a tent). Regular Kal impft. form is
יִטֶּה.

565.   וַיִּסַּע   Kal jussive imperfect from verb root

נֹסַע (pull up tent pegs), hence "break camp."

566.   נָ ס ו עַ   Kal infinitive absolute of the above verb.

567.   הַ נֶּ גְ בָּ ה   "the" plus "south" plus "ward" (He-directive).

II. Grammar

1. The inflection of Ayin-Waw and Ayin-Yodh nouns.

These are first class nouns. The second radical combines with the penultimate vowel making an unchangeable long vowel in the masculine construct singular, to which *all* affixes and suffixes are added. It is thus like סוס.

E. g. מָוֶת (death) — māwĕth; contraction of ו and ָ makes מוֶת — moĕth; hence מוֹת — môth.

2. The inflection of Ayin doubled nouns.

These are first class nouns. When adding affixes or suffixes, the final radical is doubled and stem vowel is shortened since it stands in an unaccented closed syllable.

E. g.   יָם — yām   — sea

        יַמִּי — yămmî   — my sea

    יַמֵּיכֶם — yămmêkĕm — your sea

3. All feminine forms of these two classes of nouns add their pronominal suffixes to the construct after the order of סוס. If noun as אֵם (mother) is feminine in the short form, it follows the masculine order in the singular but follows the feminine in the plural. (See 4, 4 below).

4. Nouns for practice; work out in full:

Sing. *Abs.*	Sing. *Const.*	Plu. *Abs.*	Plu. *Const.*
1. מָוֶת — death	— מוֹת —	— מוֹתִים —	מוֹתֵי
2. זַיִת — olive tree	— זֵית —	— זֵיתִים —	זֵיתֵי
3. יָם — sea	— יַם —	— יַמִּים —	יַמֵּי
4. אֵם — mother	— אֵם —	— אִמּוֹת —	אִמּוֹת
5. שֵׁן — tooth	— שֵׁן —	— שִׁנַּיִם —	שִׁנֵּי

III. Vocabulary

626. אַלּוֹן oak tree

627. קָלַל he made light of, cursed. (Cf. 552)

628. רָכַשׁ he gained, acquired

629. רְכוּשׁ substance, property, wealth (m)

630. גּוּר to sojourn

631. מָגוּר sojourning, residence (m)

632. גֵּר sojourner, stranger (m)

633. עָתַק he broke camp, removed

634. עָתִיק removed, taken away, ancient (adj.)

635. נָטָה he pitched, spread, stretched out

636. מַטֶּה branch, scepter, tribe (m)

637. רָעֵב he was hungry, (adj.) has the same form

638. רָעָב famine, hunger (m)

639. כָּבֵד it was heavy, (adj.) has same form

640. כָּבוֹד honor, glory (m)

641. כֹּבֶד weight, vehemence (m)

642. מוֹלֶדֶת kindred, family (f)

מוֹלַדְתּוֹ his family)

643. בְּרָכָה blessing (f)

PART FOUR — LESSON FOURTEEN

I. Reading Lesson — Gen. 12:11–20.

568.   הִקְרִיב   "(he) caused to draw near." Hifil perfect from verb root קרב (draw near).

569.   מִצְרָיְמָה   "Egypt-ward." Note use of He directive.

570.   יְחַיּוּ   "they will let live." Piel impft. from verb root חיה (live).

571.   יִיטַב   "It may be well or good." Kal impft. from verb root יטב (be or do good or well). This is used as a subjunctive here.

572.   וַיְהַלְלוּ   "and they praised." Piel jussive impft. from verb root הלל (touch, smite), and used with waw conversive.

573.   וַיְנַגַּע   "And he plagued." Piel jussive impft. from verb root נגע (touch, smite) and used with waw conversive.

574.   וַיְצַו   "And (he) commanded." Piel jussive impft. from verb root צוה (command) and used with waw conversive.

II. Grammar — the inflection of Lamed-He nouns

These are second class nouns.

1. When adding affixes or suffixes, the final הָ֫ is dropped; the stem vowel is retained when pretonic, but reduces to Sheᵉwa when ante-pretonic.

2. In the masculine singular construct the ־ֶ becomes ־ְ.

E. g. Mas. sing. abs. — שָׂדֶה — sādĕh (field)

Mas. sing const. — שְׂדֵה — sᵉdēh (field of)

(stem vowel in open, pretonic syllable)

Stem vowel pretonic — שָׂדִי — sādî (my field)

Stem vowel ante-pretonic — שְׂדִיכֶם — sᵉdêkĕm (your field)

3. If nouns are feminine, the suffixes are added to the construct form, the rules for tone-long vowels being observed.

III. Vocabulary Lesson

644. יָפָה it was fair, beautiful (fem. adj. has same form)

645. יָפֶה fair, good (m)

646. בִּגְלַל because of, for the sake of

647. הָלַל he praised

648. תְּהִלָּה praise, hymn, psalm (f)

649. בַּיִת house (m)

650. אָחוֹת sister (f), (an irreg. plu.)

651. שַׂר prince (m)

652. שָׂרָה princess (f)

653. שִׁפְחָה maid servant (f)

654. בָּקָר cattle, oxen (c)

655. חֲמֹר donkey (m)

656. אָתוֹן she donkey (f)

657. גָּמָל camel (c)

658. צֹאן flock (m)

659. נֶגַע plague, stroke (m)

PART FOUR — Lesson Fifteen

I. Oral or written vocabulary review of words, Nos. 629–659.

II. Grammar review of inflection of ע״ו, ע״י, ע״ע and ל״ה nouns.

III. Sentences to be translated into Hebrew and written in exercise
book:

1. I sent our horses and your cattle with his men to their (f)
   queen.

2. All your (f. pl.) silver and their (f. pl.) gold will not buy
   her books.

3. Abram went to Egypt with his family and Lot also with
   his possessions.

4. My house shall be for all people to serve me in my holiness.

5. When God called Abraham he obeyed His voice and His
   words.

6. Men shall follow my righteousness and my justice all the
   days of their life.

7. Cain killed his brother when God did not look in favor
   upon his offering from the fruit of his field.

8. Noah brought his family to their ark to keep them alive
   with all their cattle and fowls.

9. God spoke His good words to her daughters in her house.

10. My mother will keep my words in her heart.

PART FOUR — Lesson Sixteen

I. Reading Lesson — Gen. 13:1–9.

575. לְמַסָּעָיו   "to journeyings his." A mas. deverbal
                      noun from verb root נָסַע (to pull up tent
                      pegs, hence to travel, journey).

576. בַּתְּחִלָּה   "in the beginning or formerly." A de-verbal noun with preposition בְּ (in) from verb root חלל (begin). It is used as an adverb.

577. נָשָׂא   "could bear." Kal pft. from verb root נשׂא (to lift up,) also, "carry, bear, endure".

578. לָשֶׁבֶת   "to dwell." Kal inf. const. from verb root ישׁב (set down, abide, dwell). Cf. טֶלֶת.

579. רִיב   "strife, quarrel, contention." A mas. de-verbal noun from verb root רִיב (contend, strive). Cf. מְרִיבָה (strife) in vs. 8.

580. אַל ־ נָא   "let not I pray thee." Interjection נָא used with negative. Cf. μή in Greek.

581. הִפָּרֶד   "separate thyself." Nifal imperative from verb root פרד (separate).

582. אַשְׂמְאִילָה   "I will turn to the left." Hifil impft. from irregular verb root שׂמאל (turn to the left).

583. אֵימִינָה   "I will turn to or take the right." Hifil impft. from verb root ימן (turn to or take the right).

II. Grammar

1. The inflection of third class nouns.

The penultimate vowel is unchangeable and the ultimate vowel, when adding affixes or suffixes, remains long when pretonic and becomes short when ante-pretonic.

An exception occurs when original ־ָ becomes ־ֵ under the tone as in אֹיֵב (enemy). This vowe l remains ־ֵ in the singular construct, reduces to Sh ͤwa before the light suffixes and throughout the plural, and shortens to ־ֶ before the grave suffixes and ךָ in the singular. E. g. Sing. abs. אֹיֵב (enemy); sing. const. אֹיֵב (enemy of); sing. with light suffix אֹיְבִי (my enemy); sing. with grave suffix אֹיִבְכֶם (your enemy). Lamed-He nouns of this class drop ה־ֶ and make additions direct, with the penultimate vowel remaining unchangeable. E. g. Sing. abs. חֹזֶה (prophet); sing. const. חֹזֵה (prophet of); sing. before suffix חֹזִי (my prophet).

2. The inflection of fourth class nouns.

The penultimate vowel being changeable must always reduce to Sh ͤwa, since it is always ante-pretonic when affixes or suffixes are added. The ultimate vowel being naturally long is unchangeable. E. g. Sing. abs. פָּקִיד (overseer); sing. const. פְּקִיד (overseer of); with light suffix פְּקִידִי (my overseer).

3. The inflection of fifth class nouns.

Since, like סוּס, their vowel or vowels are unchangeable, either because naturally long, short in an unaccented syllable, or tone-short (as Sh ͤwa's), the affixes and pronominal suffixes are added as with סוּס. (See paradigm, p. 216.)

E. g. Sing abs. תַּלְמִיד — disciple

  Sing. const. תַּלְמִיד — disciple of

  with suffix תַּלְמִידוֹ — his disciple

  sing. abs. כְּתָב — writing

  sing. const. כְּתָב — writing of

  with suffix כְּתָבוֹ — his writing

III. Vocabulary

660. נָא I pray thee
(Interj.)

661. נֶגֶב south country,
desert (m)

662. תְּחִלָּה beginning (f)

663. יָחַד he was united

664. יַחַד union (m); adv.
— together,
entirely

665. יָמַן he turned to or
took to the
right (used
only in Hif.)

666. יָמִין right hand (as to
direction) (m)

667. שָׂמְאַל he turned to or
took to the left
(used only in
Hif.)

668. רִיב to strive, contend,
quarrel. Noun
has same form —
strife, quarrel
(m)

669. מְרִיבָה strife, contention
(f)

PART FOUR — Lesson Seventeen

I. Reading Lesson — Gen. 13:10–18.

584. כִּכָּר "plain, circumjacent tract of country,
circle." Sing. const. of כִּכָּר mas. deverbal
noun from verb root כרר (leap, dance,
whirl about, hence, to surround, enclose).

585. מַשְׁקֶה "well watered." Hifil participle from verb
root שקה (drink) and is used here as an
adjective.

586. שַׁחֵת "destroyed." Piel inf. const. from verb root

שָׁחַת (spoil by rotting). The Piel stem means "to destroy".

587.   בֹּ אֲ כָ ה   "thy entering." Kal inf. const. from verb root בוא (go in) and suffix ךָ. Note use of protective ה which is sometimes at the end of a word ending in a vowel.

588.   וַ יִּ סַ ע   "and he journeyed." Kal jussive impft. from verb root נסע (pull up tent pegs). Cf. No. 575.

589.   אֶ תְּ נֶ נָּ ה   "I will give it." Kal impft. from verb root נתן (give). Note use of nun epenthetic.

590.   שַׂ מְ תִּ י   "I will establish." Kal pft. from verb root שׂים (to put, place, set, found, establish).

591.   מַ מְ רֵ א   "Mamre." A proper noun meaning "fat, strong" from verb root מרא (be well fed, or fat).

592.   חֶ בְ רוֹ ן   "Hebron." A proper noun meaning association or confederacy from verb root חבר (join or unite, as allies).

II. Grammar

1. Adverbs.

Adverbs are of two kinds, primitive and derivative.

a. Primitives: original expressions, spontaneous from experience, as. אֵי, where; אָז then; שָׁם, there; אַל, not; לֹא, not.

b. Derivatives

  (1) From pronouns and numerals.

   E. g. זֶה, here, now; הֵנָּה, hither; כֹּה, thus; כֵּן, so; שָׁלֹשׁ, thrice.

  (2) From nouns, with or without prepositions.

   E. g. מְאֹד, exceedingly; עוֹד, again; חוּץ, abroad; לְבַד, alone, מִבַּיִת, inside.

  (3) From verbs, especially Piel and Hifil infinitive absolutes, which are really verbal nouns.

   E. g. הַרְבֵּה, much; הַשְׁכֵּם, early; מַהֵר, quickly.

  (4) From adjectives, particularly in the feminine.

   E. g. טוֹב, well; רִאשׁנָה, formerly; רַבָּה, much; נִפְלָאוֹת, wonderfully.

  (5) By combinations.

   E. g. מַדּוּעַ, why, from יָדוּעַ plus מַה; מִלְמַעְלָה, from above, from מִן plus לְ plus מַעְלָה; לָמָה, wherefore, from לְ plus מָה.

  (6) Impersonal forms that have verbal idea and take pronominal suffixes, as:

   (a) הִנֵּה, here is, behold; with suffix הִנְנִי, etc.

   (b) עוֹד, still is; with suffix עוֹדִי, etc.

   (c) אַי, where is; with suffix אַיּוֹ, etc.

   (d) אַיִן, there is not; with suffix אֵינְךָ, etc.

   (e) יֵשׁ, there is; with suffix יֶשְׁךָ, etc.

2. Prepositions.

Besides the inseparable prepositions בְּ, לְ, כְּ, and מִן, there are many prepositions which are really construct forms of nouns, to which suffixes are added, or which precede regularly their nouns, in the absolute. E. g. אַחַר, after; בֵּין, between; מוּל, over against; אֶל, unto; סָבִיב, around; עַד, unto; תַּחַת, under.

There are also compound prepositions. E. g. מִתַּחַת, from under; לְמִן, since; אֶל־מוּל, toward.

3. Conjunctions.

  a. The principal conjunction is וְ, and (see p. 35), but other common, simple conjunctions are אוֹ, or; אַף, also; אִם, if; אֲשֶׁר, that; כִּי, because; פֶּן, lest.

  b. Compound forms are כִּי אִם, but if; אַף כִּי, also that; עַל־כֵּן or לְכֵן, therefore; כַּאֲשֶׁר, according as.

4. Interjections.

These are similar to those in other languages.

  a. Natural sounds expressing various emotions. E. g. אָח, and אֲהָהּ, ah! oh!; הֶאָח, aha!; הוֹי, ho! woe!; אוֹי, and אִי, woe!; אַלְלַי, alas!; הַס, hush!

  b. Regular words of speech converted into interjections. E. g. הָבָה, come!; הִנֵּה, behold!; רְאֵה, see! behold!; בִּי, pray!; נָא, I pray thee! now!

III. Vocabulary

    670. מַשְׁקֶה well watered country, drink (m)
    671. כִּכָּר circular plain, circuit (m)

672. עָר city (m)

673. צָפוֹן north (c)

674. מָנָה he numbered, appointed

675. חַטָּא sinner (m)

PART FOUR — Lesson Eighteen

I. Oral or written vocabulary review of words, Nos. 660–675.

II. Grammar

Review rules for the inflection and also the paradigm of
דָּבָר.

PART FOUR — Lesson Nineteen

I. Reading Lesson — Gen. 14:1–12.

593.   מִ לְ חָ מָ ה   "war." Fem. abs. deverbal noun from verb root לָחַם (fight).

594.   חָ בְ ר וּ   "joined together in war." Kal pft. from verb root חבר (join together).

595.   עֵ מֶ ק   "valley, low plain bordered by high ground." A deverbal segholate mas. noun from verb root עמק (sink down, be deep).

596.   הַ מִּ דְ בָּ ר   "the desert." A mas. deverbal noun from verb root דבר (Piel stem — to destroy).

597.   וַ יַּ כּ וּ   "and they smote." Hifil jussive impft.

from verb root נכה (smite) and used with waw conversive.

598.   וַיַּעַרְכוּ   "and they set in battle array." Kal jussive impft. from verb root עָרַךְ (set in order), and used with waw conversive. When used with מִלְחָמָה (war) it means as above used.

599.   בְּאֵרֹת   "pits." Plu. const. of fem. deverbal noun from verb root בָּאַר (dig).

600.   חֵמָר   "bitumen or asphalt." A mas. abs. deverbal from verb root חמר (be hot, boil, bubble). This bitumin or asphalt springs up in a turbid effervescence near the Dead sea or in its bottoms.

601.   וַיָּנֻסוּ   "and (they) fled away." Kal jussive impft. from verb root נוּס (flee away, ride swiftly) and used with waw conversive. Note defective writing of וּ (u).

II.   Grammar — Review rules for the inflection of Segholate, ע״ו, ע״י, and ל״ה nouns.

III.   Vocabulary

676. מִלְחָמָה war (f)

677. עָרַךְ he set in order, arranged

678. חָבַר he joined together, bound

679. חֶבֶר company, association (m)

680. עֵמֶק valley (m)

681. מֶלַח salt (m)

682. מָרַד he rebelled, revolted

683. נוּס to flee away, escape

684. מִדְבָּר desert (m)

685. שָׁפַט he judged

686. מִשְׁפָּט judgment (m)

687. בְּאֵר well, cistern (f)

688. חֵמָר asphalt (m)

PART FOUR — Lesson Twenty

I. Reading Lesson — Gen. 14:13–24.

602. הַפָּלִיט "the fugitive or one who escaped by flight." A deverbal adjective used as a noun and from verb root פלט (slip away, escape).

603. בַּעֲלֵי בְרִית "a confederate." Literally this form means "possessors of a covenant."

604. נִשְׁבָּה "(he) had been captured." Nifal pft. from verb root שבה (capture).

605. וַיָּרֶק "and he led out." Hifil juss. impft. from verb root רוק (lead or draw out) and used with waw conversive.

606. חֲנִיכָיו "his trained men." Plu. mas. deverbal noun from חנך (train) and used with pronominal suffix יו.

607. לִקְרָאתוֹ "to meet him." Kal inf. const. from verb root קרא (meet) and used with pronominal suffix וֹ and preposition לְ.

608. מִגֵּן "he delivered." Piel pft. from verb root מגן (enclose or shut up). Piel stem means "to deliver."

609. הֲרִמֹתִי "I cause to lift up." Hifil pft. from verb root רום (be high or lift up).

610. הֶעֱשַׁרְתִּי "I cause to make rich." Hifil pft. from verb root עשר (be rich, prosperous).

611. בִּלְעָדַי "as far as regards me." Literally יִ֫ (me) plus עַד (to) plus בַּל (not) hence "nothing to me".

II. Grammar

Review rules for the inflection of Segholate, עַ"וּ, עַ"י, and לַ"ה nouns.

III. Vocabulary

689. פָּלִיט fugitive (m)

690. פָּלַט he fled, escaped, slipped away

691. שָׁבָה he captured, took captive

692. חָנַךְ he trained, taught

693. חָנִיךְ trained or drilled men (m). Only used in plural in O. T.

694. רוּק to lead or draw out

695. קָרָא he met (same in form as, hě called)

696. חוּט thread, line, cord (m)

697. שָׂרוֹךְ lachet (m)

698. נַעַל shoe (m)

699. עָשַׁר he was rich, prosperous

700. חֵלֶק portion (m)

PART FOUR — Lesson Twenty One

I. Oral or written vocabulary review of words, Nos. 676–700.

II. Review of Gen. 12 as to reading, parsing of verbs and classification of nouns.

III. Be thorough in your preparation for the examination.

HEBREW-ENGLISH VOCABULARY

1.	אָב	(m) father (const. אֲבִי)
2.	אֶבֶן	(f) stone
3.	אֵד	(m) mist
4.	אָדֹן	(m) Lord, Master
5.	אָדָם	(m) man, mankind
6.	אֲדָמָה	(f) ground (const. אַדְמַת)
7.	אֹהֶל	(m) tent, tabernacle
7a.	אָהַל	to tent, to pitch a tent
8.	אוֹר	shine, give light (הָאִיר) Hifil inf. const. cause to shine)
9.	אוֹר	(m) light
10.	אוֹת	(f) sign
11.	אָז	then, there (adv.)
12.	אָזַן	give ear, listen
13.	אֶחָד	(m) one, same, first. For meaning of numerals see list on pp. 174, 175.
14.	אַחַת	(f) one
15.	אָח	(m) brother (const. אֲחִי)
16.	אָחוֹת	(f) sister (const. אֲחוֹת)
17.	אַחֵר	other, another (adj.)
18.	אַחַר	after (adv. and prep.)
19.	אַחֲרֵי	after (adv.)
20.	אֲחֹרַנִּית	backwards (adv.)
21.	אֵי	where (adv.)
22.	אַי	where (adv.)
23.	אִי	(m) coastland, island

24.	אֵיבָה	(f) hatred, enmity (const. אֵיבַת)
25.	אַיִן	nothing, there is not
26.	אֵימָה	(f) fear, terror
27.	אִישׁ	(m) man, husband
28.	אַךְ	surely, nothing but, only (adv.)
29.	אָכַל	eat
30.	אָכְלָה	(f) food
31.	אֵל	(m) God
31a.	אֶל	to, unto (prep.)
32.	אֵלֶּה	(m) these
33.	אֱלֹהִים	(m) God
34.	אַלּוֹן	(m) oak tree
35.	אֵם	(f) mother plural אִמּוֹת
36.	אִם	if (conj.)
37.	אַמָּה	(f) cubit
38.	אָמַר	say (וַיֹּאמֶר and he said) (יֹאמֵר he will say)
39.	אִמְרָה	(f) saying, utterance, word
40.	אֱנוֹשׁ	(m) common people, man
41.	אַף	(m) nostril, nose
42.	אַף	surely, indeed, also, yea (conj.)

43. אָסַף collect, gather
44. אֲרֻבָּה (f) window
45. אֹרֶךְ (m) length
46. אֶרֶץ (f) earth
       (הָאָרֶץ the earth)
47. אָרַר cursed
48. אֵשׁ (c) fire
49. אִשָּׁה (f) woman (const. אֵשֶׁת)
       (plu. ab. נָשִׁים)
       (plu. const. נְשֵׁי)
50. אֲשֶׁר who, which
51. אֵת sign of definite and
       direct object
52. אֵת with (prep.)
53. אָתוֹן (f) she donkey
54. בְּ in, on (inseparable
       prep.)
55. בְּאֵר (f) cistern, well
56. בִּגְלַל for sake of, because of
       (prep.)
57. בַּד (m) separation
58. בָּדַל divide, separate; Hifil
       הִבְדִּיל he caused to divide
       יַבְדִּיל he will cause to divide
       וַיַּבְדִּל and he will cause to
       divide
59. בְּדֹלַח (m) pearl, bdellium
60. בֹּהוּ (m) waste
61. בְּהֵמָה (f) cattle
       בֶּהֱמַת const. sing.
62. בּוֹא come, go in
       Hifil = to bring
63. בּוֹשׁ be ashamed

64. בָּחַר choose, examine
65. בֵּין between, among (prep.)
66. בַּיִת (m) house (const. בֵּית)
67. בְּכוֹרָה (f) first born, first fruit
68. בִּלְתִּי not, used with infinitive
       (adv.)
69. בָּלַל confound, mix, confuse
70. בֵּן (m) son
71. בָּנָה build
       וַיִּבֶן and he built
72. בַּעֲבוּר for the sake of, on
       account of (prep.)
73. בְּעַד around, behind, about
       (prep.)
74. בַּעַל (m) Lord, Master
75. בָּצַר cut off, restrain
76. בָּקַע hatch, break up, split,
       divide
77. בִּקְעָה (f) valley, plain
78. בָּקָר (c) oxen, cattle
79. בֹּקֶר (m) morning
80. בָּרָא create
81. בַּרְזֶל (m) iron
82. בְּרִית (f) league, covenant
83. בָּרַךְ bless
84. בְּרָכָה (f) blessing
85. בָּשָׂר (f) flesh
86. בַּת (f) daughter
87. בָּתַר cut in pieces, divide
88. בֶּתֶר (m) part, piece
89. גָּבוֹהַּ high, proud, majestic
       (adj.)
90. גִּבּוֹר (m) hero, mighty man

91.	גָּבַר	be mighty, be strong
92.	גָּדַל	be great, be mighty
93.	גָּדוֹל	great
94.	גּוֹי	(m) nation, people
95.	גּוֹזָל	(m) young pigeon
96.	גָּוַע	expire, die
97.	גּוּר	dwell, sojourn
98.	גֶּזֶר	(m) piece, part
99.	גָּחוֹן	(m) stomach, belly
100.	גִּיחוֹן	(m) Gihon river
101.	גָּלָה	make bare, uncover
102.	גַּם	even also (adv. and conj.)
103.	גָּמָל	(c) camel
104.	גַּן	(c) garden
105.	גֹּפֶר	(m) gopher tree, pine tree
106.	גֵּר	(m) sojourner, stranger, foreigner
107.	גָּרַשׁ	drive out, cast out
108.	גֶּשֶׁם	(m) rain (heavy shower)
109.	דָּבַק	cleave, cling
110.	דָּבַר	speak
111.	דָּבָר	(m) speech, word
112.	דָּג	(m) fish
113.	דָּגָה	(f) fish
114.	דִּין	judge, strive, contend
115.	דּוֹר	(m) generation, age
116.	דָּם	(m) blood
117.	דְּמוּת	(f) likeness
118.	דַּמֶּשֶׂק	Damascus (proper name)

119.	דַּעַת	(f) knowledge, understand
120.	דַּרְדַּר	(m) thistle
121.	דֶּרֶךְ	(c) path, way
122.	דָּרַשׁ	require, seek, demand
123.	דָּשָׁא	sprout
124.	דֶּשֶׁא	(m) grass
125.	הַ,, הַ, הָ	the (definite article)
126.	הַ	interrogative particle
127.	הֶבֶל	Abel, proper name
128.	הוּא	he (pronoun) See table of pronouns.
128a.	הוּא	that (demonstrative)
129.	הָיָה	become, exist, to be, And he was וַיְהִי, She was הָיְתָה, He will be or let be יְהִי, to be לִהְיוֹת
130.	הָלַךְ	go
131.	הָלַל	praise
132.	הֵן	behold (interj.)
133.	הִנֵּה	behold (interj.)
134.	הָפַךְ	turn
135.	הַר	(m) mountain
136.	הָרַג	kill
137.	הָרָה	conceive וַתַּהַר and it conceived
137a.	הֵרוֹן	(m) conception
138.	וְ	but, and Other forms וְ, וַ, וֶ, וִ, depending upon accent or following letter. וָ waw conversive used

with impft. וְ waw con-
versive used with pft.

139. זֶה (m) this (See table on p. 57)

140. זָהָב (m) gold

141. זַיִת (m) olive

142. זָכַר (m) remember

143. זָכָר (m) male

144. זָמַם consider, purpose, meditate, think, plan

145. זֵעָה (f) sweat (const. זֵעַת)

146. זָרַע sow (Hifil participle מַזְרִיעַ)

147. זֶרַע (m) seed

148. חָבָא hide

149. חַבּוּרָה (f) bruise, hurt

150. חָבַר join together, bind

151. חֲגוֹרָה (f) girdle

152. חָדַל cease, leave off

153. חִדֶּקֶל Tigris

154. חֹדֶשׁ (m) new moon, month

155. חַוָּה (f) Eve, life

156. חוּט (m) thread, cord

157. חוּל cease, stay, wait

158. חוּץ (m) field street, outside

159. חַטָּא (m) sinner

160. חַטָּאת (f) sin, sin offering

161. חַי living, alive (adj.)

162. חָיָה live
וַיְחִי and he lived

163. חַיָּה (f) life, beast, living creature. const. חַיַּת, חַיְתוֹ

164. חָיַי live (Used twice in O. T.)

165. חֵלֶב (m) fatness, fat

166. חַלּוֹן (m) window, opening

167. חָלַל begin

168. חָלַק divide

169. חֵלֶק portion, part

170. חָם Ham

171. חֹם (m) warmth, heat

172. חָמַד desire

173. חֲמִישִׁי fifth (ordinal)

174. חָמָס (m) injury, violence

174a. חֲמֹר (m) donkey

175. חֵמָר (m) bitumen, asphalt

176. חֹמֶר (m) mud, mire

177. חֵן (m) favor, grace

178. חֲנוֹךְ Enoch

179. חָנִיךְ trained (adj.)

180. חָסַר decrease, diminish

181. חָרֵב drain, be dry, be desolate

182. חֶרֶב (f) sword

183. חָרָבָה (f) dry land

184. חָרָה kindle, burn
וַיִּחַר and it burned

185. חֹרֶף (m) autumn (frequently winter)

186. חָרַשׁ plow, engrave, scratch

187. חֹרֶשׁ (m) cutting instrument

188. חָשַׁב reckon

189. חֹשֶׁךְ (m) darkness

190. חֲשֵׁכָה (f) darkness

191.	חַת	terrified, dismayed (adj.)	219.	יָמִין	(m) right hand
192.	חַת	(m) dread, fear	220.	יָמַן	turn to the right, take to the right.
193.	טָהוֹר	(m) pure, clean (adj.)	221.	יָסַף	add
194.	טוֹב	good, pleasant (adj.)	222.	יָפָה	beautiful, fair (const. יְפַת)
195.	טוֹב	well (adv.)			
196.	טוֹבָה	(f) benefit, blessing, good	223.	יָצָא	go out, go forth
			224.	יָצַר	make, fashion, form
197.	טֶרֶם	not yet (adv.)	225.	יֵצֶר	(m) image, thought
198.	טָרָף	new, freshly plucked (adj.)	226.	יְקוּם	(m) living thing, standing thing, a being
199.	יָבֵשׁ	be dry	227.	יָקַץ	awake
200.	יַבָּשָׁה	(f) dry·land	228.	יָרֵא	fear, be afraid, tremble
201.	יָד	(c) hand	229.	יָרַד	go down
202.	יָדַע	know	230.	יֶרֶק	(m) greenness
203.	יָהַב	give, come, go	231.	יָרֵשׁ	inherit, possess
204.	יְהֹוָה	Jehovah	232.	יָשַׁב	sit, dwell
205.	יוֹם	(m) day	233.	יָשֵׁן	sleep
206.	יוֹמָם	daily (adv.)	234.	כְּ	as, like (inseparable prep.)
207.	יוֹנָה	dove (f)			
208.	יָחַד	unite	235.	כָּבֵד	be heavy
209.	יַחְדָּו	mutually together (adv.)	236.	כָּבֵד	heavy, abounding (adj.)
210.	יָחַל	wait, stay	237.	כָּבַשׁ	subject, subdue
211.	יָטַב	do good, do well, do right	238.	כֹּהֵן	(m) priest
			239.	כּוֹכָב	(m) star
212.	יַיִן	(m) wine	240.	כֹּחַ	(m) vigor, strength
213.	יָכֹל	be able, bear	241.	כִּי	that, when, because, for (conj.)
214.	יָלַד	bring forth, bear			
215.	יֶלֶד	(m) child, boy, lad	242.	כִּכָּר	(f) circuit (of land), a circular plain
216.	יָלִיד	born (adj.)			
217.	יָלַךְ	go	243.	כֹּל	every, all (adj.)
218.	יָם	(m) sea	244.	כָּלָא	withhold, restrain

245.	כָּלָה	end, complete, finish
246.	כֵּן	thus so (adv.)
247.	כִּנּוֹר	(m) harp
248.	כָּנָף	(f) wing
249.	כָּסָה	cover, conceal
250.	כֶּסֶף	(m) silver
251.	כַּף	(f) palm of hand, hollow of hand, sole of foot
252.	כָּפַר	cover, pardon
253.	כֹּפֶר	(m) bitumen pitch
254.	כְּרוּב	(m) cherub
255.	כֶּרֶם	(m) vineyard, orchard
256.	כָּרַת	destroy, cut off
257.	כְּתֹנֶת	(f) garment, tunic
258.	לְ	to, towards, for (inseparable prep.)
259.	לֹא	not (adv.)
260.	לֵב	(m) heart
261.	לָבֵן	make brick
262.	לְבֵנָה	(f) tile, brick
263.	לָבַשׁ	put on, clothe
264.	לַהַט	(m) glittering blade, flame
265.	לוּד	Lydia
266.	לֶחֶם	(c) bread, food
267.	לָטַשׁ	forge, sharpen, hammer
268.	לַיְלָה	(m) night
269.	לָמָּה	why? (adv.)
270.	לֶמֶךְ	Lamech
270a.	לְמַעַן	that (relative particle)
271.	לָקַח	receive, take
272.	לָשׁוֹן	(c) tongue, language
273.	מְאֹד	exceedingly, very (adv.)
274.	מֵאָה	(f) hundred (const. מְאַת)
275.	מָאוֹר	(m) luminary, light
276.	מַאֲכָל	(m) food
277.	מַבְדִּיל	(Hifil participle) division
278.	מָבוֹא	(m) entrance
279.	מַבּוּל	(m) flood
280.	מִבַּיִת	inside (adv.)
281.	מִגְדָּל	(m) fortress, tower
282.	מָגַן	deliver (Kal not used) Piel
283.	מִדְבָּר	(m) large plain, desert
284.	מָה	what?
285.	מוֹלֶדֶת	(f) native land, family, kindred
286.	מוֹעֵד	(m) season
287.	מוֹרָא	(m) fear, reverence
288.	מוֹשָׁב	(m) dwelling
289.	מוּת	die
290.	מִזְבֵּחַ	(m) altar
291.	מָחָה	blot out, destroy, wipe out
292.	מָחוּץ	outside (adv.)
293.	מַחֲזֶה	(m) vision
294.	מַחֲשָׁבָה	(f) design, thought
295.	מָטַר	rain
296.	מִי	who? (interrogative pronoun)
297.	מַיִם	(m) waters (const. מֵי)

298.	מִין (m) species, kind		323.	מָשַׁל rule
299.	מִכְסֶה (m) covering		324.	מִשְׁפָּחָה (f) clan, family,
300.	מָלֵא be full			const. מִשְׁפַּחַת
301.	מְלָאכָה (f) work, service		325.	מִשְׁפָּט (m) judgment
302.	מֶלַח (m) salt		326.	מַשְׁקֶה (m) well watered
303.	מִלְחָמָה (f) battle, war, fight			country
304.	מֶלֶךְ (m) king		327.	נָא I pray thee (a particle,
305.	מַמְלָכָה (f) kingdom			interjection)
306.	מֶמְשָׁלָה (f) dominion, rule		328.	נָבַט look (Kal not used)
	(const. מֶמְשֶׁלֶת)			in Piel and Hifil
307.	מִן from (prep.)		329.	נֶ גֶ ב (m) desert, south
308.	מָנָה number			country
309.	מָנוֹחַ (m) resting place		330.	נָגַד tell, declare, show
310.	מִנְחָה (f) offering, present			Hifil (Kal not used)
311.	מַסָּע (m) a removing		331.	נֶ גֶ ד opposite to, before,
	journey			over against (prep.)
312.	מֵעֶה (m) bowels (only in		332.	נָגַע touch, (Piel to plague)
	plural מֵעִים)		333.	נֶ גַ ע (m) blow, stroke,
313.	מַעְיָן (m) fountain. Uses			plague
	either m. or f.		334.	נָד (m) fugitive
	plural affixes		335.	נָהָר (m) river
314.	מַעַל above (adv.)		336.	נוּד be driven about
315.	מַעֲשֶׂה (m) work, labor		337.	נוֹד (m) Nod (proper
316.	מָצָא find			name), A wandering
317.	מִקְוֶה (m) collection,		338.	נוּחַ to rest
	gathering			וַ יָּ נַ ח and he rested
318.	מָקוֹם (m) place		339.	נֹחַ Noah (proper name)
319.	מִקְנֶה (m) wealth, possession,			(m), quiet, rest
	substance		340.	נוּס escape, flee away
320.	מַרְאֶה (m) appearance sight,		341.	נוּעַ wander
	vision		342.	נָחַם Kal not used. Nifal
321.	מָרַד rebel, revolt			grieve over, repent,
322.	מְרִיבָה (f) strife, contention			comfort, sigh

343.	נָחָשׁ (m) serpent	
344.	נְחֹשֶׁת (c) copper, brass	
345.	נָטָה spread out, stretch out, pitch	
	וַיֵּט and he stretched out	
346.	נָטַע plant	
347.	נִיחֹחַ (m) pleasantness, delight	
348.	נָכָה strike, smite	
349.	נָסַע travel, journey, pull up tent pegs	
350.	נָע (m) wanderer	
351.	נְעוּרִים (m) youth, childhood	
352.	נָפַח blow, breath	
353.	נְפִילִים (m) giants, fallers upon (i. e. robbers) plu. only	
354.	נָפַל fall	
355.	נָפַץ spread abroad, scatter	
356.	נֶפֶשׁ (f) soul, breath	
357.	נְקֵבָה (f) female	
358.	נָקַם revenge, avenge	
359.	נָשָׂא lift up, to bear	
360.	נָשָׁא lead astray, deceive	
361.	נָשַׁב frighten; Hifil, blow	
362.	נְשָׁמָה (f) breath (const. נִשְׁמַת)	
363.	נָתַן give	
	יִתֵּן he will give	
	וַיִּתֵּן and he gave	
364.	סָבַב encompass, surround	
365.	סָגַר shut	
366.	סוּר to turn aside, to remove	

367.	סָכַר stop, shut	
368.	סָפַר write, number	
369.	סֵפֶר (m) writing, book	
370.	סָתַר hide	
371.	עָבַד he served	
372.	עֶבֶד (m) servant, slave	
373.	עָבַר he passed over	
374.	עַד until, till, unto (prep.)	
375.	עֵדֶן (m) delight, Eden	
376.	עוּגָב (m) pipe, flute, organ	
377.	עוֹד yet, still (adv.)	
378.	עָווֹן (m) iniquity, guilt, full form	
	עָוֹן (short form)	
379.	עוֹלָה (f) burnt offering (const. עוֹלַת)	
380.	עוֹלָם (m) age, eternity	
381.	עוּף do fly	
	וַיָּעָף and he flew	
382.	עוֹף (m) fowl	
383.	עוֹף (m) bird	
384.	עוֹר (m) skin	
385.	עָזַב forsake, leave	
386.	עֵזֶר (m) helper, help	
387.	עַיִן (f) fountain, eye	
388.	עִיר (f) city	
389.	עָרֹם naked (adj.)	
390.	עַל upon (prep.)	
391.	עַל־כֵּן therefore	
392.	עָלָה ascend, go up; Hifil to offer up	
	וַיַּעַל and he went up or	

offered. Both Kal and
Hifil have same form.

393. עָלֶה (m) leaf (const. עֲלֵה)

394. עֲלָטָה (f) thick darkness

395. עַם (c) people, kindred,
nation

396. עִם with (prep.)

397. עִמָּד with (prep.)

398. עֵמֶק (m) valley

399. עָנָה be bowed down;
Hifil, oppress, afflict

400. עָנַן (Piel) cloud, cast over

401. עָנָן (m) cloud

402. עָפָר (m) dust

403. עֵץ (m) tree, wood

404. עָצַב suffer pain

405. עֶצֶב (m) pain, travail

406. עִצָּבוֹן (m) travail, pain

407. עֶצֶם (f) bone

408. עָקֵב (m) heel

409. עָקָר barren (adj.)

410. עָר (f) city (Old form of
of עִיר; only used in
plural.)

411. עֶרֶב (m) evening

412. עֹרֵב (f) raven

413. עֶרְוָה (f) nakedness

414. עָרוֹם naked (adj.)

415. עָרוּם cunning, crafty (adj.)

416. עֲרִירִי childless, forsaken
(adj.)

417. עָרַךְ arrange, set in order

418. עֵשֶׂב (m) herb

419. עָשָׂה do, make; ע ש ו and וַיַּעַשׂ and
he did or made. (Kal
impf. jussive with waw
conversive); יַעֲשֶׂה he
will make (Kal impf.)

420. עֲשִׂירִי tenth (ordinal)

421. עָשָׂר ten. (cardinal form
used only in com-
pound with units.)

422. עֶשֶׂר (m) ten (cardinal)
עֲשָׂרָה (f)

423. עָשָׁן (m) smoke

424. עָשַׁר make or become rich

425. עֵת (c) time

426. עַתָּה now (adv.)

427. עָתַק break camp, remove

428. פֶּגֶר (m) corpse

429. פֶּה (m) mouth (const. פִּי)

430. פּוּץ scatter, disperse

431. פָּלַג divide (Kal not used),
Nifal divide

432. פָּלִיט (m) escaped one,
fugitive

433. פֶּן־ lest (conj.)

434. פָּנִים (m) faces (constr. פְּנֵי)

435. פַּעַם (f) stroke, anvil, step

436. פָּצָה open, rend

437. פֶּצַע (m) wound

438. פָּקַח open

439. פָּרַד divide, separate, disjoin

440. פָּרָה bear fruit, be fruitful

441. פְּרִי (m) fruit

442. פָּתַח open
443. פֶּתַח (m) opening, door, gate
444. צֹאן (c) flock
445. צָבָא (m) host, army
446. צַד (m) side
447. צְדָקָה (f) righteousness
448. צַדִּיק blameless, righteous, just (adj.)
449. צֹהַר (f) window
450. צָוָה command (Kal not used)

וַיְצַו and he commanded (Piel)

451. צַיִד (m) hunting, game
452. צֶלֶם (m) image
453. צֵלָע (f) rib, side
454. צָמַח spring forth, sprout
455. צָעַק cry out
456. צָפוֹן (c) north
457. צִפּוֹר (c) sparrow little bird
458. צַר (m) enemy, adversary
459. קָבַר bury
460. קֶדֶם (m) east
461. קִדְמָה (f) eastward
462. קָדַשׁ separate, be holy
463. קָוָה collect, wait
464. קוֹל (m) cry, voice, sound
465. קוּם stand, rise

וַיָּקָם and he arose

466. קוֹמָה (f) height, stature
467. קוֹץ (m) thorn
468. קָטָן little, small, young (adj.)

469. קָטֹן little, small, young (adj.)
470. קַיִן Cain
471. קַיִץ (m) summer, fruit, harvest
472. קָלַל curse (in Piel), lessen, made light of, diminish, be light
473. קֵן (m) room, nesting place
474. קָנָה buy, purchase, acquire, gain, obtain
475. קֵץ (m) end
476. קָצֶה (m) end
477. קָצִיר (m) harvest
478. קֹר (m) cold
479. קָרָא call
480. קְרָאָה (f) an encountering or meeting; (const. קְרַאת with לְ used as a prep. against, towards, with)
481. קָרַב approach, draw near
482. קֶשֶׁת (c) bow, rainbow
483. רָאָה see, Kal impf. jussive with waw conversive; וַיַּרְא and he saw
484. רֹאשׁ (m) head (plu. רָאשִׁים)
485. רִאשׁוֹן first (adj.)
486. רֵאשִׁית (f) beginning
487. רַב (m) numerous (f רַבָּה) many, much (adj.)
488. רָבַב multiply

וַיִּרֶב and be multiplied

489. רָבָה multiply
490. רְבִיעִי fourth (ordinal)
491. רָבַץ crouch, lie down
492. רֶגֶל (m) foot
493. רָדָה rule
494. רָדַף pursue
495. רוּחַ inhale, smell, in Hifil (Kal not used.)
496. רוּחַ (f) wind, spirit
497. רוּם be high, be lofty
498. רֹחַב (m) breadth, width
499. רָחַף brood, hover over
500. רִיב contend, quarrel, strive
501. רִיב (m) strife, quarrel
502. רֵיחַ (m) odor, smell, fragrance
503. רְכוּשׁ (m) property, wealth, substance
504. רָכַשׁ acquire, gain
505. רָמַשׂ creep
506. רֶמֶשׂ (m) creeper, creeping thing
507. רַע (m) evil, injury (adj.)
508. רֵעַ (m) neighbor, friend
509. רָעָב (m) famine
510. רָעָה (f) badness, wickedness
511. רָעָה (m) feed, tend
512. רֹעֶה (m) feeder, herdsman
513. רָעַע be hurtful, be evil
514. רָפָא (m) giant (plu. רְפָאִים)
515. רַק only (adv.)
516. רָקִיעַ (m) expanse

517. שַׁ, שֶׁ which, what, who, (shortened form of אֲשֶׁר)
518. שָׁאַר remain, be left (Nifal)
519. שְׁבִיעִי seventh (ordinal)
520. שִׁבְעָתַיִם (c) sevenfold
521. שָׁבַת cease, rest
522. שַׁג (m) wandering (used with suffix ◌ָם, Gen. 6:3)
523. שָׂדֶה (m) field
524. שֹׁהַם (m) onyx
525. שׁוּב return, to turn
526. שׁוּף bruise, wound
527. שׁוּת put, set, place (שִׁית)
528. שָׁחַת spoil by rotting, (Kal not used); (Nifal) corrupt (Hifil) destroy
529. שֵׂיבָה (f) old age
530. שִׂיחַ (m) shrub
531. שִׂים to put, place וַיָּשֶׂם and he placed
532. שָׁכַךְ abate, assuage, decrease, subside
533. שָׂכַל look at, be wise (Hifil)
534. שְׁכֶם (m) shoulder
535. שָׁכַן dwell, abide
536. שָׂכָר (m) hire, wage
537. שָׁכַר be drunk
538. שָׁלַח send
539. שְׁלִישִׁי third (ordinal)
540. שָׁלֵם full, complete (adj.)

541.	שָׁלוֹם (m) peace	563.	שָׁרַץ swarm
542.	שָׁם there (adv.)	564.	שֶׁרֶץ (m) swarm
543.	שֵׁם (m) name, fame (plu. שֵׁמוֹת)	565.	שִׁשִּׁי sixth (ordinal)
		566.	שָׁתָה drink, banquet
544.	שָׂמְאַל turn to the left take to the left		וַיֵּשְׁתְּ and he drank
		567.	שְׁתַּיִם (f) two
545.	שָׁמַיִם (m) heavens	568.	תַּאֲוָה (f) delight
546.	שִׂמְלָה (f) garment	569.	תְּאֵנָה (f) fig tree
547.	שָׁמַע listen, hear, obey	570.	תֵּבָה (f) ark, chest
548.	שָׁמַר watch, keep	571.	תֹּהוּ (m) desolation
549.	שֶׁמֶשׁ (m) sun	572.	תְּהוֹם (c) abyss
550.	שָׁנָה (f) year	573.	תָּוֶךְ (m) midst (const. תּוֹךְ) middle
551.	שְׁנַיִם two (const. שְׁנֵי)		
552.	שֵׁנִי second (ordinal)	574.	תּוֹלְדוֹת (f) generations (only in plural)
553.	שָׁעָה looked with favor, regard		
		575.	תְּחִלָּה (f) beginning
553a.	שַׁעַר (f) gate	576.	תַּחַת under (prep.)
554.	שָׂפָה (f) shore, tip, language	577.	תַּחְתִּי lower of two, lowest of three (adj.)
555.	שִׁפְחָה (f) maid servant	578.	תָּמִים perfect, complete (adj.)
556.	שָׁפַךְ shed, pour out		
557.	שָׁקָה drink Hifil (Kal not used)	579.	תַּנּוּר (m) furnace, oven
		580.	תַּנִּין (m) serpent, great fish, sea monster
558.	שַׂר (m) prince		
559.	שָׂרָה (f) princess	581.	תָּפַר stitch, sew together
560.	שְׂרוֹךְ (m) shoe lachet	582.	תָּפַשׂ lay hold of, perform
561.	שָׂרַף burn	583.	תַּרְדֵּמָה (f) deep sleep
562.	שְׂרֵפָה (f) burning	584.	תְּשׁוּקָה (f) longing, desire

ENGLISH-HEBREW VOCABULARY

Number indicates Hebrew word in Hebrew-English Vocabulary

abate, 532
Abel, 127
abide, 535
able (be) 213
abounding, 236
above, 314
about, 73
abyss, 572
account of (on) 72
acquire, 474, 504
add, 221
adversary, 458
afflict, 399
afraid (be), 228
after, 18, 19
again, 377
against, 480
age, 115, 380
alive, 161
all, 243
also, 42, 102
altar, 290
anvil, 435
among, 65
and, 138
another, 17
appearance, 320
ark, 570
around, 73
army, 445
arrange, 417
as, 234
ascend, 392
ashamed (be), 63
asphalt, 175
assuage, 532
autumn, 185

avenge, 358
awake, 227

backwards, 20
badness, 510
banquet, 566
bare, 101
barren, 409
battle, 303
bdellium, 59
be (to), 129
bear, 213, 214, 359
bear fruit, 440
beast, 163
beautiful, 222
because, 241
because of, 56
become, 129
before, 331
begin, 167
beginning, 486, 575
behind, 73
behold, 132, 133
being, 226
belly, 99
benefit, 196
between, 65
bind, 150
bird, 383
bird (little) 457
bitumen, 175, 253
blade (glittering), 264
blameless, 448
bless, 83
blessing, 84, 196
blood, 116
blot out, 291

blow, 333, 352, 361
bone, 407
book, 369
born, 216
bow, 482
bowed down, 399
bowels, 312
boy, 215
brass, 344
bread, 266
breadth, 498
break camp, 427
break up, 76
breath, 352, 356, 562
brick, 262
bring, 62
bring forth, 214
brood, 499
brother, 15
bruise, 149, 526
build, 71
burn, 184, 561
burning, 562
burnt offering, 379
bury, 459
but, 138
buy, 474

Cain, 470
call, 479
camel, 103
cast out, 107
cast over, 400
cattle, 61, 78
cease, 152, 157, 521
cherub, 254
chest, 570
child, 215
childhood, 351
childless, 416
choose, 64
circuit (of land), 242
circular plain, 242
cistern, 55
city, 388, 410
clan, 324

clean, 193
cleave, 109
cling, 109
clothe, 263
cloud, 400, 401
coastland, 23
cold, 478
collect, 43, 463
collection, 317
come, 62, 203
comfort, 342
command, 450
complete, 245, 540, 578
conceal, 249
conceive, 137
conception, 137a
confound, 69
confuse, 69
consider, 144
contend, 114, 500
contention, 322
copper, 344
cord, 156
corpse, 428
corrupt, 528
country, (well watered), 326
covenant, 82
cover, 249, 252
covering, 299
crafty, 415
create, 80
creep, 505
creeper, (creeping things) 506
crouch, 491
cry, 464
cry out, 455
cubit, 37
cunning, 415
curse, 47, 472
cut, (in pieces), 87
cut off, 75, 256
cutting instrument, 187

daily, 206
Damascus, 118
darkness, 189, 190

darkness, (thick), 394
daughter, 86
day, 205
deceive, 360
declare, 330
decrease, 180, 532
delight, 347, 375, 568
deliver, 282
demand, 122
desert, 283, 329
design, 294
desire, 172, 584
desolate, (be) 181
desolation, 571
destroy, 256, 291, 528
die, 96, 289
diminish, 180, 472
disjoin, 439
dismayed, 191
disperse, 430
divide, 58, 76, 87, 168, 431, 439
division, 277
do, 419
door, 443
do good, 211
do right, 211
do well, 211
donkey, (she) 53; (he) 174a
dominion, 306
dominion (have) 493
dove, 207
drain, 181
draw near, 481
dread, 192
drink, 557, 566
drive out, 107
driven about, (be) 336
drunk, (be) 537
dry, (be) or dry up, 181, 199
dry land, 183, 200
dwell, 97, 232, 535
dwelling, 288
dust, 402

earth, 46
east, 460

eastward, 461
eat, 29
Eden, 375
encompass, 364
end, 245, 475, 476
enemy, 458
engrave, 186
enmity, 24
Enoch, 178
entrance, 278
escape, 340
escaped one, 432
eternity, 380
Eve, 155
even, 102
evening, 411
every, 243
evil, 507
evil (be), 513
examine, 64
exceedingly, 273
exist, 129
expanse, 516
expire, 96
eye, 387

faces, 434
fair, 222
fall, 354
fallers upon (robbers), 353
fame, 543
family, 285, 324
famine, 509
fashion, 224
fat, 165
father, 1
fatness, 165
favor, 177
fear, 26, 192, 228, 287
feed, 511
feeder, 512
female, 357
field, 158, 523
fifth, 173
fig tree, 569
fight, 303

find, 316
finish, 245
fire, 48
first, 13, 485
first born, 67
first fruit, 67
fish, 112, 113
fish (great), 580
flame, 264
flee, 336
flee away, 340
flesh, 85
flock, 444
flood, 279
flute, 376
fly, 381
food, 30, 266, 276
foot, 492
for, 241, 258
for sake of, 56, 72
foreigner, 106
forge, 267
form, 224
forsake, 385
forsaken, 416
fortress, 281
fountain, 313, 387
fourth, 490
fowl, 382
fragrance, 502
fresh, 198
friend, 508
frighten, 361
from, 307
fruit, 441
fruitful (to be), 440
fruit harvest, 471
fugitive, 334, 432
full, 540
full (be), 300
furnace, 579

gain, 474, 504
garden, 104
garment, 257, 546
gate, 443, 553a

gather, 43
gathering, 317
generation, 115
generations, 574
giant, 514
giants, 353
Gihon River, 100
girdle, 151
give, 203, 363
give ear (listen), 12
glittering blade, 264
go, 130, 203, 217
God, 31, 33
go down, 229
go forth, 223
go in, 62
gold, 140
good, 194, 196
good (do), 211
go out, 223
gopher tree, 105
go up, 392
grace, 177
grass, 124
great (be), 92
great, 93
greenness, 230
grieve over, 342
ground, 6
guilt, 378

Ham, 170
hammer, 267
hand, 201
harp, 247
harvest, 477
hatch, 76
hatred, 24
he, 128
head, 484
hear, 547
heart, 260
heat, 171
heavens, 545
heavy, 236
heavy (be), 235

take to the right, 220
tell, 330
ten, 421, 422
tend, 511
tent, 7, 7a
tenth, 420
terrified, 191
terror, 26
that,128a, 241, 270a
the, 125
there, 542
therefore, 391
there is not, 25
then, 11
these, 32
think, 144, 188.
third, 539
this, 139
thistle, 120
thorn, 467
thought, 225, 294
thread, 156
thus, 246
Tigris, 153
tile, 262
till, 374
time, 425
to, 31a, 258
together, 209
tongue, 272
touch, 332
towards, 258, 480
tower, 281
trained, 179
travel, 349
travail, 405, 406
tree, 403
tremble, 228
tunic, 257
turn, 134, 525
turn aside, 366
turn to the left, 544
turn to the right, 220
two, 551, 567

uncover, 101
under, 576
understanding, 119
unite, 208
until, 374
unto, 31a, 374
upon, 390
utterance, 39

valley, 77, 398
very, 273
vigor, 240
vineyard, 255
violence, 174
vision, 293, 320
voice, 464

wage, 536
wait, 157, 210, 463
wander, 341
wanderer, 350
wandering, 337, 522
war, 303
warmth, 171
waste, 60
watch, 548
waters, 297
way, 121
wealth, 319, 503
well, 55, 195
well (do), 211
well watered country, 326
what?, 284
what, 517
when, 241
where, 21, 22
which, 50, 517
who?, 296
who, 50, 517
why?, 269
wickedness, 510
width, 498
wind, 496
window, 44, 166, 449

INDEX

(Numbers refer to pages)

271